Louis XIV's Architect

Louis XIV's Architect

Louis Le Vau, France's Most Important Builder

Richard Ballard

First published in Great Britain in 2023 by
Pen & Sword History
An imprint of Pen & Sword Books Limited
Yorkshire – Philadelphia

Copyright © Richard Ballard 2023

ISBN 978 1 39905 419 5

The right of Richard Ballard to be identified as
Author of this Work has been asserted by him in accordance
with the Copyright, Designs and Patents Act 1988.

A CIP catalogue record for this book is
available from the British Library

All rights reserved. No part of this book may be reproduced or
transmitted in any form or by any means, electronic or mechanical
including photocopying, recording or by any information storage and
retrieval system, without permission from the Publisher in writing.

Typeset by Mac Style
Printed in the UK by CPI Group (UK) Ltd, Croydon, CR0 4YY.

Pen & Sword Books Limited incorporates the imprints of After
the Battle, Atlas, Archaeology, Aviation, Discovery, Family History,
Fiction, History, Maritime, Military, Military Classics, Politics,
Select, Transport, True Crime, Air World, Frontline Publishing, Leo
Cooper, Remember When, Seaforth Publishing, The Praetorian Press,
Wharncliffe Local History, Wharncliffe Transport, Wharncliffe True
Crime and White Owl.

For a complete list of Pen & Sword titles please contact

PEN & SWORD BOOKS LIMITED
47 Church Street, Barnsley, South Yorkshire, S70 2AS, England
E-mail: enquiries@pen-and-sword.co.uk
Website: www.pen-and-sword.co.uk
or
PEN AND SWORD BOOKS
1950 Lawrence Rd, Havertown, PA 19083, USA
E-mail: Uspen-and-sword@casematepublishers.com
Website: www.penandswordbooks.com

For my grandson Samuel,
who made his first visit to Versailles when he was six

Contents

Preface		viii
Chapter 1	A Family in the Building Trade	1
Chapter 2	The Architect and his Clients	21
Chapter 3	Vincennes: A Royal Project	40
Chapter 4	Mazarin's Louvre	55
Chapter 5	Vaux-le-Vicomte: Fouquet	66
Chapter 6	Colbert: A Difficult Taskmaster	88
Chapter 7	The King in All His Glory	104
Chapter 8	Mazarin's Memorial	135
Chapter 9	A Metallurgical Disaster	153
Chapter 10	In the Shadow of his Successors	172
A Glossary of Architectural Terms		201
Notes to the Text		206
Acknowledgements		207
Notes		209
Select Bibliography		227
Index		229

Preface

Louis Le Vau's achievement was obscured at Versailles by the work of his successor but one, Jules Hardouin-Mansart, who added the enormous north and south wings to the palace, to say nothing of the Hall of Mirrors, the wonder of its time. He was also overshadowed in Paris, where his work on the eastern Colonnade of the Louvre was compromised by having, on Colbert's instructions, to draw up plans for it in committee with Charles Le Brun and Claude Perrault – after a visit to Paris by the internationally celebrated Gian Lorenzo Bernini – and tradition gave the credit for it to Perrault. The College of the Four Nations, later established as the *Institut de France* by Napoleon I, facing the Louvre across the Seine is, however, his creation, finished after he died in 1670 by his faithful pupil François d'Orbay.

And yet his status as a great architect was again compromised by charges of embezzlement brought against him for diverting funds from the building of the College into a project he had undertaken in the Nivernais for making tinplate to replace lead as a roofing material and cannon for Colbert's expanding navy. He had been a speculator ever since the time he was working with his father and site managers on the Île Saint-Louis during the building boom of the 1630s when he was a young man becoming a businessman architect by practising as one.

He never went to Italy, yet the college built with Mazarin's legacy to honour the cardinal's place as Louis XIV's chief minister, godfather and mentor is his baroque masterpiece, with all its imitative originality and, just by turning your head through 180 degrees while standing in the middle of the Pont des Arts, you can see that Le Vau could embrace the distinctions between that style and classicism without diminishing either by mingling them.

There do not seem to be any extant personal letters, there is not even a portrait of him.[1] He was too active on commissions and in commitments and there was no calm retirement to allow him to write memoirs, even had he been disposed to do so. He has not been the victim of any continuous account of his life, despite the countless articles written about particular aspects of his work that have accumulated in the last hundred years.

He lived for fifty-eight years, and we shall follow the progress of his career as an architect and speculator who met the needs of state officials and bankers who wanted to have mirrors turned inwards upon their newly found enormous wealth. He then worked for one particular state official, Nicolas Fouquet, Superintendent of Finances, who made the mistake of turning his mirror outwards in his palace of art and culture at Vaux-le-Vicomte designed for him by Le Vau in all its extravagant beauty – as well as committing the more important error of fortifying a harbour for his private navy to protect his overseas commercial interests on Belle-Île, off the Breton coast, which had all the appearances of treasonable behaviour.

After Fouquet's trial and official disgrace and a decent interval, Le Vau made the *enveloppe* for the late Louis XIII's little palace, built originally as a hunting lodge for his inner circle of courtiers and for giving hospitality to ambassadors, turning it into the first stage of what was to become the capital of France. This gave rise to the misleadingly persistent legend that the nobles would be subdued to Louis XIV's style of monarchy by the necessity to take part in the inner circle or lose their influence. As an American historian of culture says, 'Versailles [was] revolutionary not despite its bourgeois roots, but because of them.' The palace was to become Louis XIV's 'laboratory of absolutism'.[2]

Louis Le Vau was an autodidact from among the tribe of stonecutters (literally, 'tailors of stone') who gathered every day in the place de Grève in front of the Hôtel de Ville in Paris to be taken on for work.[3] The craft of an architect was not yet closely defined by the standards of a recognised profession – the Academy of Architecture was not founded until the year after his death and it was his younger brother François who profited from being a member of it. Young Louis learned his craft from the overseers of the building sites he worked on, along with his stonecutter, then master mason, father. He moved, also with his father, into the market in building land in his twenties and, by 1637 when he was twenty-five, became autonomous – or as autonomous as you could have been – as an architect to the King. It was not long before he was living in his own *hôtel particulier* (for which an acceptable translation is mansion), where members of his extended family lived together.[4]

Thereafter, he was close to the King's ministers, Mazarin, Fouquet, and then Colbert, and this meant that the King was his client too. The King set the tone and for a time the architect set the style. When the First Architect to the King, Jacques Lemercier, who was responsible for designing the clock tower at the Louvre, died in office in 1654, Louis Le Vau, who had been assisting him there, took his place in what seems to have been a seamless handover: one day Lemercier was signing contracts, and the next, Le Vau.[5] In contrast with what happened to Fouquet, the only way for Le Vau was upwards – until the posthumous corruption charges from which his death saved the man himself, but not his family nor his memory.[6]

A continuous account of Louis Le Vau's life has not yet been compiled, though some have been undertaken without being completed. A great deal of material exists, however, digested in morsels, by as many writers who are listed in numerous bibliographies. There are the plans he sketched and had made into drawings and engravings in the agency that he set up in his successive homes or, once his buildings were in being, by artists such as Israël Silvestre and Jean Marot. Enough of these buildings survive to enable an assessment of the quality of his vision.

The flesh and blood man is difficult to find but gradually, as books from the last hundred years make their presence known – books from art historians and architects like Louis Hautecœur, Anthony Blunt, Hilary Barron, Maurice Dumolin, Jean-Claude Le Guillou, Alexandre Cojannot, Alexandre Gady, Cyril Bordier – as well as books by commentators of his own time, including André Félibien, who was at Fouquet's Vaux-le-Vicomte with him, or in the next century such as Henri Sauvel and Jaques-François Blondel – the man appears in his own setting. In the history of culture, the observation made by Ardis Butterfield, a historian of music, that the past has a special allure when it is imagined as present, is an authentic one.[7]

To stand in the quadrangle of the Louvre looking at the inner facades of the east and south wings, and through the carriage entrance across the Seine to the dome and portico of his building that houses the Institute of France on a strangely rare quiet Sunday afternoon in autumn was for me an occasion to share Louis Le Vau's vision of the majestic grandeur that Louis XIV wanted from him. Colbert, after one of the extravagant fêtes held by the King before any large-scale permanent building began at Versailles, said that Le Vau and Le Nôtre were the architect and garden designer only for the King's *divertissements*, while what was needed was an artist who could express of his *Grandeur*. What Le Vau eventually did at Versailles to enhance the King's and Queen's apartments does not assert itself against later versions what Anthony Blunt was acerbic enough to call 'that most expensive of toys',[8] while at the Louvre, behind the facades that emerged from Le Vau's drawing office, there is a sense of cheerful awe, enhanced nowadays by the performances of young musicians and the enthusiasm of their small, impromptu audiences.

Whatever could or should be said against absolute monarchy, it cannot be criticised for the beauty that appeared as its setting. Once Versailles was in being, the Louvre could do no more than echo a majesty that had decided not to live there any longer.

Chapter 1

A Family in the Building Trade

Henri IV brought religious toleration into being with his edict of Nantes, political stability with his establishment of the Bourbon dynasty, and urbanisation of Paris with a building programme carried out from the time he entered his capital in 1589 until he was assassinated in 1610.

The establishment of a new ruling dynasty was an essential element in the new-found stability of the French state. The Papal Curia allowed the King's marriage to Catherine de' Medici's daughter to be annulled. Queen Margot received a generous financial settlement. She and Henri had no children together, and an heir was needed to establish a dynasty in the name of the Bourbons without any Valois participation. Within a year, Henri IV had married again: this time with Marie de' Medici – a distant relative of his ex but nobody seemed to mind. The Medici of Florence were Henri's principal creditors and Marie brought a substantial dowry with her. An heir – the future Louis XIII – arrived a year after the marriage. Other children followed, including the troublesome Gaston of Orleans and Henrietta-Maria, who would marry Charles I of England.

Henri IV was stabbed while in his carriage by François Ravaillac, a Catholic fanatic, and died from the wound, but he had provided opportunity in the capital for an ambitious building programme by unleashing investment in his building projects. The subsequent careers of architects like Jacques Lemercier, François Mansart and Louis Le Vau fitted into the new conditions. New stability brought the realisation of a new artistic potential: there was to be stylish, even beautiful, building. Henri IV's interest in Paris is the most significant domestic feature of his reign.

One of his first decisions after gaining access to his capital in 1594 was to order the repair and continuation of the Louvre Palace and join it to the Tuileries, a process already begun under Catherine de' Medici. Jean de Fourcy was his *Intendant des Bâtiments,* part of a hierarchy responsible for all the King's buildings, and he held an adjudication on 7 January 1595 about the construction of the gallery that the King wanted to build along the right bank of the Seine from the Tuileries to the Louvre.

The author of the original design had been Pierre Lescot. He remained as architect to François II and Charles IX, who wanted their father's project finished. Lescot died in 1578, and the work was taken over by Baptiste Androuet du Cerceau, whom Henri III ordered to keep to Lescot's design. All had been brought to a standstill by the wars of religion, during which what had been built fell into ruin. So Henry IV undertook a policy of making good before beginning on his own project. In Louis XIII's reign, all this continued on Pierre Lescot's design, and not until Louis XIV began his career of personal rule in March 1661 was the plan modified for completion.

Henri's next building project was to be the Place Royale (known since 1800 as the Place des Vosges), which was, at first, part of an economic project designed by the King himself to allow French capital, currently being spent lavishly in Italy to pay for silk, to remain in France. Great encouragement was exerted on French agriculturalists towards the development of mulberry tree plantations and upon the mercantile class to import silkworms so that the weaving of gold and silver threads into the silk to make an even more luxurious product would be achieved in Paris.

To this end, silk manufacturing was established in the Place Turenne. The King acquired extra land there and gave it to aristocratic developers, who would build three sides of a square, leaving the silk weavers in occupation of its north side. The other sides had their facades developed in a uniform pattern on nine pavilions, each four bays wide, with arcades at street level, behind which there were to be shops, two higher floors, and high roofs incorporating an attic with *lucarnes*. The developers had to preserve the uniformity of the fronts, but they could do what they liked with the interiors of the pavilions.

The design in brick and dressed stone with dark slate roofs was realised with a certain anonymity, perpetuated by an almost complete absence of ground plans and elevations. It is surmised that the most likely designers were the usual royal architects of the reign: Jacques II Androuet du Cerceau and Louis Métezeau, with possible participation in the King's Pavilion by Salomon de Brosse – designer of the Luxembourg Palace for Marie de' Medici.[1] The King hoped to develop the Place Royale for clearly designated purposes, expressed in his edict of July 1605.

The Place Royale was intended to support his venture into silk manufacturing, providing accommodation for skilled artisans, most of whom would have to be enticed to Paris from other countries with the double bait of prestigious housing and association with the crown. The King's second intention was to provide a large and attractive open space for the city population to enjoy a leisurely stroll, described as 'a distinctively urban recreation' in an area of increasingly dense population since 'strolling required an architecturally defined space.' This was not merely for those who lived in the quarter: it was to be for the whole of Paris. It was also to serve as a marketplace, again, not a local one, but serving as a 'city-wide magnet for trade in precious goods'. The final purpose for the Place Royale in the King's plan was as a setting for court ceremonies and public celebrations for which space would be needed.

'The appropriation of public space for the periodic staging of royal ceremonies was hardly an unusual practice, but what is distinctive here was the crown's interest in sharing the space with the ignoble pursuits of manufacturing and trade. In effect the crown was lending its prestige to commerce: that identification of the monarchy with artisanal activity distinguished Henri IV's court and his urbanism from that of the Valois kings who preceded him and the Bourbon kings that were to follow.'[2]

Unfortunately the nobles did not share this vision, and in April 1607 the plan to develop silk manufacturing there was abandoned, and the pavilions were developed as dwellings for royal office holders and other members of the *noblesse de robe*.[3] Prominent among these was Pierre Fougeu d'Escures, who held a post in the administration of waterways in Sully's government. He had been granted a building plot next to the royal pavilion in 1605, on which he provided shops in the arcades, as was originally intended, and stables in a courtyard behind the house. He did not intend to live there, but to let it out to shopkeepers and traders. It cost him a sum that he could afford but the artisans could not have. Then, in March 1607, he was given five plots on the west side of the square as a reward for his rapid construction of his first house. He used two of these to provide a larger house for his own use, and sold the other three, together with the one he had finished, to pay for it. A year later, he closed the shop arcades off, in the interests of improving his house as a private dwelling, and then sold it at a profit. With the money, he bought another property comprising two pavilions in the square and enlarged its garden behind it. He lived there until his death in 1621. What had been intended as housing for a bourgeois became a nobleman's *hôtel particulier*.

There were five artisan homeowners, but it was the royal office holders who predominated. The rich owners of the silk workshops who had begun the project, men like Pierre Sainctot and Charles Marchant, still developed properties, but profited from letting them to others. After Henri IV's death, however, the Bourbon court preferred the Louvre as its Paris base, and the officials lost interest in the Place Royale.

The construction of the Pont Neuf and the Place Dauphine at the western tip of the Île de la Cité was another stage in Henri IV's urbanisation of his capital. The last Valois, Henri III, had made plans that were changed more than once for the bridge, but the outbreak of civil war in 1588 prevented them from being carried out. Henri IV decided to take them up again ten years afterwards, though he would abandon the idea of building houses on it in order to make it a vantage point for the expanded Tuileries, the Cité and the river. Marie de' Medici would order the equestrian statue of him in the middle of the bridge from Florentine artists, but the Florentine element was not influential in the King's vision for his project of urban development in the capital while he intended to settle in the Tuileries. His design to create the Place Dauphine at the end of the island emerged over the next seven years.

Construction of the bridge recommenced in 1599 under the direction of the masons François Petit and Guillaume Marchant. The quays on the island were to be developed to enhance their aesthetic appearance and the buildings to be raised above them were to have a monumental aspect, despite the later tendency to regard them as too small for that purpose – more recently rectified by their restoration. The Pont Neuf was opened in 1604 and completed in 1606. The statue was erected in 1614 and became the King's memorial.

On 10 March 1607 the King gave the western tip of the island to President Harlay of the *Parlement* as a reward for his loyalty during the wars of religion, with the proviso that he would carry out plans drawn up by Sully for a tribute to the heir to the throne, Louis XIII, who had been born in 1601, and have them completed within three years. Harlay was empowered to sell the building lots, transfer the requirement of speedy completion to the new owners and keep his profits from the sale of the land.

The form of the *place* was dictated by the irregular, triangular site, with its point at the side of the Pont Neuf and its two arms diverging eastward to the street that was to bear Harlay's name. According to a drawing made by Robert de Cotte nearly eighty years afterwards in 1685, while he was making recommendations to realign the statue with the *place*, there were fifty-eight independent buildings there. The two new quays in front of these buildings had the purpose of directing the expected increased traffic to the commercial centres on the island and to the law courts, the cathedral and the hospital, while preserving calm for the people who would occupy houses that should be 'public on one side and private on the other'.[4] The appearance of the buildings depends upon the same materials as were used in the Place Royale: the stone arcades in front of the shops and the brick with stone decoration on the higher floors, and the high roofs in slate, which previously had elegant chimneys also in brick and stone.

* * *

Besides these projects undertaken on the King's initiative there was a new phenomenon during the reigns of Henri IV and Louis XIII in the adoption of the town mansion (*hôtel particulier*) by wealthy royal officials and the new financial class. The new situation was exemplified under Louis XIII on the Île Saint-Louis with its stone embankments lined with mansions and its internal shopping streets – a mixture of medieval survival and contemporary style for businesses and large houses incorporating garden spaces.[5]

The development of the Île Saint-Louis is what concerns us most for this study of Louis Le Vau. It began in 1614 and it went on for thirty years. The way it was developed by speculating builders followed the success of the Place Royale and of the Place Dauphine under Sully's administration, the impulse of the growing demand for housing for courtiers now that the monarchy was stabilised in the Île de France, and a vigorous market in real estate.[6] In 1600 there were two islets in the Seine to the east of the Île de la Cité, one called Île Notre-Dame and the other Île des Vaches, divided from each other when a north–south ditch was dug between them for defensive purposes under Charles V for a chain to be drawn across the river at night. The two islets remained uninhabited even after the chain disappeared, used only for storing trade goods for the port Saint-Paul close by or let to a butcher as pasture for his beef on the hoof. They were the property of the canons of Notre-Dame. Many a duel took place on them.

In 1600, the only bridges across the Seine were from either bank to the Île de la Cité. Otherwise there were ferries large enough to take carts and carriages at Neuilly, Chatou and at Pecq. There was nearly a national disaster on the Neuilly ferry on 9 June 1606 when Henri IV, Marie de' Medici, the Duke of Montpensier and the Princess of Conti were nearly drowned as their heavy carriage slid into the river.

Christophe Marie, a financier who would later be responsible for all the bridges of France,[7] proposed a system that he claimed to have been his own invention to the King for constructing wooden bridges capable of carrying all loads – even artillery. One like it could be built over a great river in no more than four months, he said, and he offered to build it at his own expense in return for a concession of twenty years' rights of tolls equal to those of the ferry that it would replace. Henry IV accepted the proposal by letters patent with any future disputes about the matter to be referred to the *Parlement*. Marie completed the Pont de Neuilly by September 1611. His outlay was 42,000 livres and it brought him in 12,000 a year, which he had to share with the associates he had accrued during the two years it took to complete. Moreover, there would be financial complications involving claims by local landowners for the rest of Marie's life.

As early as 1577, in Henri III's reign, there had been a plan to construct a bridge to take the pressure of traffic away from the Île de la Cité that would reach from the Celestins to the Île des Vaches with houses on it, and continued from the Île to the Pont de la Tournelle on the left bank. It was not selected at the time but kept for future consideration and re-emerged when Henri IV had completed the Place Royale. Its construction was entrusted to Christophe Marie. Henri IV's assassination on 14 May 1610 put everything on hold for several months. Marie then formed an association on 7 February 1611 with Lugles Poulletier, *commissaire des guerres*, who took on the part of banker to the enterprise.[8]

The two islets that were going to be united by filling in the ditch between them were the property of the canons of Notre-Dame, and as soon as they heard of the project, they took up the cudgels against it. Christophe Marie had offered to build the bridge to the left bank within a year at his own expense in return for the concession yielded to him and his inheritors of the first sales of building plots on the united Île Saint-Louis. He was to build houses on the bridge, together with six water mills in places where boat traffic would not be hindered.

Experts, including Louis Marchant, visited the sites but the choice was regarded with disfavour because of the sloping banks of the island, which would make the bridge too long, the creation of obstacles for boatmen, the likelihood of flooding and the losses to the established ferrymen. Nevertheless, Marie persuaded the traders of the *quartier* to support his proposals unanimously in an agreement dated 12 March 1612 on condition that the bridge was built of stone and not of wood. Marie agreed that the pillars should be high enough not to hinder the boats. Measurements and costings were made in August. Louis XIII granted the islets to Marie, all except for the roads, and he was to have local taxes for sixty years. 'Sieur Christophe Marie, *entrepreneur-général des ponts de France*, living in the rue des Prouvelles', signed his contract before the notaries on 19 April 1614. A year later, François Le Regrattier was associated with Marie and Poulletier in the project. Poulletier held a half share and Marie and Legrattier a quarter each. Marie was regarded by the other two as the technician.

It was all very well for the King's Council and the *echevins* to have given their approval – the King and Queen laid the first stone of the bridge on 11 October 1614 – but two major opposition groups remained: the boatmen and the canons of Notre-Dame, who had not been consulted. They intimidated potential purchasers of building plots on the island and the three entrepreneurs had to bear all the costs of construction of the bridge without yet having made any sales by which they would have been recompensed. The canons of Notre-

Dame began their offensive even before the stone laying in June 1614 and after a year they threatened to have destroyed whatever had already been built. The Paris *Parlement* supported them.

Their arguments against the project were that unnecessary floods would be provoked and that, as the former owners of the islets, compensation was due to them for their loss of revenue. The Royal Council decreed that Marie should construct dressed stone quays around the islets to keep flooding to a minimum, and that, after the sixty years of revenue granted to him and his heirs, those revenues should revert to the Dean and Chapter. The canons demanded that this should be rescinded, especially since Marie was planning to build a huge hexagonal commercial enterprise on the bridge that would disfigure the environs of the old city.[9]

The dispute dragged on and on until Marie's associates could no longer cope with their creditors calling in their loans. In 1624, the King's Council took away Marie's contract and awarded it to a speculator named Jean de La Grange and his associates, Philippe de Coulanges and Claude Charlot, who undertook to finish the bridges and the quays by 1629.[10] They were awarded the same recompenses as Marie, also for sixty years, in return for indemnities for work already done, but this was too expensive for La Grange, and the contract reverted to Marie and associates by a decree of 24 July 1627 with the same stipulations as before.

The works went ahead, despite disputes among the triumvirs about the appointment of builders for the plots that were sold for building. Meanwhile, the canons accepted an indemnity of 50,000 livres for the loss of their revenue at Richelieu's suggestion in 1634. Disputes were not at an end, but the Pont Marie was open to traffic and potential purchasers of building plots were reassured. One of these was Claude de Ragois de Bretonvilliers who, in February 1635, ordered the construction of his huge *hôtel particulier* to the designs of Jean Androuet du Cerceau at the eastern point of the island. This was the signal for the intensive development of the plots that gathered momentum from then onwards.

* * *

Louis Le Vau's father, also Louis, was designated in legal documents signed in the presence of notaries between 1622 and 1634 as 'a stonecutter living in Paris', and so held a subordinate position in the building trade. He cut the stone received from the quarry on the orders of the master masons who carried out the construction, but it is not known in which sites or for which employers he worked before 1634. He signed himself as Louis Le Veau.

Only one of Louis Le Veau's relations is known by name: his sister Claude, who married a companion carpenter called Pierre Moret in 1603. She had been a servant in the household of Guillaume Marchant (a member of the entrepreneurial dynasty that has already appeared in this narrative), who sold pigs in the Paris market, and she was not able to sign her name. Her parents (and therefore her brothers) are not mentioned in her marriage contract. Louis Le Veau was witness to Moret's second marriage in 1628 after his sister had died. The inventory made after her death speaks of her modest possessions.[11]

There is no surviving contract for Louis Le Veau's own marriage to Étiennette Louette in the papers found after her death in 1648, nor after his own in 1661, which in itself is another clue to their working-class status that did not warrant such niceties. On their mother's side, the Le Veau children were descended from country people living in the Vexin near Beauvais. Their grandfather was Charles Louette, a blacksmith, owner of several parcels of land and part of a house at Montagny-en-Vexin, which enabled him to buy fifty-one vines when he sold it. It is assumed that on their father's side the Le Veau children came from a family with roots in Paris reaching back for several generations and living in the parish of Saint-Jean-en-Grève. Proof is lacking that Louis and Étiennette lived in Paris before 1620, but tradition maintains that their eldest son (of three) was born there in about 1612. The date is vague because young Louis's birth certificate from the parish church was lost in a fire, but enough antiquarians recorded it before it was lost to vouch for its existence.

His mother apprenticed Louis to another stonecutter, Marin Louette, probably his uncle, at Montagny. Marin had bought the family house there in 1628. A further family connection in the building trade was that his Aunt Claude, Mme Moret, was married to a master carpenter in Paris, so there was a link with the powerful Marchant family who owned a building firm. The Marchants seem to have been pleased to help Claude because they gave her a dowry of 130 livres between them when she married the carpenter. The head of the firm, Guillaume, seems to have gone on from selling porkers after 1603 to play a major role in the urbanisation of Paris under Henri IV and Louis XIII, eventually holding the eminent post of Master of the King's Masonry Works. His gift to Claude might suggest larger patronage to the Le Veaus. Perhaps her brother worked regularly for him on his sites. The family unit and its wealthier patrons were the usual building blocks of business in the organisation of work in the trade in this epoch.

Until the mid-1630s, Louis and Etiennette Le Veau lived near the Hôtel de Ville – made apparent by contracts in the National Archives for his work – in a rented property in the rue de Saint-Jean-en-Grève, where tortuous narrow roads crossed, and the address for the same building changed regularly. It was in the neighbourhood of the former rue de La Mortellerie, which recalled the medieval word for masons, *mortelliers,* and it was near the place de Grève, where the builders took on the tradesmen for their various sites.

There are signs that Louis Le Veau's ambitions were the forerunners of those of his eldest son. When the building boom had started, he made his own modest speculation by means of the purchase of a building plot near the Porte Saint-Denis by a deed drawn up with the sisters of the Filles-Dieu Convent on 10 October 1622. This was in a new quarter called Villeneuf-sur-Gravois, so-called because it was where masons used to deposit the rubble that they took away from the sites they were developing. Le Veau built a little house with a shop on the ground floor on the site, and let it out to a bourgeois called Robert Burnouf for 60 livres a year, who sublet it to a master carpenter. It was soon sold on. 'This modest investment shows that the stonecutter had his part in the prosperity which the professionals in the building trade had in the first decades of the golden century.'[12] Building was in the blood and speculation in the bone of his eldest son and his youngest, François; the middle one, Antoine, was a master mason, and two of the three sisters married into the trade. Anne's husband was Charles Thoison, a mason who will figure large in this narrative, Marie's was Etienne Monnard, a carpenter.[13] They took part in the motivations of this period of intense change.

There were ten years between Louis and François, and François followed in Louis's footsteps as well as being a civil engineer working on bridges and highways. The Duchess of Montpensier commissioned him in 1653, when she was exiled from court for her part in the Fronde, to embellish and remodel the enormous dilapidated chateau in brick and dressed stone that she had inherited at Saint-Fargeau near Cosne-sur-Loire, for which he achieved a striking similarity with his brother's mature work at Vaux-le-Vicomte. It is easy to conjecture that the designs for both buildings reflect a certain co-operation between the two brothers. François was also a founder member of the Royal Academy of Architecture when Louis had been dead a year. This meant that the profession of architect was defined in a way that it had not been during Louis's lifetime. When it was up and running, those entrepreneurs in the building trade who wanted to be recognised as belonging to the profession of architects had to obtain formal qualifications, which those of Louis Le Vau's age group did not.

* * *

Le Vau's first independent design is taken to have been for the Hôtel Bautru. The decade of the 1630s was the occasion of a massive building boom in the *quartier* known as Richelieu or the Fossés Jaunes, between the Louvre, the royal residence in Paris, and what we know as the Palais-Royal, where Cardinal Richelieu lived. The leasing out of this area was entrusted to the financier Louis de Barbier. The plots were being taken up by courtiers and the great officials of the state. One of these was Guillaume Bautru, Baron de Segré, then Comte de Serraut, who presented foreign ambassadors to the King, and had himself been an ambassador several times. In April 1634 he had bought a large building plot at the corner of the rue Neuve Petits-Champs and the rue Vivienne measuring 42.8 x 79.7m. In July 1635, Michel Villedo signed a contract for the construction of a large house in dressed stone, comprising large central living quarters (*corps de logis*), two pavilions, two wings, a *basse cour* with stabling, a large courtyard and a garden. A second contract was signed in June 1636 for a gallery along the garden and the rue Vivienne, and a first floor above the long stable block.

Louis Le Vau the younger had learned architecture on the building sites where he worked, probably from the site managers, men like Michel Villedo, but whose identities are largely unknown. Villedo himself was still young when he was entrusted with the construction of the Bautru mansion in 1634. He had been working in the Île de France since 1626. He was a master mason and lived in rue de Verbois in the parish of Saint-Paul. He worked on several of Mansart's contracts and in the King's service at the Bastille. He bought the office of Master General of the King's Masonry Works from one René Fleury. Guillaume Marchant, Claude Le Veau's patron, had held this office in 1603. Under a decree of 1645, there were three masters general, of whom Michel Villedo was one (it was a hereditary office and it remained in his family for two generations after him) and their task, as judges responsible to the Treasurers General of the kingdom, was to regulate the craft in the entire nation.[14] So, if anyone was in a position to find occupation for an ambitious young architect it would be Villedo, and he found it for him in Bautru's project for his mansion in 1634.

The work was completed on 16 August 1636 when the final receipt was signed. Disputes about the difference between the estimate and the price lasted for some time, and Bautru drew up a list of complaints against Villedo in 1641. There was an inspection by experts in February 1643 that found defective materials, fragile masonry, and insufficient foundations. These complaints would be repeated in 1665 when Colbert bought the house and wanted an upstairs storey on the wings. He told his Italian guest Bernini all about it, to Le Vau's discredit. Although the 1655 engraving of the mansion by Jean Marot identifies Le Vau as its creator, he was not credited as its designer until Henri Sauval gave him a paragraph in his account of the buildings in the quarter in the 1650s (though published much later).[15] Very little of the building remains to be seen in our time.

The importance of this work by the young Le Vau is that he was working within a few years of buildings being designed by the big names of the period: Jacques Lemercier at the Palais-Richelieu (1628), Jean Thiriot at the Hôtels Duret and Chevry, and François Mansart at the Hôtel de La Vrillière. It is certain that the Hôtel Bautru was very derivative, and has been called 'an astonishing mixture of very archaic elements and innovative features', but the style can be recognised as that which he would still be employing at the Louvre as First Architect to Louis XIV twenty years afterwards.[16] There was a textbook of models for budding architects by Pierre Le Muet, published in 1625, which Le Vau is known to have possessed[17] and which he pillaged[18] for the *corps de logis* at the mansion for Bautru: the differences between an illustration in Le Muet and the engraving by Jean Marot are 'no more than adjustments'.[19]

However, we can appreciate the innovations of the fledgeling architect who was learning his craft by the practice of it. The exterior appearance of the *corps de logis* flanked by the two taller pavilions with high roofs is lifted straight from a model in Le Muet's textbook, but the treatment of the interior disposition of the rooms is innovative. Instead of the staircase being in the centre of the *corps de logis*, as had been usual, Le Vau placed it in the pavilion at the right of it, thus allowing for a linear progression of the elements in the large *appartement* on the first floor. These elements were a large room, an ante-chamber and a large bedroom, from which a small office and a chapel opened into the pavilion on the left above the court, and a large office and a dressing room in another pavilion above the garden front together with a long gallery above the stables. The rooms opened out of each other in a single *enfilade*. A further innovatory feature was the balcony with iron railings in the centre of the apartment's garden front, opening from the ante-chamber.[20]

* * *

If, as is usually supposed, after his apprenticeship with his uncle Marin, that Louis the younger's principal teacher was his father, then Louis the elder profited by becoming better professionally qualified himself and was rewarded accordingly with more interesting work since he went on from being a stonecutter to recognition as a master mason. From 1634 onwards, when his son had received his first commission as an architect, he was working for himself: a candidate for repairing a bridge over the lake at Rampillou on the road from Paris to Troyes, then a candidate for repairing the prison at Gournay-sur-Marne and in 1635 for building a road from the ferry over the Oise at Neufville. He was employed on bridge repair at L'Isle Adam. In April 1637, he was a candidate for constructing a drain on the rue de Seine in Paris. He was not successful, but kept the right to be designated as a *maçon entrepreneur*. He also made sub-contracts with other artisans, and established himself as available for short-term projects.

The birth of the family business as such was signalled by the signing of a contract on 2 September 1634 between Louis *père* and Henri Le Prebtre, a councillor at the *Cour des aides*, to build a house in the rue de la Fromagerie in which he was described for the first time as a master mason. Moreover, he had become an *entrepreneur de maçonnerie*, that is, a jobbing builder. Soon afterwards, he made contracts with two sub-contractors for knocking down Le Prebtre's house and building another on the same site using salvaged materials. For this, he engaged a master carpenter, Jean Leclerc, to work with him, as well as two companion masons, named as Liénard Bertel and Michel Morin, who was his nephew by marriage, husband of Marguerite Muret, daughter of his deceased sister Claude. This modest structure with a shopfront was to have rubble stone walls with external surfaces made good with plaster and painted to look like brick.

Louis the younger could well have taken part in this work. It becomes certain that he worked on projects with his father because his signature is also on the contract signed for building three houses for Pierre Pontheron, 'painter in ordinary to the King', at a site on the corner of the rue de Deux-Ponts and the quai d'Anjou at the island end of the Pont Marie. The estimate for these houses carries his signature. This was part of the urbanisation plan undertaken earlier by Christophe Marie in which it was stipulated that all the houses built on this particular site should have facades identical with those built on the Pont Marie itself (now demolished but plainly visible on the famous Turgot map of 1739). The houses were finished after the due date had expired, but were accepted after an inspection by Michel Villedo in October 1637.

Then the Le Veaus undertook to complete some half-finished houses known as the Hôtel de Pellevé in the rue du Roi de Sicile near the Hôtel de Ville for the Controller-General Extraordinary for War, Jean Desmaretz. Louis the elder made 5,000 livres out of this contract.[21] The work carried out was an example of the speculative nature of these jobs. The works were financed by credit and the costs covered by the sale of the completed buildings. When Le Veau the elder took on some small works in 1637, he agreed that payment for them would not be in cash, but in the form of the control of a stone quarry at Créteil. We shall see this characteristic of the building trade repeated again and again during Louis Le Vau's career both as architect and as speculator since you could not be the one without also being the other.

Jean Desmaretz was one of the witnesses at Louis Le Vau's marriage in 1637, and Le Vau was taken on for a restoration project by Nicolas Fourrel, a legal official in the Paris *Parlement*, in the same year so, even before he attained his majority at the age of twenty-five and was legally qualified to accept responsibility for work in his own right, he had patrons among officials of state under the guidance of his father.

In the stratified society of seventeenth-century Paris, Le Vau's education appears exceptional. He had an elegant hand for writing, as numerous contracts and estimates show, and he would not have acquired that at the parochial school, which was all his artisan father could have afforded. His lack of Greek or Latin suggests that he had not been sent to a college like Clermont where the Jesuits would have provided such a curriculum. The library that he acquired for himself over the years, inventoried after his death, does not include much in the way of classical authors, and usually in translation, such as his copy of the four-volume edition of Plutarch by Jacques Amyot, or of Ovid's *Metamorphoses* by Nicolas Renouard.[22]

His knowledge was practical, acquired through working with his father, such as how to draw up a contract, which he knew perfectly well how to do by the time he was twenty-three in 1635. Yet it was his association with Michel Villedo that gave him a more sophisticated training as an architect, and it seems that it was his father who introduced them to each other. Working on Bautru's mansion was the beginning of an association that lasted for thirty years until Villedo's death. Respective children of theirs married into René Mignon's family. Villedo had already formed professional links with the prominent pictorial artists and sculptors of the time. Several people close to Villedo called themselves architects – like his namesake son or his son-in-law Michel Noblet – there were no legal limits on doing that provided the projects were delivered. So Villedo's recommendation of his young friend to Bautru opened Le Vau's specialisation for the foreseeable future into commissions offered by royal officials and financiers on which he built his reputation, which in turn led to contracts at royal palaces and the notice taken of him by Mazarin and then Colbert.

* * *

Louis Le Veau decided to move his family from their lodgings in the La Grève quarter to a house on the quai Celestins opposite the right bank end of the newly opened Pont Marie. The new address appears for the first time in a contract signed by Le Veau on 11 May 1637.[23] The removal suggests both a new-found modest prosperity and seizing new opportunities in the obvious growth area of the Île Saint-Louis. New commissions came in for small houses for artisans on the island that had parts attached to them that could be rented out to others. Some were constructed to be rented as soon as they were completed and were the property of influential people like Antoine Le Marier, procurator at the Chatelet; that is, a high-up in the Paris police.[24]

Building plots were typically being bought by royal court officials, one of them being Melchior Le Gillier, *seigneur* of Lagny, and *maître d'hôtel* in ordinary to the King. He bought a prime site on the corner of the quai d'Anjou and the rue Poullettier measuring 19.4 x 27.2m and commissioned a large house for it from Le Veau father and son in August 1637. This is the Hôtel de Gillier, 23 quai d'Anjou. All the bills for construction – amounting to a total of 28,200 livres – were paid by July 1639.

This building is particularly remarkable for being the work of a recently accredited master mason and his tyro son at the time when architecture was dominated by François Mansart, who began working at Maisons (now Maisons-Laffitte) in 1640. The outside is dignified, comprising a ground floor and three upper storeys, with a Doric frieze above the first one and with the third floor set in the type of *combles brisés* (literally: 'broken eaves'), similar to those used by Louis Le Vau fifteen years later at Vincennes. But the 'wow factor' is the interior staircase hanging over an empty space and supported by vaulting. At the upper levels the construction is of wood covered in plaster, presumably to reduce the weight. The ironwork of the bannisters is probably a replacement of stone originals, which would accord more readily to the taste of the 1630s.[25]

Louis Le Veau *fils* cut his teeth, as it were, on Le Gillier's mansion, in collaboration with his father, but his ambition drove him to work with other builders on sites in the other area of rapid urbanisation in Paris, the Marais. One of these was inevitably Michel Villedo, and another Claude Dublet, whose qualification as a master carpenter complemented Villedo's work as a master mason.

Dublet's astonishing personal history cannot be disregarded. His son was convicted of certain criminal activities, so he shot him to save him from facing a shameful death on the gallows or being broken on a wheel. However, he managed to obtain a royal pardon both for his son's crimes and his own in shooting him.[26] Dublet, Villedo and Le Vau often worked together until 1660.

Villedo and Dublet had acquired an interest in building plots around the Place Royale from Nicolas Le Jay, first president of the Paris *Parlement* who died in 1640. Some of the plots had already been sold for development in 1637, but much was left from the medieval market gardens maintained by the hospitallers of Saint-Gervais, part of which Henri IV had taken over for his new development. Villedo and Dublet were the builders of houses that were commissioned on these plots, and the contract made between Dublet and one of the owners, François Petit, a royal official who gradually accumulated posts at court, indicates that Louis Le Vau was involved, by then recognised as an architect to the King. Many of the annotations in the margins of the document are in Le Vau's own hand. Once more, traits can be recognised from the models of Pierre Le Muet and the methods used by Le Vau in the Hôtel Bautru to separate the rooms used by the bourgeois owners from the rest of the house.

This Hôtel Petit has a staircase designed on similar principles to the one in the Hôtel Bautru. An innovation was a dining room on the ground floor easily accessible from the kitchens, another importation from Le Muet, not generally adopted in Parisian houses until the 1650s. It is very likely, though there is no extant documentation, that the next-door house, the Hôtel Boulin, is also built to Le Vau's design (Pierre Boulin and François Petit were brothers-in-law). Whether or not Le Vau designed the Hôtel de Balsac at the corner of the street that contains these two houses, it is certain that Villedo, the master mason, and Dublet, the master carpenter, had recognised the skills of the young architect and were prepared to work from his designs.

Louis Phélypeaux de La Vrillière was the secretary of state for the Reformed Church in France, with a great deal of responsibility in the Midi. He was associated through his daughter's marriage to the very rich intendant of the King's finances, Michel Particelli d'Hémery. These men were both appointed by Cardinal Richelieu. François Petit was the latter's personal assistant, and when the need arose for designs in La Vrillière's hôtel, opposite d'Hémery's and near the Hôtel Bautru, he recommended Le Vau. The architect of La Vrillière's mansion was François Mansart and one of the building contractors was Claude Dublet, whose associate, Jean Pastel, was made responsible in 1639, the date when Le Vau arrived on the site, for the interior arrangements of the living quarters.

Le Vau had already incorporated an alcove bedroom in the Hôtel Bautru and this feature of domestic design was something of a novelty in France. The first example of it is in François I's Château de Madrid in the Bois de Boulogne, built after his return from captivity in Spain in 1527 and developed until he died in 1547. It was also a feature of the Marquise de Rambouillet's house near the Louvre, installed not long before La Vrillière's house was being built. She had brought an appreciation of Spanish taste into French society – it was she who was the hostess of the influential intellectual salon held in her famous 'Blue Room'. Guillaume Bautru, Member of the French Academy and diplomat, and a frequenter of her salon, wanted an alcove for his mansion, and ordered it from Le Vau in 1636–37. Then one was ordered for the Luxembourg Palace, where Villedo was working. All the prominent French architects took up the idea in their projects – Lemercier, Le Muet, Mansart – and alcove bedrooms were all the rage; but the credit for this Spanish feature being incorporated into Parisian mansions via the route of Italian influence should be accorded to Le Vau. Le Vau's ability in the matter of interior planning in these mansions 'constituted one of the principal pillars of his professional success, inscribing him within the general context of the renewal of the arts of decoration in Paris'.[27]

* * *

In the inventories of La Vrillière's and his wife's property after their deaths in 1681 and 1682 respectively, this bedroom is described as *à l'italienne*. Such a room was also provided in the renovations at Louis Hesselin's newly acquired country house at Chantemèsle. Hesselin, a royal official on the edge of court life, knew Le Vau, and would confide the design of his *hôtel* on the Île Saint-Louis to him in 1640. These Italian bedrooms were designed on the basis of leaving out the ceiling so as to take the room right up into the roof, rounding off the spaces where the walls met that roof with rounded *voussures* (arched walls, in a section shaped as a quarter of a circle's circumference), based on salons in Italian palaces and villas. That is the characteristic of the rooms in La Vrillière's mansion and Hesselin's country house. Both the Italian bedrooms and the French alcoves appear as part of the young architect's repertoire. The effect was of a room both spectacular and decorative at the same time. Le Vau gave the officials and financiers what they wanted for their dwellings, proclaiming their wealth and success to all who were admitted inside.[28]

* * *

Le Vau was making his money out of modest bourgeois dwellings, but his reputation was made from designing prestigious mansions for the new rich who were constantly networking with one another. As the 1630s came to an end, Le Vau was asserting himself among his professional colleagues and was appreciated by the increasing number of his clients who understood his aspiration to participate in their social milieu. It does seem that Louis Le Vau admired what they had achieved for themselves and wanted to emulate it. In former times, a young man with no family money could rise through the ranks of the Church. That still happened, but now the professional route was also open to the talents, long before Bonaparte made it official.

Normally, to have the right to practise a profession that was in any way artistic and be paid for it, necessitated receiving a royal brevet, and this gave you the right to call yourself Painter, Sculptor, Architect in ordinary to the King. Yet, unlike François Mansart at his coming of age, Le Vau did not seem to possess such a document, though he names himself with the title on all contracts he made from 5 May 1638 onwards until 1654, when he acquired a different one. Was this merely ambitious bravado, or did he have some grounds for claiming the qualification? His close association through Villedo with Guillaume Bautru, who had the ear of Cardinal Richelieu, may have allowed him to make certain assumptions about his status upon which to capitalise.[29]

It was no use just being styled as an architect. Since there was no Academy of Architecture yet, there was no recognition as such for practitioners of the profession, so the role of entrepreneur had to go along with it. Le Vau had to be a businessman, handling his own affairs as well as being a consultant designer. By 1638, when he was regarded as having come of age, he was asserting his independence. He demonstrated this by leaving out the letter 'e' in his family name. The French dictionary published in 1680 by César-Pierre Richelet[30] relates that 'to play the calf' (*faire le veau*), used about a little boy or young man, meant 'to be a simpleton (*niais*) or a silly person (*sot*)'. If that was already the case, more than forty years before, no wonder his name was an embarrassment to someone who wanted to make a professional reputation for himself. 'Le Vau' would suggest a place name derived from the word for valley, and would cause no such problems. His brothers and sisters followed him in this change, and, after 1658, his father did so too. His signature on documents, surrounded by extravagant flourishes, underlines the point he had made. Le Vau was now a gentleman, like many a *parvenu* who was to be found in the ranks of the *nouveau riche* financiers who were to be his clients.

Father and son lived under the same roof: from 1637 in the quai Celestins. Then, from August 1639, they lived on the Île Saint-Louis, in what is now the rue Saint-Louis en l'Île.

On 22 July 1638 he had bought a building site at the end of the quai d'Anjou (at the time quai d'Alencon), an awkwardly shaped plot at a price he could afford, allowing him at some future time – not to be long delayed – to live next door to some of his richest clients. The artisans lived in the centre of the island but the quality on the quays.[31]

The next step of Le Vau's gentrification was to be an advantageous marriage, and a contract to this end was signed before a notary on 2 May 1639. His bride was Jeanne Laisné, whose father had been Marshal of the Duchess of Orleans's household: Marguerite of Lorraine, wife of Gaston d'Orleans, Louis XIII's brother. Jeanne brought with her a dowry that amounted to 11,000 livres, not exactly riches, but enough to give a good lift to the ambitious young man with his sights fixed on high.

Jeanne Laisné was an orphan, and her guardian was her uncle, Henri, abbé Laisné, and he held a variety of church appointments besides being attached to the parish of Saint Jean de Grève in which Le Vau had grown up. Jeanne lived in her uncle's house in the rue de la Tissanderie, not far away. One of Louis's witnesses at the signing of his marriage contract was the equivalent of a churchwarden in this parish, and one of his father's clients, Nicolas Pontheron, was also a prominent member of the congregation. The marriage was arranged within the social group to which the Le Veaus belonged, for which these *notables* provided leadership, and there were others, former clients of Louis *père*, of this higher social status, who acted as witnesses, among whom was Jean Blanchard. He was an established artist, representative of the milieu of artists and craftsmen found in this quarter of the capital and he appears to have been a close family friend. Louis Le Vau had begun his social ascension, but his parents' contacts had provided him with a reasonable launch pad. He had not exactly come from nowhere now that he was starting to be everywhere.

Other professional contacts for Louis Le Vau were established in contracts for the King. One was Guillaume Veniat, a cabinetmaker, who had been working on the royal furniture since 1631 and had built up a significant private clientele as a specialist in interior decoration. Another master cabinetmaker was Étienne Le Hongre, and Louis Le Vau was godfather to at least two of his children. This gifted woodcarver often worked with Le Vau on his projects, notably the doors for the carriage entrance at the Hôtel Hesselin (the only feature of the mansion that is still there). Another interior decoration specialist, especially for ceilings, Jean Cotelle, chose Louis Le Vau as a godfather. 'The links established with and around Le Vau point to a socio-professional milieu [which was] relatively narrow, but close and coherent.'[32]

* * *

This was a time in Paris when there was a quest for novelty in art and design and enough people with enough money to pay for buildings, for paintings and for sculpture in settings enhanced with stucco and carved woodwork. There was also enormous influence from across the Alps in Italy, particularly from Rome, whence architects from France including Jacques Lemercier had recently returned after a period of study there. Roland Fréart de Chambray, also returned from Italy, was involved in the process of making the Four Books of Architecture of the Venetian Andrea Palladio known in France under the benign influence of François Sublet de Noyers, who was Louis XIII's appointee as Superintendent of the King's Buildings until his retirement enforced by Mazarin in 1644.

Le Vau would read the Palladio volumes assiduously once they were available and he eventually had them in his own library. He was influenced by Italian taste from his reading and his appreciation of the beautiful plates that came with the books after 1650. The painter Nicolas Poussin returned from Rome, but he went back there as soon as he possibly could to maintain his influence from afar on his compatriots. It was a mark of success for the French financiers that they had a Poussin original on a wall somewhere. Of course, while the Italian Mazarin was prime minister during the regency of Anne of Austria and the very early years of Louis XIV, there was no doubt of this influence, but Mazarin had the good sense not to press too hard for Parisians to take to it.

Not only novelty, then, but Italian novelty, known in France as Baroque, a term derived from the Portuguese word for a deformed pearl, was being taken seriously by creative spirits in the Île de France. It was an extravagant style, rooted in the triumph of the Counter-Reformation in Italy and Spain. Louis Le Vau was part of this tendency, but he too had learned to be discreet about it.

* * *

Louis had three sisters, two called Marie, and Anne. One Marie was nearly blind, remained single and lived after her father died in her brother François's household – he married in 1658 and Louis *père* died in 1661. Anne married in 1642 at a time close to her mother's death in 1642. Her husband was a master mason, Charles Thoison, who lived in the parish of Sainte-Étienne du Mont, in the rue de la Bûcherie. The other Marie married a master carpenter, Étienne Monnard, in 1645. Louis's brother Antoine married Jeanne Cerizier, orphan daughter of a master spur manufacturer. The family all stayed together for a long time in the homes they shared on the Île Saint-Louis. By the end of 1641, Louis Le Vau and his father had finished building the home they would share on the quai d'Anjou and they all moved in, subsequently taking in Charles Thoison for three years when he married Anne, as agreed in the marriage contract. Louis's own children were born there. After Jeanne, who had arrived in the rue Saint-Louis-dans-l'Île in 1640, there was Marie-Marguerite, then Marie, then Nicolas. The girls had close relations for their godparents, but Nicolas was held over the font by Nicolas Lambert, master in ordinary to the Chambre des comptes in Paris, the brother and heir of Jean-Baptiste Lambert, for whom Louis Le Vau was building the Hôtel Lambert next door to his own home. What does that tell us?

Antoine seems to have been the only Le Vau brother to have been content with that state in life unto which it had pleased God to call him (the great brake on social mobility in near-contemporary England expressed in the 1662 Prayer Book Catechism!). He remained a companion mason and moved away from the rest of his socially ambitious relations to live in the Faubourg Saint-Antoine, not involved in the professional activities of his brothers or brothers-in-law.

Louis *père* has '*honorable homme*' before his name in the estimates and contracts that he signed after 1637, which was the usual designation for his rank. Louis *fils*, however, in the documents he signed, has an upward progression of qualities. In 1639 he had the ambiguous word '*sieur*' before his name, no more than Mr., perhaps. Then in 1641, he was '*maître*', denoting a step up in the social order. When a notary wrote '*honorable homme*' on a particular document in March 1641, he changed it himself, in his own hand, to '*maître*', appropriate to the rank above. From May of the same year onwards he was designated as '*noble homme*', strangely the highest rank possible for anyone not actually from the nobility, but behaving as though he were.[33] He lived in a fashionable house, he wore elegant clothes, and he possibly owned a carriage and horses. Louis Le Vau had become what we used to call a self-made man.

Chapter 2

The Architect and his Clients

From a young age, Louis Le Vau collected his clients from among the class of financiers and officers of state who had gathered around the royal court that settled in Paris or the Île de France after Henri IV brought the wars of religion to an end. With the monarch established in the Louvre or not far away at Saint-Germain-en-Laye or Fontainebleau, the financiers and higher officials of the state needed to live near the unique centre of power. It was they who financed the urbanisation for which those named as architects to the king, like François Mansart and Louis Le Vau, designed town houses (*hôtels particuliers*) within the city limits or manor houses (chateaux) in the adjacent countryside for them to live in.

These clients were often from the new class of financiers who became prominent during the wartime conditions of the reign of Louis XIII under the aegis of the minister Cardinal Richelieu, whose collaborators were a prestigious team, men like Nicolas Colbert, father of Louis XIV's future alter ego.[1] The royal treasury was the conduit for between a third and a half of all the money in circulation within France. The sum involved was more than an eighth of the French national product and the management of it was a mammoth task since the arms dealers and other creditors of the state had to be paid in gold or silver coin. The financiers of the state became a socio-economic (or perhaps socio-political) grouping composed of a limited number of specialists whose main function was to collect the urgently needed revenues at a time of international conflict. Their function 'placed them, in the monetary and economic system alike, at the centre of the State'.[2]

They were private individuals who acted as agents uniquely for the King. They were known as 'projectors' because they proposed new ways of selling salt, or of state offices, or of paying wages to the *trésoriers de France*. An alternative activity for them was to take up the farm of indirect taxes and, having paid the sums due to the King, became entitled to a portion of the profit they gained from transactions during the time that the money from *gabelles, aides* and so on was in their possession.

Some acted in accordance with 'treaties' that they negotiated with the royal council. These were called *traitants*. They collected the land tax (*taille*) or a loan due to the crown or taxes on individual offices in a designated region. There were a large number of these deals struck in the years 1630 to 1646, during which there was hidden or open warfare when such expedients were required.

Other financiers were lenders (*prêteurs*) who advanced huge sums to the state for major operations such as recruiting Swedish and Dutch allies or building warships. They counted upon having their money back in due course from sources that the treasury designated. This spent the revenues of the state before they were received but the financiers were eventually enriched by the process. This new financial class was made up mostly of French nationals who replaced the Italian bankers of Lyon.

'They were all rich but, albeit with some exceptions, they were not amongst the very rich. Their origins were often quite lowly, sometimes fairly modest; so they took it upon themselves to acquire letters of personal nobility as a step towards hereditary nobility. Such social ascension rendered them detested and sometimes discriminated against. Yet they were as essential to the functioning of the monarchical system as the king's armies. They provided the means whereby it could function efficiently and thus overawe its neighbours.'[3]

This system of state finance was developed under Richelieu's successors, Mazarin and then Colbert, and carried over as the basis for administration into peacetime after 1659.

How did the system work? After the amount of tax to be raised on a given commodity had been decided upon in Council, the right to collect it was put up for auction in each generality. The time taken to complete the procedure varied from region to region, depending on how many bidders presented themselves, and whether the taxable commodities had reached their point of distribution.[4]

The holders (*titulaires*) of farms emerged from the processes of the auctions and the majority of them made no bid at all unless they were confident of being successful. Some made use of borrowed names to conceal their identities as they made their bid and it was acceptable that a good number of the holders had made successful bids for more than one or even several farms. More than 64 per cent of *titulaires* were resident in Paris, the remainder coming from places relatively remote from the capital.[5] So to be a holder of a tax farm meant you were probably a bourgeois who owned, or came to own, a domicile within the increasingly urbanised zone of Paris. The aristocracy were already established in the Faubourg Saint-Germain, so the developing areas were principally the Marais or the Île Saint-Louis, where investors such as Christophe Marie at first, and Louis Le Vau later on, understood what their speculating clients wanted and shared their ambitions. These speculators wanted town mansions that to some extent concealed their wealth from passers-by in the street but flaunted it indoors with lavish decorations and ornaments in order to give confidence about their substantial finances when their customers were invited indoors.

The leaseholders of farms were given guarantees (*cautions*), sometimes by more than one person. They often sought the security of having someone who would offer proof of the transaction at the auction (*certificateur*). So there was a hierarchy among the financiers and some holders of farms had more weight than others, depending upon how long the leases were intended to last, although only a few leases were intended to last for more than twenty years. This meant that a lease could be profitable in financial terms for its holder during the time that it was held, and guarantors were found for them, sometimes in association with other leaseholders.[6]

* * *

We can regard the fledgeling years of Le Vau as architect to be defined as extending between 1634, when he designed the Hôtel Bautru, until 1644, when his designs for the Hôtels of Jean Tambonnier, Antoine Boyer, and François Luillier were implemented in the area of the Pré-des-Clercs at the western end of the Faubourg Saint-Germain, henceforth to be the rue de la Université on the left bank of the Seine, sold off directly to these individual financiers by the University just previously. Tambonneau was Président of the *Chambre des comptes de Paris*, a leading *parlementaire* and 'the largest money-lender of the tax-farmers',[7] who, on 31 August 1639, bought 7,500 sq m to build two mansions, a large one for himself and a smaller one attached, together with two other plots nearby on which to build houses for his Boyer and Luillier relations, who were dependent upon him. The construction of these was commissioned from Charles Thoison, Le Vau's sister's husband, and Claude Dublet, with Le Vau himself as the financial guarantor, on the basis of Louis XIII's letters patent of 13 June 1642.

None of these buildings still exists. Tambonneau's houses were demolished when the rue de Pré-des-clercs was pierced in 1844, but Jean Marot's print from around 1664 demonstrates the maturity of Le Vau's concept for them.[8] This one was built around a large rectangular court bordered on the side of the street with a wall made up of linked partitions with central, double carriage doors surmounted with a balustrade. On either side of the court there were nine arcades containing windows on the ground floor; on the left-hand side there is a first floor and high roofs with chimneys, but no such thing on the right, where, after the wall behind, is the small house's *basse cour*. The residential part of the large house spans the rear of the court. It has a double depth of rooms and the central portion, with its triple arcade, projected forward – a device known as *avant corps*. The roof was large with a higher section in the middle with a triangular *fronton* before it, with the top of the wall issuing in balustrades. The roof itself is of the type known as 'broken eaves' (*combles brisés*). The attic space has six round lights (*lucarnes*), and the central portion has a round window light (*œil de bœuf*). Features of these houses would be repeated in the later buildings of Le Vau's *œuvre*.[9]

* * *

Jacques Bordier was one of Le Vau's clients, a typical financier. His origins were humble, like those of many of the financiers. His father manufactured candles in the Place Maubert,[10] but we find him later on with a portrait of the queen on the wall of his house in the rue Royale,[11] and the king visited the chateau at Raincy, which he commissioned from Le Vau in 1648.[12] Along with three others, he obtained one of four new offices of Intendant of finances during the regency of Anne of Austria in 1649 at the price of a million livres, for which he took his time over settling the payment. Hence he became a royal office holder,[13] while remaining active in commerce and urban construction.[14] He had a bathroom, the ultimate luxury, at Raincy,[15] and another indication of opulence there was his stock of bed linen recorded in 1652.[16]

He had married Catherine Lybault in 1614 and thereby attached himself to a family of notaries well settled in the capital, who were members of a circle of connoisseurs of fine art, financiers and investors, all providers of state loans and guarantees, the Macquarts, the Quentins and the Margonnes. In 1624 Bordier had become deputy to Antoine Feydeau, who held the two largest tax farms in France, those of the *aides* and the *gabelles*, lived sumptuously in his chateau at Bois-le-Vicomte, and had a picture gallery that was universally admired. Bordier wanted nothing more than to follow the example of Feydeau's way of life and set out to do so.

The most important outward and visible sign of Bordier's wealth was his own collection of fine art exhibited in his town house, and what is now 10 rue du Parc Royal is typical of the *hôtels particuliers* that were built from the time of Louis XIII onwards in the Marais and on the Île Saint-Louis. He bought the house from Charles Margonne on 30 March 1628 as a way of signalling to others that he had arrived in the world of high finance. It had been built in 1618 by the architect Thiriot for Margonne with the living area between the court and the garden and two wings enclosing the court: a model Le Vau would use for town houses he would build for his other clients, like Tambonneau. Le Vau was commissioned to enlarge Bordier's house in 1642–43, modify the wings, add a large staircase, a chapel, and a small bathroom. The staircase is particularly notable for the ironwork, which serves both as a guard rail (*garde corps*) and banisters (*rampe*). It is elaborately wrought, intricate and sturdy.[17] His work there lasted until 1648 but he was never troubled about taking on several projects at the same time. A great salon was provided, together with a spacious bedroom. Bordier had expensive furniture installed: ebony Chinese cabinets, Venetian mirrors, Turkish carpets, and luxurious tapestries for the walls. Wall paintings by contemporary big names were added above the interior doors. There was panelling with *grisaille* paintings, and lavish bases for the lamps. Le Vau's activities on the Île Saint-Louis also had Bordier's financial support.

Louis Le Vau's rise as a successful architect, from the mid-1630s to his first commission for a chateau given him by Bordier, shows that he was working for a whole range of clients, from artisans who occupied his apartment buildings in the rue de l'Île Saint-Louis to the bourgeois businessmen, holders of royal offices, king's secretaries, and members of tax or accounting jurisdictions. Le Vau's clients were neither nobles nor ecclesiastics.

So, at the same time as the Fronde against Mazarin was fomenting – the summer of 1643 – Le Vau accepted the commission at Le Raincy in the village of Livry-en-Brie, to the north-east of Paris, which Bordier had acquired in 1639. This was to be a magnificent house completed in 1645 and designated as a chateau in 1660. Members of the nobility detested this type of *parvenu* who had qualified as a lawyer, obtained employment from the *Parlement* as such, then undertaken business ventures and bought the office of King's secretary, which for many like him, turned out to be the first step towards becoming a member of the *noblesse de robe*. Bordier had grown rich as a result of lending money to the crown, and made himself accepted after shouldering his way in as secretary to the Council of state and finances.

The building site was in operation by the end of August 1643, when Bordier signed the contract for the provision of large stone blocks for walls and for flights of steps. Then, in the following February, he took on the master carpenter from Sucy-en-Brie for all the woodwork that was going to be necessary: a large-scale contract considering all the load-bearing timber that would be needed. Le Vau is designated in the contract as being in charge of the entire works, with his assumed title as Architect in ordinary to the King. By June 1645 there was a contract for making the locks and keys. The boy king and his court paid two visits for the inauguration of the house on 2 and 24 August 1648 (at the same time as the Frondeurs were beginning their revolt), the second time accompanied by Anne of Austria at a banquet that Bordier offered them. It is worth noting that the second of these occasions preceded the Days of the Barricades in Paris[18] by a mere two days.

The works were certified as complete in a document dated 6 August 1651, on which the name of Michel Villedo appears as site manager. It took so long to complete the project because it was conceived on a vast scale, with gardens that were not finished even ten years later, and massive projects of interior decoration in the hands of François Perrier until he died in 1649.

The appearance of the chateau is known from contemporary engravings – particularly those by Israël Silvestre and Jean Marot – an inventory drawn up when Bordier's wife died in 1653, and descriptions made in the following century, as presented Alexander Cojannot's lavish book on Le Vau's early years published in 2012, copiously referenced from the central collection of notaries' minutes kept under his direction at the *Archives nationales*.

There was a great court laid out in front of a rectangular platform and its counter-scarps were topped off with balustrades; the principal entrance was a portal between two pillars decorated with *termes* and trophies, the work of Philippe de Buyster. There were pavilions at the corners of the building, linked to this portal by low walls, which left the house with a frontage 60m wide. The ground floor of the central pavilion was taken up by an oval vestibule that, when repeated at Vaux-le-Vicomte, would become a characteristic of Le Vau's buildings. It was decorated by Gérard van Obstal with a ceiling supported by thirty-six Doric columns. A flight of steps to the left of the vestibule led to the great staircase, with three flights leading to the salon above following its proportions. There was a view over Le Nôtre's gardens at the rear of the building. On the other side of the oval from the staircase was the 'Italian' bedroom.

The interior decoration was François Perrier's work with bas-reliefs made from stucco on the theme of the story of Medea set in seventeen compartments between the pilasters. In the 'Italian' bedroom also, Perrier was responsible for the fresco of bacchic, festive, open-air scenes. Carrara marble sculptures by Jacques Sarrazin were placed on the floor of the salon. The vaults in the cupola's roof were painted by Perrier, who also painted Venus in her chariot preceded by the graces and some cupids (always called '*amours*' in French), for the great bedroom on the first floor.[19]

Both in Bordier's house in the Marais and in the chateau, there were collections of easel paintings inventoried when his relations sold his properties after his death. The best pieces in the collections are paintings and sculptures by Jacques Sarrazin exhibited in the Louvre after the destruction of Raincy in 1807, and a painting by Valentin de Boulogne of the Four Ages of Man now in the National Gallery in London. In the salon at Raincy there were portraits of Louis XIII and Anne of Austria by Perrier, who also collaborated with Le Vau and Le Sueur at the Hôtel Lambert.[20] Then there were his laurel bushes, and his library of 1,054 books whose titles are unknown and a further 925, expensively bound, with titles ranging from theology to history and global exploration listed in his inventory. There was a private chapel under the authorisation of the diocesan bishop, and endowments for requiems to be said.[21]

It is no wonder then, that on 12 August 1647, a year before the inauguration, all this magnificent opulence – the measure of the wealth of its owner – provoked a fierce protest just before the outbreak of the Fronde. The Viscount of Fontrailles, one of the Fronde's also-ran leaders, came to Le Raincy with a handful of other landowners who resented this bourgeois upstart's prominence and set about breaking all the newly installed windows. They admired the building and its setting well enough, but it was the ambitions of its proprietor that enraged them.[22]

Le Vau's buildings were usually showcases for the visual arts. He provided them for this new class of office holders and financiers out of his own contacts with the artists themselves, thus managing to provide his clients with the good taste they were demanding. It may have been new money, but it bought artefacts that satisfied educated and sophisticated tastes, which means that Le Vau had acquired these tastes for himself as well.

* * *

Jean-Baptiste Lambert was another of the earlier patrons of Louis Le Vau as an architect. His father was President of Accounts, then secretary to the King and ennobled in 1642. Jean-Baptiste emerged from under the tutelage of Claude de Bullion, Superintendent of Finances, after ten years working for Bullion's agent, Gaspard de Fieubet, whose house was on the quai des Célestins, opposite the Île Saint-Louis on the right bank, near the Le Veaus' house. De Bullion entrusted a portfolio of 26 million livres of his savings to Lambert to administer for him, and Lambert managed to accrue his own fortune, estimated at his death in 1644 at 4 million livres.[23]

It is worth glancing at de Bullion as a patron of the contemporary artistic scene before we go any further because he sets the tone for the commissions being considered in this chapter. Françoise Bayard's presentation of the indications of the wealth of these financiers allows the measure of this man's fortune to appear. Like Bordier, he had pictures by Jacques Sarrazin. His collection of curiosities had a value of 20,000 livres. He owned expensive tapestries and displayed them in his house in the rue Plastrière. He owned 221 tablecloths, and 256 dozen napkins valued at 5,067 livres, while his kitchen linen was worth 82 livres. At his death, his estate was valued at 7,826,864 livres.[24] He had donated 10,000 livres to Catholic charitable causes.[25]

For Lambert then, de Bullion was a man to be emulated and he set out to do so when he made his contract with Louis Le Vau for the construction of his *hôtel* on the eastern end of the Île Saint-Louis. Jean-Baptiste Lambert de Thorigny was an assistant to the *Trésorier de l'Épargne*. He was one of the 'new men, the thirty-somethings to whom everything seemed possible'.[26] He offered an example to the ambitious Louis Le Vau. Lambert had gained a great deal from his uncle, Jean Guillemeau, who was a King's secretary, but he had built his own fortune too. In 1645, shortly after his death, the doctor who had attended him noted that he had three sources of wealth: his employment by Bullion, his being assistant to Treasurer Fieubet for eighteen years, and from his household management, only having had his mansion on the Île Saint-Louis since the Easter before he died.[27] However, he had ploughed his own furrow as well, buying the offices of King's councillor and secretary to the King in 1636, and then he bought the lordship of Thorigny-sur-Oreuse in 1641, thus establishing himself among the nobility. He was one of the speculators in the new building sites on the Île Saint-Louis at the same time, for his own *hôtel particulier* and several houses to rent out. He had just installed himself in the former when he died in December 1644 aged only thirty-nine, leaving all to his brother Nicolas Lambert de Thorigny.

For Le Vau, acquiring a substantial property on the *île* was a step similar to leaving out the second letter of his father's name. It gave him the status he needed to be on look-me-in-the-eye terms with his clients. His property was to go up alongside the Hôtel Lambert and at the same time, with him ordering the same materials, incorporating the same ground plan by the length of a wrought-iron balcony of identical design. Originally, it is suggested, Le Vau's house had colossal orders similar to those on the garden facade of Lambert's. His part of the building, the three bays on the quai d'Anjou, has been modified by subsequent proprietors and the original connection is no longer obvious.[28]

Le Vau's own next acquisition underlined his association with Lambert. Since the financier had bought the lordship of Sucy-en-Brie near Créteil, it was appropriate for Le Vau to have a country house there and he bought one in 1640. He had intended to buy a house at Neuilly-sur-Seine, but that deal fell through and he bought a small estate at Brévannes in the parish of Limay instead, and this was very near Sucy. Michel Villedo had had a property in the same village until 1646, which may have influenced Le Vau's decision to buy Brévannes. Villedo had a son, also Michel, who had married Anne, daughter of René Mignon, and Le Vau's daughter Louise had married Anne's brother Jacques Mignon, so there was some kind of marriage tie between the two families.[29]

Jean-Baptiste Lambert's house at Sucy was nothing remarkable, and it was improved by Le Vau on Nicolas Lambert's instructions only in 1660. However, Jean-Baptiste enlarged the park that went with the property, which involved him in disputes with the villagers because the walls he wanted in order to make the park private involved the destruction of some public fountains. Le Vau was commissioned to prepare the terrain with avenues and provide these walls.

Brévannes, like Sucy, was a proper manor house, with stables and other outbuildings and extensive gardens, so Le Vau had become gentry, though there is no suggestion that he bought a title to go with it – that was saved for later when he bought the lordship of Beaumont-la-Ferrière in the Nivernais. He added some agricultural land to his manor after another two years, so he was an employer as well as a man of substance. Pierre Dupré managed the farmland and livestock belonging to Lambert and Le Vau together. Le Vau made frequent use of Brévannes, especially towards the end of his life.[30]

This upward social mobility was to continue according to his ambition. He was a thruster with an eye to the main chance. He shared the values that he seemed to admire in people like Bordier and Lambert, the new men of the reign of Louis XIII and of Anne of Austria's regency. He had the land and the houses: now he needed the rank that came from office holding. For that, you did not wait to be appointed: you saw the opportunity and you paid good money for it. At the end of 1642 he installed his extended family in his house next door to Lambert's in the quai d'Anjou. He had arrived among the Parisian notables: owner of a capacious town house, a *manoir* in the Brie countryside, and several houses to let on the Île Saint-Louis. In 1644 he bought – for 25,000 livres – the office of councillor and secretary to the King, following what Lambert had done in 1636. That price was worth paying to fulfil his ambition and he managed to afford it.

There were all sorts of responsibilities involved in being one of the secretaries to the King in terms of tax privileges as well as social prestige attached to the office. If a King's secretary had held his office for twenty years, his son could inherit it upon his death. Le Vau did not fulfil the functions of his office, but what was important was that he held it as if it were another property, as indeed it was. Furthermore, he tended to dissociate his office as architect in ordinary to the King, which was carried as a personal title for his professional doings, from his public rank as secretary to the King, which was official and carried prestige with it.[31]

Le Vau bought the building plot that was to contain his own *hôtel* and Lambert's in the north-east corner of the Île Saint-Louis on 22 July 1638, when he was only twenty-six. The sellers were Christophe Marie and François Le Regattier, the original developers of the island. It was an awkward, triangular site of 30 *toises*, whereas most of the others up for sale were square or rectilinear. His own site was the upper part of the triangle with its entrance on the quai d'Alençon (now quai d'Anjou) and then Lambert bought the rest of the site between Le Vau's plot and the rue de l'Île Saint-Louis from him on 21 February 1639, thus providing him with some necessary funds to begin building. By July 1640, the foundations of both houses were in place and a party wall was raised between them. Le Vau's house was finished and he moved his family in on 12 December 1641, as a notary's deed confirms.[32]

Le Vau gained a certain reputation for solving the problems posed by awkwardly shaped sites. For his own section of this one he provided three facades with two 'elbows' between them on the riverside front, which still exist in spite of the complete transformation of the building in the eighteenth century, The construction contract[33] provides for four square floors and an attic above cellar level behind the middle facade. Le Vau arranged a sort of lookout in this attic space to the advantage of the views over the countryside across the river. His family's accommodation was to be on the second floor and an apartment to be rented out was on the first, the two living spaces having separate entrances. The architect and the speculator, since Le Vau was both, were in agreement on this decision. The most important aspect of his plan is that his house and Lambert's were conceived as a single entity, with the possibility that Lambert might have eventually decided to amalgamate the two buildings into one for himself, thereby providing Le Vau with extra working capital for other projects.

The contract says that the colossal pilasters – which were decorative and not part of the construction – should be made of mortar covered in plaster. Extracting and transporting finished stone blocks from the quarries around Paris was very expensive and, for his own house, Le Vau cut costs by using cheaper materials. There was a royal edict preventing the use of bare wood in order to avoid fire risk, and plaster had been used since the Middle Ages to protect timber from the effects of weather. Nevertheless, rain water would crack the plaster and shorten the life of the constructions. Cyril Bordier suggests that this is what happened in the case of Le Vau's house and why its frontage was replaced with stone after a comparatively short time. The owner of the Hôtel Lambert in 1747, Martin de la Haye, acquired Le Vau's house and made many alterations. Others were made subsequently.[34]

When we come to examine the Hôtel Lambert itself, we see how Le Vau made economic use of the space available on the curiously shaped site. To look at the house from the rue de l'Île de Saint-Louis, its monumental coach entrance gives no idea of what will be found beyond it. Anthony Blunt gave a very clear account of what a visitor might find. Once past the entrance, he would be in the court looking straight at the curved far end that contains the staircase. Le Vau set two wings on the side of this court with sets pf private rooms on the first floor. Both are approached from the great staircase, the one on the left by a hexagonal antechamber and the one on the right by an oval vestibule, which past, gives a view over the garden to the Seine. If the visitor had not turned right after the oval vestibule but gone straight on, he would be in the long gallery, which ended in an apse giving directly on to the river, with windows at the side that looked onto the garden. On the left at the end was the door to the chapel. These arrangements gave Le Vau 'the opportunity for a brilliant and dramatic disposition of the staircase and gallery'.

Since this is not a coffee table book and access to illustrations is limited, it is good to be able to rely upon Blunt's word picture of Le Vau's innovative staircase:

> The staircase is a highly personal invention, conceived on almost theatrical principles entirely opposed to those applied by [François] Mansart in his staircase at Maisons. There the visitor realises at first glance the whole plan and spacing of the staircase; at the Hôtel Lambert these are only gradually revealed as he goes up the steps, encountering as he does so a series of surprises. After going up a few steps from the court the staircase divides into two flights, of which that on the left leads only to the lower of the two main floors, while that on the right, after taking the visitor to this level, doubles back and leads him to the upper floor. Gradually, as he goes up this second stage, he moves from the narrow, confined flight into the main cage of the staircase, three times the width of the flight, lit by big windows on the next floor and continued upwards past a gallery through the whole height of the building. The effect of emerging from a dark tunnel into a well-lit open space is deliberately prepared and elaborately carried out in an almost Baroque spirit. However, this is not the end, because as the visitor turns on to the upper landing he will see – if the door is open – a long vista through the oval vestibule, along the gallery and out on the river landscape beyond. This is the kind of dramatic effect of which Le Vau is the master.[35]

Cyril Bordier points out that:

> Le Vau moves the main buildings to the side of the court and raises it to the first floor level: on one side, the house overlooks the court and on the other side is level with the garden. So the combination is achieved by positioning the different buildings vertically above each other and breaking away from the axis. On the ground floor, in the court, the

kitchens are to the right and the service area to the left. On the first floor, to the right and on the same level as the garden, are the formal apartments and, to the left, the private ones ... Stabling and a secondary court are situated underneath the gallery and ... direct access to the quai d'Alençon is gained.[36]

This staircase pavilion in its innovative quality is derived from Andrea Palladio: Le Vau's inspiration, which he had recently discovered in the engravings in *The Four Books of Architecture*. In the middle of the pavilion is the embryonic appearance of the triple arcading that will become one of his trademarks in other commissions. Here it is somewhat lost under the unifying classical cornice that serves to hold the whole building together.

An important derived innovative feature is to be seen at the Hôtel Lambert: Le Vau's decision to raise the whole garden to the level of the first floor with only three steps down from the formal apartment to enter it. The construction of the suspended garden at the Hôtel Petit-Luxembourg (17 rue Vaugirard), built several weeks before, had been entrusted to a group of building experts, one of whom was Le Vau's associate, Michel Villedo. The main feature of the ground floor over there was that the garden could be entered directly from the salon, the alcove bedroom and the winter bedroom that, on three sides, surrounded it. 'The transformation of the Hôtel Petit-Luxembourg was without any doubt a veritable event in Parisian architecture ... an idea of an originality too exceptional to remain unappreciated.'[37]

At the Hôtel Lambert, Le Vau conceived the garden as an independent unit of space in architectural terms: the colossal Ionic pilasters surrounding the garden at the Petit-Luxembourg were only painted decoration, but at the Hôtel Lambert they are an integral feature pointing to the difference between the walls of the garden and those of the court on the garden side; the gallery wall with its colossal pilasters defines the limits of the garden rather than of the gallery, and the garden is incorporated into the building as a whole, not merely an adjunct to it. The novelty of this is that the garden corresponds to the structure of the buildings surrounding the terrace of the island above its embankments and the inverted image of it in the mirror of the Seine. So, if we take the ground level of the island above the embankment as the first terrace, the garden becomes the second and the house itself the third, especially since there is no raised roof. The building is thus related to the environment, which became another distinctive feature of Le Vau's buildings whereby living and recreational space complemented each other.[38]

There is also innovation in the roofing on Lambert's house. The building which contains the porch and staircase and the two wings in the court has high-pitched roofs in French style, but on the garden side, the roof is low-pitched, more Italianate.[39] There is also another first time use here of what is known in England as the French window, a window that is also a double door. A iron balcony, soon to become fashionable, was also a recent invention.

'Closed with a half-moon, these galleries enjoy the possibility of access to pleasing views, both out to the garden and the Seine. The Hôtel Lambert otherwise played an important role in the history of interior decoration. Arching ceilings (*voussures*) and painted decorations characteristic of rooms "*à l'italienne*" make their first appearance.'[40]

Le Vau was eager to challenge accepted tradition in his buildings. For the purposes of an attempt at a continuous account of his life, we can see at the eastern tip of the Île Saint-Louis evidence of his own personal evolution as he follows in the steps of the financier Jean-Baptiste Lambert – his character as a speculator taking risks and the boldness of his architectural ideas. This leads him from the urbanisation he carried out on green sites to what he would achieve later at Vaux-le-Vicomte, at Versailles, at the College of the Four Nations and at the Louvre, where his patrons were no longer bourgeois chancers but Cardinal Mazarin, the minister whose chances seemed to have already paid off, Jean-Baptiste Colbert, and then the King himself, whose main public preoccupation was his monarchy's unique grandeur.

We cannot leave the Hôtel Lambert without remarking upon the artistic splendour of its various rooms. Anthony Blunt can still be our guide. The decorations of the *Cabinet d'Amour* have been moved to the Louvre but there remains an engraving by Bernard Picart.[41] The walls were divided into dado and frieze, with the former decorated by painted panels by Pierre Patel, Herman van Swanevelt, and Jan Asselyn, and the latter with mythological subjects by François Perrier, Giovanni Francesco Romanelli and Eustache Le Sueur, who also painted the panels for the ceiling. There was also the *Cabinet des Muses*, with more works from Perrier and Le Sueur.

But 'the finest room of the period to survive' is the gallery.[42] The walls are decorated with reliefs in stucco, coloured bronze and gold by Gérard van Obstal representing the Labours of Hercules, and these reliefs alternate with landscape paintings by Jacques Rousseau. Charles Le Brun was entrusted with the ceiling, also on the theme of Hercules, 'which was in its time the most ambitious piece of Baroque illusionism to be executed in France'.

A great deal depends upon Blunt's word 'presumably' when he asserts that Le Vau was 'the controlling mind behind this magnificent scheme'.[43] The assembly of such talent in his building by an architect who was not long out of his twenties is astonishing, even if he was working in close co-operation with his knowledgeable client and colleagues with their reputations as artists already established.

* * *

A third client who demands our attention in relation to the architect he chose for his house is Louis Hesselin, although he does not fit in the same categories as Bordier or Lambert, except for being wealthy. He had a great reputation as an art collector whose property on the Île Saint-Louis was as remarkable for its exterior as its indoors. He had refined tastes and specialised in the production of performances of ballets and *divertissements*, so much in vogue at the time. There was never any question of him being included among the financiers. He came from an established, armigerous family, the Cauchons, who originated in the Champagne region, first mentioned as living in Paris in 1297. (One cannot resist asking whether one of these Cauchons was the Bishop of Beauvais who presided at Joan of Arc's trial in Rouen in 1431.)

His father was Pierre Cauchon, *seigneur* of Condé, auditor of the *chambre des comptes*, who died in 1614. His godfather was Louis Cauchon's great-uncle, his grandmother's bachelor brother, who treated him as his son and left him his fortune by his will of 18 August 1620 on condition that he assumed his family name. He signed himself as Hesselin on a document in 1623, but the change was not made official until royal letters patent signed on 1 December were registered in the *Parlement* in the same month as his appointment as *Maître de la chambre aux deniers*. This meant that, in rotation with two others of the same rank, he was retained at court with the specific occupation of settling the King's catering bills out of public funds. He was not caught sight of again until 6 July 1634, when he signed his cousin's marriage contract at Reims, adding his title as *conselleur au roi, maître d'hôtel ordinaire du roi et maître de sa Chambre aux deniers*.

Having inherited a large fortune, he spent a good deal of it on his collection of curiosities, and took part in the purchase of building land on the Île Saint-Louis in about 1638, along with Thomas de Comans, sieur d'Astry and Nicolas de Sainctot, who would become his neighbours. In 1641, he commissioned Le Vau to prepare designs for a house on the corner of the quai du Dauphin as it was then called and the rue Poulettier (24 quai de Béthune), and it was ready for him to occupy five years later, a showcase for works by the sculptors Étienne Le Hongre, Gilles Guérin, Jacques Blanchard and Gérard van Obstal and the painters Simon Vouet, Charles Le Brun, Eustache Le Sueur and Jacques Sarrazin – all of them prominent in the artistic world of the young Louis XIV.

It was an innovative building in its own right. The owners of the building plots on the river embankment agreed to leave the other side of their plots open to provide a good view towards the west over more than 130m.[44] Le Vau intended to make the most of Hesselin's site being at a street corner. He was creating two hôtels at the same time, one for Hesselin, on the corner, and another for Sainctot next door. Since Le Vau's building was condemned as too dilapidated to repair in 1932 and was replaced for an American proprietor with a new design by Louis Süe, an engraving from 1684 by Jean Marot helps us to appreciate the quality of Le Vau's conception of the two buildings.[45] Both are planned on three floors with an attic, and in between them is the perfect square facade of the entrance to Hesselin's. There are three separate roofs, not identical but deliberately similar, and the roof over the front door is without ornament on the exterior, as opposed to the two over the attics that have three lucarnes. Two plain friezes unite the three buildings, the lower one under the first floor windows having balconies. Only the middle building has what could be taken for colossal pilasters uniting the storeys, but they are not really pilasters and they are the only parts of the facade to have *refonds*. The window frames on the two buildings are deliberately a little different so as to prevent the larger Hesselin from overwhelming the smaller Sainctot.

The great double door, with its woodcarving by Le Hongre – the only feature preserved in the rebuilding – led to the court, which was entered by means of a vestibule giving on to it, decorated by Gilles Guérin with eight termes – figures mounted on plinths[46] – and a sculpture of Atlas whose globe recorded the passage of the hours of the day (Guérin had been trained by the sculptor Nicolas Le Brun, Charles Le Brun's father[47]). There were mirrors – the imported luxury items par excellence forty years before they were produced in France for the Hall of Mirrors at Versailles – reflected the columns and the staircase. On the ground floor, an apartment looked out on to the rue Poulettier but the dining room and the salon took their light from the river front. Works by van Obstal and more by Guérin decorated the salon, including the chimney piece bas-reliefs and paintings. A bedroom in Italian style, as usual taking up two floors, was full of more mirrors, pieces of porcelain, and paintings by the same artists, based on drawings by Jacques Sarrazin.

The rectangular court ended in a rounded structure filled with niches and then there was the garden flanked by the rue Poulletier on one side and the *basse-cour* and the stabling on the other. Above the inside of the entrance there was a sculpted bas-relief nearly 3m square taking up the whole space of the first floor in the newly established tradition of either using moulds of antique models brought from Italy[48] or creating new ones on classical themes. Here it is the latter where Gilles Guérin created a relief with sixteen figures about 2ft high that represent Apollo on Parnassus with the muses of sculpture, painting and architecture as well as Homer and Virgil. The work can be seen from a distance on Jean Marot's seventeenth-century engraving but the details are given in Henri Sauval's later description of the interior of Hesselin's house.

Sauval gives us other details as well, such as of Guérin's figure of Atlas, which 'enriched' the vestibule and had a 'very crafty' (*artificielle*) clock, as did more bas-reliefs, this time by Jacques Blanchard. The light from the lantern was reflected in the mirrors on the walls, as was the double staircase. The great salon had a painted ceiling, also the work of Blanchard and Guido Reni, but it was Gilles Guérin again who placed bas-reliefs of two angels, a Venus with Cupid, and a Bacchus with a Satyr, all in plaster, and two other satyrs in stone, on the chimney piece. The middle of the mantel was decorated with another bas-relief, this time by Gérard van Obstal.

The room 'in Italian style' was lit by windows on two storeys, and the pillars of what would have been upstairs, had there been a floor, framed Italian paintings. The cornice has large porcelain vases upon it and, at ground-floor level, the decorations would have cost 30,000 livres, says Sauval. The mantelpiece above the fireplace had two vestal virgins 'of very considerable beauty' standing on it. They were executed by Guérin and van Obstal to a design of Jacques Sarrazin. Charles Le Brun painted the walls of one of the bedrooms, and Le Sueur the chapel, in a way that suggested that Hesselin wanted this house to be his own masterpiece.[49]

The inner court was surmounted by a frontal curved inwards with balustrades and full-centred arcading.[50] This presented an advantage: residents and guests could dismount from their horses or descend from their carriages under cover at the foot of the staircase, since their living accommodation was on the first floor and the entrance was underneath it. The young Le Vau was the first to make use of this system in the houses he built for Nicolas de Sainctot and Thomas Comans d'Astry in the years 1643 to 1647, where the passages bulge out into the shape of the oval vestibule in front of the staircase, an idea imported from Italy.[51]

* * *

Hesselin owned a country estate 6 miles from Troyes, where he commissioned the chateau of Saint-Sépulchre from Le Vau that is represented in another engraving by Jean Marot. It was raised on the usual plan for such a building, with large living areas, joined by two wings to two pavilions by a curved wall attached to a great entrance, such as we shall see again on Mazarin's College ten years later. The semicircular jointure was in François Mansart's repertoire, and Le Vau adapted it for his own entrances.

A design from Le Vau's own stock-in-trade was used again at Saint-Sépulchre: a vestibule giving access to a salon where a view of the garden presented itself. This will occur again at Vaux-le-Vicomte and was in turn used and adopted by others after him. The staircase retreats into an angle to make room for reception areas. On the court side, the ground level is raised up on a platform – to be used again at Vaux – with its facade topped by a high roof. This gave the house a massive aspect, but Le Vau tried to limit this by topping off two Ionic columns with an entablature. However, on the garden side, he gave the chateau two storeys unequal in size. Here is where he diverges from the tradition from Lescot and Philibert de l'Orme, maintained by Mansart, of projected bays with superimposed orders that serve for decoration but not much else. Le Vau's pillars really do support the building, holding up the entablatures in open peristyles. The chapel has a cupola like the ones he had seen in engravings of contemporary Roman churches, but, says Hautecœur, there is in Le Vau's work 'a constant concern for simplicity'.[52]

Another country mansion, this time at Essonnes between Paris and Fontainebleau, was also Hesselin's property. It was called Chantemèsle after the family name of the man from whom he bought it sometime before 1638, He carried out improvements there, including developing the garden and installing fountains, if the description beneath Israël Silvestre's engraving of it is correct. It can be presumed that Louis Le Vau had a hand in the designs.[53]

The property was described by John Evelyn in his *Journal*, which mentions a collection of pictures, gardens, fountains one of which 'sends up a jet of water in the form of serpents which intertwine around a globe', a cascade 'with pretty baths'.[54] Hesselin had installed machines on the watercourses to make his fountains work. Inside the house, Le Brun had been commissioned for ceilings and there were several sculptures by Gilles Guérin made from drawings by Jacques Sarrazin. The *hôtel* on the *île* and the house at Essonne were both expressions of the same flamboyant personality.

The purpose of Chantemèsle was to provide an annexe to the King's court for diversions, spectacles and entertainments on a lavish scale. Hesselin's occupation for a third of the year as the bursar for the king's table kept him at wherever the court was, but for the rest of the year he was in charge of the entertainments as *Intendant des plaisirs du roi*, and he often performed that office at his own Chantemèsle, as reported in the *Mercure* in the late 1640s and the 1650s. What is surprising is that some of these lavish undertakings were offered in the years of the Fronde, almost as a provocation to the court's opponents. It is presumed by commentators that Hesselin paid the bills himself.[55]

He is named first in the *Gazette* on 30 August 1646 in a report that Queen Henrietta-Maria of England with the Prince of Wales and Prince Rupert of the Rhine, together with a suite of three hundred others, were his guests. There was a banquet, a ball and an improvised ballet. Down the years, it was as an organiser and, before he became too corpulent, a performer in ballets that he made his mark. Soon after, in October, the Swedish ambassador made a visit to Chantemèsle, where he was lavishly entertained, after which he was brought to the house on the Île Saint-Louis, where there was music, a ballet and a ball followed by fireworks on the Seine. In 1651, Hesselin played the role of Harlequin in a ballet called *The Festivals of Bacchus*, with the King in the leading role, at the Palais-Royal.

The court stopped for dinner at Chantemèsle on the way back from Fontainebleau in May 1653 and the King came in person in the following year. When one of Cardinal Mazarin's nieces, Laure Martinozzi, married the Prince of Modena, the couple stayed at Chantemèsle to see a ballet that Hesselin devised and presented himself. Three months later, the Prince of Mantua paid a visit, and then, in September, the whole court paid visits on two occasions. But, to avoid a tedious list of these junketings, let us be content with just two more that confirm the character of this office holder at the edge of royal life with whom our Le Vau was associated.

The first of these visits was made on 24 July 1656 by *La Grande Mademoiselle*, the Duchess of Montpensier, daughter of Gaston d'Orleans, reinstated at court after her internal exile for her part in the Fronde, who related what happened on her visit to Chantemèsle in her memoirs.[56] Mademoiselle and the Duke of Guise passed through a grotto when they heard shouting, because 'the ingenious Hesselin' had opened the water jets in the grotto floor and the Princess of Lixein was covered in mud. Next day, Mademoiselle and the princess had a good laugh together about it.

Six weeks later, she was there again at the same time as Queen Christina of Sweden who had abdicated from her throne in 1654 and made her visit to France as part of an intrigue organised by Mazarin to offer her the vacant throne of Naples so that she could rule there in the interests of France in order to embarrass Philip IV of Spain and his ally Pope Alexander VII. On 4 September 1656, Christina stayed at Fontainebleau. The *Gazette* announced that the King had commanded Hesselin to entertain her sumptuously at Chantemèsle.[57]

A fuller account given in a semi-official publication that reported on ballets authorised at court says that Christina admired the splendour of the house and gardens, after which her host appeared in person during a spectacle involving a column of fire and 'an Italian chamber stopping only at a very high vaulted ceiling' (who could have arranged that?), which was then replaced in illusion by an empty room where 'all of a sudden a flaming cloud full of thunder and lightning appeared zooming over the ruins of a town on fire'. There followed songs and ballets, with several scene changes involving grottoes and mountain scenery, rivers and clouds, with a musical accompaniment. A banquet was followed by a play and it all ended with fireworks. Christina spent the night at Chantemèsle, and in the morning there was more music, poetry readings, and the King's twenty-four violins accompanied lunch. She left satisfied, expressing gratitude to her host.[58] She watched the spectacles with *La Grande Mademoiselle*,[59] and the two misfit royal personalities found a certain affinity towards each other.

* * *

Towards 1660, Hesselin's money was beginning to run out. He still wanted to be taken into the heart of the royal court, but always remained on its edges. He died on 8 august 1662. He had a reputation for overeating and his death is said to have been the result of gobbling down 294 walnut halves to win a bet.[60]

'Rich, and spending without counting, a man of taste and intellect, but above all an epicurean, loving from his egoism to amuse himself and from his vanity to amuse others, he was toadied to by the people, caressed by the great, and exploited by everyone. At bottom he was little enough considered and little enough admired, and he did not leave a friend to respect his memory … only two lines in the *Gazette* recorded his death.'[61]

This presentation of Hesselin at Chantemèsle has been a diversion, but included because there is a coincidental similarity between him and Le Vau at the end of their respective lives. Without anticipating what should be kept for an account of the aftershock to his family of Le Vau's business ventures, it is enough to draw attention to what happened after Hesselin's death.

He had died near to financial ruin. His will, dated on the day before his death during the short illness that provoked it – whatever the truth was about the walnut halves – named his cousin, Henri Godet, who was dean of the auditors of the *Chambre des comptes*, as his heir. The dean's brother, Viscount Antoine Godet, raised a long dispute in the Great Council, where one Martin Tabouret, sieur de Tourny, was accused of 'calumnious accusations against the late Hesselin', relating to misconduct of the accounts he kept as *Maître des deniers*.[62] Le Vau did not know Hesselin well enough to want to imitate his way of life as was the case with Bordier and Lambert, but there is a certain correspondence between their posthumous reputations that is worth noticing.

Chapter 3

Vincennes: A Royal Project

Cardinal Jules Mazarin, prince of the Church, did not fit into the pattern of French great nobles among whom he took his place as a duke, both of Mayenne and Nivernais. The normal acquisitiveness of a new French noble led to the purchase of one or more landed estates and the building of a great house on one of them. The governor of the chateau at Vincennes, Bouthillier de Chavigny, died in October 1652 at the same time as Mazarin was back in Paris to re-join the court after the Fronde, and Jean-Baptiste Colbert, who had acted as his eyes and ears during his exile,[1] suggested that he should ask the King for the largely honorific vacant post. The royal chateau was 9 miles to the east of Paris in the countryside, a defensible fortress out of the reach of Parisian demonstrators, and it would give him a place to keep his fortune safe in the care of someone trusted from his household. Mazarin's enormously rich collection of art objects, especially his library, had been pillaged in Paris during the Fronde and some of it sold off. He easily obtained his request,[2] and so, rather than building his own new country chateau, as his illustrious predecessor Richelieu had done, Mazarin moved into one of the King's old ones.

Mazarin kept most of his fortune in liquidities in places where he had lodgings. He had 766,000 livres in his apartment in the Louvre and was to keep 1.46 million at Vincennes. At first he occupied the governor's apartments that were at the side of the Sainte-Chapelle, as was appropriate for a cardinal, and came and went from there, at the same time as he began to re-establish Vincennes as a royal residence, a suitable refuge should there be any recrudescence of the recent disturbances.[3] Vincennes was where privileged prisoners detained on political or religious grounds were held.[4] It was already a safe stronghold surrounded with curtain walls and Mazarin's intention was to make it a royal palace on a footing with Fontainebleau or Saint-Germain-en-Laye with buildings appropriately stylish.

Colbert undertook building works at Vincennes in Mazarin's name. They were of considerable magnitude, intended to provide living space within the chateau for the royal family and a good number of members of the court. The King's lodging that was already there was cramped and unfinished. It was only one storey high, but with a high roof, running along the inside of the curtain wall that joins the keep enclosure to the so-called King's Tower to the southwest of the enclosure, as an engraving by Israël Silvestre shows in the distance. Louis XIII had laid its foundation stone in 1610, the first year of his reign, but it had not been completed by the time of his death in 1643.

Colbert offered a choice of three architects to Mazarin: Louis Le Vau, François Mansart, and Pierre Le Muet. It was known that Le Vau was taking an interest in Italian architectural developments represented in engravings available to him. This appealed to Mazarin, who had already facilitated their discreet introduction in his own palace in the capital by means of the work of Giovanni Francesco Romanelli, whom he had invited to come from Rome for the purpose. Le Vau's co-operation with increasingly prominent artists on building projects for financiers and fringe members of the court also appealed to Mazarin. Le Vau was becoming involved in royal building sites, especially at the Louvre, where he was working with Jacques Lemercier and replaced him as the King's First Architect in 1654, although he appeared as late as 1656 only in third position in the *États des gages* (the list of those engaged in the King's service).[5] By 1656 he was also working for Colbert's rival, Nicolas Fouquet, at Vaux-le-Vicomte, which is a more likely cause of Colbert's dislike of him than his poor supervision of the mortar used in the foundations of the Hôtel Bautru, which Colbert was soon to acquire as his own town house.

Le Vau made four designs for the King's apartments in succession, the fourth one being accepted by Colbert and Mazarin.[6] It was to occupy the same western side of what would later become the courtyard, but its ground plan was doubled, and it was to have two storeys united by colossal pillars with Tuscan capitals and an attic above a classically decorated frieze. Earth from the excavation of the moat on the western side of the King's apartment was intended to be used for laying out a garden.

Before Le Vau's enlargements, Vincennes was too cramped for the King since he had to have the Queen Mother and his brother, known as Monsieur (then Duke of Anjou, but soon to be Duke of Orleans) and the cardinal himself living under the same roof. The King preferred to have the latter accessible to him for advice, as he was when the court was at the Louvre. The Louis XIII building was kept in its integrity and refurbished for the King's sole use. Le Vau added two extra storeys to it, replaced its roof and provided ceremonial rooms and an office for the King. There was thus more room for the royals and their staffs. The wall facing the inner court became one side of the interior of a much larger building when Le Vau added extra *enfilades* within three stories and the roof space. The Queen Mother would have her separate apartments, complete with a bathroom, which was an important requirement for her with marble for the non-porous surfaces. (Did it involve innovative plumbing or was it labour intensive with jugs of hot water?). Monsieur would be accommodated in the other half of the new first floor. The space in the building would be doubled under the same roof, the ground floor of it providing lodgings for gentlemen of the court, besides kitchens, storerooms and other services. Between the old ground floor and the new, there was a corridor (*enfilade*) with openings on both sides – a new feature in French great houses.[7]

Le Vau provided a ceremonial staircase with three flights inside the end of the building nearest Charles V's keep. At the other end, the King's Tower was carefully made stable. An engraving made near the time of building shows the corner towers twice as high as they are now, but it is important to note that the site available was determined by the dimensions of the medieval fortifications, and in the years between 1654 and the preparations for the King's marriage, it would be developed within these limits. The whole building was covered, not by a high roof such as was going out of fashion, but with what was becoming known as *combles brisés* pierced with dormer windows and decorated with the fashionably stylish urns elongated upwards with flames issuing from them. This is the building that we see today, gloriously cleaned. When it was first built, it stood alone with the garden laid out where the Queen's wing, raised by Le Vau in 1658, now faces it on the eastern side of a quadrangle.

The contracts for these works were found among Mazarin's papers, but they give no information about the decorations arranged by Le Vau as are extant for many of his other buildings.[8] Once Colbert and Mazarin had agreed to adopt Le Vau's final design for the King's Pavilion, they signed a contract with him and with two master masons who had the King's licence to operate as such. They were Jean Pastel and François Levé, the latter of whom was working at the Arsenal, and they signed it on the same day as the *ne varietur* – the agreement not to change anything in the architect's designs – was finalised on 7 June 1654. Detailed estimates of costs and quantities of materials were agreed upon.

A contract was signed with Claude Dublet on 16 June for roof timbers. A roofer from central Paris, Denis Hébert, signed his contract with Colbert on 3 July for the provision of slates from distant Angers and setting them in place on the *charpente*. Colbert's fidelity to Mazarin all through the time the Fronde had lasted was rewarded with the confidence placed in him by his patron and the readiness with which he listened to his ideas. Colbert's signature on deeds and on the back of plans often henceforth was to be seen in place of the absent Mazarin's. Colbert sent him frequent reports, like this one sent as early as 7 July 1654 which tells him that 'the great building at Vincennes is coming along. The foundations will soon be at ground level, and every effort is being made to have them ready by next Lent, provided that the money doesn't run out. The part for Your Eminence's own lodgings goes quicker, and I hope it will be finished by the end of October ... The King's chamber and his office are in progress; but without a certain diligence the chamber cannot be painted and gilded by then.'

The King's building was not, however, finished by Lent because the money did run out.[9] In the spring of 1655, the dilatory Pastel and Levé were replaced as contractors by other master masons, Antoine Bergeron and Michel Villedo, the latter having been an associate of Le Vau's mason father and his own mentor and guide for more than ten years. Besides what they were about to accomplish at Vincennes, these two also had a contract with Nicolas Fouquet and completed the chateau for him at Vaux-le-Vicomte in an astonishingly short time. Villedo held the rank of General of the King's Buildings and the Bridges and Roads of France. They took over their predecessors' stock of tools and materials and signed a new contract with Colbert. By 14 June 1657 they had given their receipt for 247,650 livres 10 sols and 6 deniers (£ s d!) to Mazarin's treasurer for masonry work on the King's Pavilion and other buildings at Vincennes 'alongside the Sainte-Chapelle and at other locations, terraces and gardens, fountains in the garden, at the lake in the park opposite the menagerie, and the enclosure wall'. So, in 1658, the King's wing was up and ready.[10]

* * *

There is a somewhat bizarre antiquarian's guide to this period of the building site at the Château de Vincennes to be found in the second volume of a book in octavo called *Mémoires intéressans pour servir à l'histoire de France, ou Tableau historique chronologique, pittoresque, ecclésiastique, civil et militaire, Des Maisons royales, Châteaux et Parcs des Rois de France*.[11] It is the work of a retired lawyer at the Admiralty whose name was Guillaume Poncet de la Grave (1725–1803?). He settled in Vincennes in 1770 and collected information that he turned into a catalogue of happenings. He had it published in 1788 just before things changed forever. He survived the Terror, but his account of the ceremonies and activities of the King and Queen and Court in their sojourns at Vincennes in the 1650s and after are completely uncritical of the Bourbons, even to the point of sycophancy. Nevertheless, his account allows some appreciation of the palace of Vincennes in the eyes of the youthful King, who came to the palace for the '*divertissement de la chasse*' at least from November 1654, and often stayed there, though it is not said where his lodgings were within the perimeter.

As Governor, Mazarin entertained the bachelor King and the Queen Mother several times at Vincennes 'with magnificent collations'.

They came there on 24 January 1656 'to give orders to speed up the construction and the ornamentation of the two pavilions for the royal court'. These are the two larger buildings at either end of Le Vau's new construction with their shallow projections from the building line of the central *corps de logis*. On 3 April the King came there again, and expressed his appreciation of the palace and his new apartments: 'When I feel myself heavy-laden (*pesant*), I am assured of recovering my health at Vincennes.' Once more, on 6 November 1657, returning from making war, he came to hunt 'and to visit the new buildings, which he found very advanced'. On 24 January 1658, he was with his godfather again, and stayed the best part of a month, conducting business, hunting in the *bois*, and 'giving orders to the director of his buildings'.

This was to be a foretaste of two later phenomena at Versailles: first, the King's desire to be out of the stinking capital – even if the drains were being covered over one by one – where his childhood memories of mob violence in the Fronde still frightened him, and, secondly, his tendency, here and later, to breathe down his First Architect's neck while he was working. On 18 October 1658, we find him arriving at Vincennes with the whole Court intending 'to examine the considerable works which have to be done there'.

Vincennes came into its own when, after their marriage at Saint-Jean-de-Luz and their journeys in the south and midlands of France, the King and his Spanish bride Marie-Therese came to stay in the completed King's and Queen's apartments on the sides of the quadrangle. 'It's just like an Oxford or Cambridge College,' say some of the English visitors – with a triumphal arch leading to the park in the south arcade and its bas-relief celebrating peace on absolutist terms after the Fronde and with Spain. Every architectural achievement had its political context.

Poncet's 'interesting memoirs' relate many occasions when deputations from French towns came to congratulate the royal couple on their marriage and the peace that had been made that their union represented. The young Queen had to sit through a seemingly endless parade by the Paris militia, and then make her triumphal entry into the ville de Paris itself a few days later; part of the ceremony for this was having to sit on her throne next to the King on a temporary structure in what later became the place de la Nation for five hours hearing speeches.[12] On the other hand, she probably enjoyed her visits to the Sainte-Chapelle in the old part of the chateau, and to the Minimes' convent in the Park, where, on both occasions, the canons and the monks offered her the best of their harvested summer fruits.

Except for these last weeks when the young royals took up residence, the King, his mother, the Cardinal, and the whole assembly of courtiers had had to live for part of the year in places where they had the builders in. It must have been a relief to find themselves at Fontainebleau or Saint-Germain-en-Laye where rebuilding or major modifications were not being carried out. It would take another twenty years for the court to settle down – for just over a century and two more Kings' reigns – at the greatly enlarged Versailles.

* * *

It was worth anticipating events a little, but there is more to be said about Le Vau's development of the terrain at Vincennes. The designs he had submitted to Colbert, before the one that this parsimonious factotum of Mazarin accepted, had been much more elaborate, and the King's apartments as they stand are thought by some to be severe[13] by comparison. He had wanted to insert his trademark projections, known in French as *avant-corps,* to give the facades to east and west much more alternating light and dark, but the estimates were too costly, and he was able to provide no more than rather shallow projections for the pavilions at both ends. He also wanted to provide three pediments for the wings but these ended in the reject file as well.

Between the completion of the King's apartments, doubled in width and raised up as they are, and the provision of other buildings, much was accomplished before the great welcoming that followed the royal wedding and the formal homecoming of the royal couple to the capital. If the exterior was to be relatively simple in appearance, indoors it was to be as sumptuous as the mansions built on the Île Saint-Louis for Lambert and Hesselin. The King himself issued the commission for directing the decorations to Philippe de Champaigne.[14] Works were also commissioned to decorate the rooms Le Vau was providing from de Champaigne's nephew, Jean-Baptiste, the Flemish artist Manchole, Michel Dorigny, a local lad born not far away at Saint-Quentin in 1616,[15] and an Italian, Marie-François Borzone, born in Genoa.

On the ground floor, there were the kitchens with their storerooms, and at the end nearest the enclosure for the keep (*donjon*) accommodation for several courtiers. The itinerant court needed no more than temporary lodgings, however lavishly decorated they might be. The royal apartments were on the first floor, and on the second were those for the great officers of state and bedrooms for the chateau staff. The King – and soon the Queen also – had five great rooms, one after the other in an *enfilade* reached by the grand staircase at the northern end of the pavilion, similar to what Le Vau had previously provided in his bourgeois town houses. There was a *grande galerie,* which had been part of the

Louis XIII pavilion, left unchanged as to its dignified proportions, lit by four great windows overlooking the park. What the decorations consisted of is not known. Next came the dining room with paintings of Alexander the Great's battles by Manchole. The throne room followed, which, after 1659, had its ceiling decorated with an allegory of the King as Jupiter ordering France to embrace Peace. It was a theatrical setting resembling the one Fouquet wanted the King to accept at Vaux-le-Vicomte, contemporary with it in construction, meant for the daily ceremonies of *lever* and *coucher* that Jupiter and Juno would watch from the ceiling. The King's office was the final room of his suite, and then came five more rooms for the Queen, later decorated for Marie-Thérèse with suitable mythological themes. These were rediscovered during the Second Empire when the whitewash covering them from the First Empire, the pavilion being used then as a women's prison, was removed. Paintings by Luciano Borzone decorated the Queen's concert room. Her *salle de gardes* had paintings of the muses and cherubs, which are called *amours* in French. The preliminary drawings for these were provided by Le Vau's long-time associate Eustache Le Sueur.[16]

* * *

Before that could happen, it was decided to make what was, at least externally, a mirror image of the King's wing to the south of the Sainte-Chapelle for the Queen Mother, construction of which was begun in 1658. Le Vau's plan for it was adopted *ne varietur* in a contract signed by Colbert and the two contractors, Claude Dublet and Charles Thoison, on 27 May.[17] It stipulated that the building must be completed by 31 May 1660 at the latest, but it is known that the Queen Mother moved out of the King's wing to live in this new building a good while before that.

The master mason Thoison had married Le Vau's sister,[18] and the contract says he lived in Paris in the rue du Roi de Sicile. Le Vau had bought the house near the Hôtel de Ville from Jerome de Nouveau, who was *superintendant des Postes*, on 6 February 1646,[19] moving out of the mansion he had built for himself next door to Lambert's on the Île Saint-Louis to profit from its rentability. It was in this new tall house that he developed his drawing office, soon to be entrusted to his apprentice when this latter had qualified and returned from his educational stay in Rome. Presumably Le Vau provided lodging for his brother-in-law in the same way as he had previously housed his extended family in the quai d'Alençon. The Parisian building trade was nothing if not clannish. We can perhaps deduce that it was in this house that Le Vau was living while he was working in his early days at the Louvre, at

Vincennes and at Vaux, though it is known that Fouquet put him up in this last place for periods of time. In 1664, the inner Le Vau family moved into a tied apartment for the better performance of the architect's duties in the Hôtel de Longueville in the space between the Louvre eastern facade and Saint-Germain-l'Auxerrois, which was destined for demolition once the palace was finished. It is a pity that Le Vau's personal life can rarely be seen except through the way he worked. Why are there so few signed personal letters, only documents signed in the presence of lawyers, or his speculative thoughts for his projects?

The eastern exterior of the Queen's wing was Charles V's rampart, which Le Vau pierced with an arcade opening on to the park. This encloses a court behind the main building (*corps de logis*) that has end pavilions corresponding with those on the *aile du Roi* facing them. The rooms on the two floors and the attic above the frieze were arranged in a single *enfilade* with each room opening on to the next since there was no doubling here. The original intention was that Anne of Austria and Cardinal Mazarin would each have half of the first floor for their respective apartments, but from 1659 it was Monsieur, who took the rooms in the north part, while Mazarin had the south part for the two years that remained to him.

The Queen Mother had only a small lodging facing on to the park, yet the whole building is still called the Queen's wing. The north and south apartments were separated by the great staircase with its stone balustrade. Monsieur, the Cardinal and the Queen Mother each had their own separate kitchens on the ground floor. Their officials, guards and domestics had the remaining accommodation: the *entresol*, the second floor and under the eaves.

As for decoration, not a great deal is recorded, beyond the subject of the pictures such as female figures who are holding serpents and pressing on crowned medallions and the fact that one ceiling painting was on a canvas in the form of an oval – also chosen by Le Vau in his plans for the Louvre and Vaux-le-Vicomte – surrounded by representations of the world's continents. Much of this decoration was later taken in the mid-nineteenth century to be kept in the Louvre on Louis-Philippe's orders. There was a meeting room, the ceiling of which was decorated with a representation of a prince attended by the Muses.

The Queen Mother's bedroom ceiling was the work of Michel Dorigny, portraying the Pauline virtues of Faith, Hope and Charity framed with palm fronds, birds and horns of plenty. There were also more of Borzone's landscapes on wall panels. The main feature was the bed in an alcove, becoming the usual solution in royal and noble apartments at the time and often used by Le

Vau who had been instrumental in its adoption in France. There was also a small oratory.

When we came upstairs to Monsieur's apartments, we would have seen a *salle de garde*, then a dining room decorated with historical themes with woodcarvings of his crowned heraldic device. His bedroom was gilded throughout, with a painted ceiling in compartments depicting cheerful nymphs. This connected with his office, whose ceiling had Michel Dorigny's painting of Fame carrying Philippe of Orleans' portrait with the legend, 'I speak only of great events.' His painting of Zephyrus and Flore was destroyed by the Nazis in 1944.[20] The *enfilade* concluded with a meeting room decorated by Philippe de Champaigne with Mars and Bellona presented together on the ceiling.

We have to imagine what the entire interior decor was like – the painted walls and ceilings with their *voussures* – since the whole chateau has changed its use, though there was some replacement of it in the post-1944 restoration under the sensitive direction of Jean Trouvelot.[21] Under the Fourth Republic it became the army's artillery school and it now houses the archives of the French army and navy with their associated centres of research.

Monsieur did not keep his apartment at Vincennes for very long. Once Louis XIV's engagement to Marie-Thérèse was announced, it was decided that the Queen Mother should move to the Queen's wing, and that Mazarin should occupy the other half of it. This arrangement helped to re-stimulate the rumour at court that Mazarin and Anne of Austria were lovers or, perhaps, secretly married.[22] It is certain that they had, at an earlier time, sent each other letters in secret code,[23] but there is no real evidence for the truth of either rumour. Since they were together responsible for bringing up a child as his mother and godfather, and the child was the King and his mother was regent for him, it is no wonder that they wanted a code to keep their arrangements for him from prying eyes. It was here, in this building that Mazarin breathed his last on 9 March 1661.

On a more banal level, provision was necessary for the stabling of at least two hundred horses with their *palfreniers*, and for the garaging of the carriages. Le Vau accomplished this along the curtain walls near the canons' residences by the Saint-Chapelle. It was all ready before the Court's return in 1660. Perhaps a few canons' noses were more than put out of joint, but Louis XIV liked what he found.

Vincennes was used by the court in its progresses until 1668, but then it was rejected and left abandoned, apart for occasional use by foreign ambassadors,[24] in favour of the new building that Le Vau was called away from the Louvre to provide at Versailles.

Vincennes: A Royal Project

* * *

The contract that provided the resources for the Queen's Pavilion took into account the area intended for the Royal Court between the two large buildings to east and west, and the arcades to north and south. It also included the triumphal arch proposed for the middle of the south arcade that was to be the principal entrance from the park once it was in being, complete with guard posts, and cannon in each one of the full-centred arches as seen in the engraving by Ransonnelte that Poncet de le Grave included in his *Mémoires*.

The young King – he was twenty in 1658 – was taking an interest in developments being undertaken in his name at Vincennes to enlarge, improve and embellish the ancient fortress on its south side, standing as it was amidst open country. As at Versailles later, he was respectful towards the past, but a determined innovator where he saw fit. He respected his cardinal-minister, and approved of this project. It seems that, at this stage, Colbert was doing what his patron told him to. The King accepted the Italian tendency, which Le Vau was discreetly demonstrating in his designs.

The whole terrain was to be enriched. It already had the two distinct enclosures to the north: the first court, which contained the services – kitchens and stables, lodgings for the dean and chapter of the Sainte-Chapelle, which reflected the one on the Île de la Cité with its own piece of the True Cross, and their cloister. Then there was the imposing chapel, itself founded in 1379 by Charles V, opposite the *donjon* in its defensive enclosure begun by Philip VI at the outbreak of the Hundred Years War, continued by Jean II, who was defeated by the English and captured at Poitiers, and completed by Charles V. A third space was where Mazarin, with Louis XIV's active consent, resided while he was making all his arrangements to provide for the King's grandeur, attended by his courtiers, whenever he was in residence. The whole enclosure was surrounded by curtain walls and dry moats. Le Vau was entrusted with the designs for extending what he had begun with his double *enfilade* between the keep and the south-western tower. This area was to be separated from the keep and the Sainte-Chapelle by arcades with iron grilles on either side of a grand portico surmounted by balustrades. He was using almost free-standing pillars as well as the triple arch he often enjoyed using in other works.

To delimit the south side of the court, along the line of the medieval curtain wall and moat, Le Vau had already supplied the full-centred arcading, and its most imposing feature was to be a gate of honour – the main entrance to the palace coming from Paris through the park. This was in essence an *arc de Triomphe*, commemorating the royal victory over the Fronde.

There was already a medieval tower in the place where Le Vau intended to put this gate. His first project was restrained, but he soon replaced it with something more exuberant, as it appears in the 1658 contract. He took the tower down as far as the balustrade that was at the top of the arcade and the contract states what would be seen on the inside of the gate:

> a great doorway of six columns ... in the Tuscan order, crowned in the middle with a great pediment, on which some famous personages (*renommés*) shall be seated, who shall hold the King's emblems, and in the tympanum shall be Mazarin's heraldic arms. Above this Tuscan order shall be another attic [frieze] with pilasters on which there shall be a balustrade and pedestals which shall carry antique figures, and the sides shall have bas-reliefs.[25]

What Le Vau actually provided did not correspond in detail with what was intended at the time of the contract being signed. The interior side shows what has been lost in destruction – only one of the bas-reliefs remains, under the alcove on the left, and the statues are elsewhere[26] – and reconstruction in succeeding centuries. Jean Marot's contemporary engraving of the exterior gives a better representation of what Le Vau actually had built.

This was meant to be the triumphal arch for the King's and Mazarin's victory over the Fronde, with the cardinal's emblems represented upon it with equal prominence as the Fleur-de-lys and the Crown. The statues and the cornucopia represent the prosperity and peace that their triumph over their adversaries was seen by them to have brought to the state.[27]

Before we pass on from it, however, it is important to notice that one of its features is that 'the six columns in the Tuscan order' on the inside and the outside of the arch set four of them in pairs. This, together with Le Vau's alterations to Mansart's ground-plan sketch for the eastern frontage of the Louvre that dates from 1663, suggests that placing columns, rather than colossal orders that he has used previously, on monuments had been in his mind at least since 1658 at Vincennes. The appearance of similar columns on Claude Perrault's accepted design for the triumphal arch to be erected after the peace of Aix-la-Chapelle in 1668 may show no more than that columns were becoming fashionable.[28]

* * *

There was to be what we call a home farm in the grounds towards the village of Saint-Mandé, where Fouquet was having a house built for himself out of several existing ones. Elm trees were brought and planted in an avenue, while Mazarin devised a plan to divert the course of the Marne with a double waterway to assist in the victualling of Paris. The convent of the Minimes in the park was not ignored in the spiritual life of the chateau, and took its place alongside the worship provided in the Saint-Chapelle.

Mazarin's papers also contained a plan for a *serail* and the contract for building it. This was not the term for an Ottoman harem, but a translation into French of the Italian word *seraglio*, used for a set-up where wild beasts were kept alongside an arena where they would be induced to fight for the entertainment of spectators. Guillaume Poncet de la Grave once again leaps to our assistance, where he recounts that:

> On 28 March 1665, the Duke of Mazarini, [the late cardinal's nephew-in-law who had inherited the governorship of the chateau] having been to collect the Prince of Denmark on the King's orders from his Paris hôtel, brought him to Vincennes [...] for the pleasures of the chase and of the combat between a lion and a bull at the menagerie [...], where they found the ambassador and ambassadress of Denmark, and this was followed by a superb collation.
>
> On 18 July [...] arrived at Vincennes, the Queen had first the pleasure of a combat of a lion with a bull and then between other animals, then a hunt in the park ...[29]

The first animals had been brought from the menagerie at the Tuileries, then replacements were purchased in African countries.[30]

The building of this *seraglio* issues from exchanges made by Mazarin with contacts in his native Italy, in this case with the principal secretary of the Grand Duke of Tuscany, Ferdinand II, who had his court at Florence. Mazarin had asked, through the good offices of the Tuscan representative at the French court, the abbé Pietro Bonsi, for help with providing distractions for Louis XIV in the park at Vincennes. After initial confusion about the exact nature of the cardinal's ambiguous request, in late 1657 it became clear that he wanted someone to come to Vincennes to organise combats between the lions, tigers and other animals that were already there (apparently kept in a section of the dry moat[31]), and to advise about how best to house them in the vicinity of the palace.[32]

The result was that a courtier called Ottavio Ricci, one of the Grand Duke's hunting companions, came to Vincennes. He was accompanied by Francesco Guiloni, an expert on the wild animal fights, for which the Tuscan court was well known, who brought information about how to maintain these exotic animals, the possession of which was a distinguishing mark of their owner's magnificence. European rulers in the Middle Ages had kept lions as such. Street names, the *via de' Leoni* in Florence and the *rue des Lions* in Paris near where Charles V had his menagerie, bear this out. The lions in Florence were maintained at the Republic's expense from 1350 onwards in cages near the *Podesta*, behind the *Palazzo Vecchia*. The well-being of the state was thought by the citizens to be related to the good health of these animals, not unlike the connection of ravens with the Tower of London.

The lions were made to fight each other for the first time in Florence when Pope Pius II, Aeneas Sylvius Piccolomini, and Galeazzo Sforza of Milan made a state visit in 1459. Cosimo dei Medici sought to profit from this association with the customs of Roman antiquity. As long as the Medicis remained in power in Florence, there were lion fights on important diplomatic occasions, and they were maintained in readiness near the ducal palace. Mazarin's Florentine visitors, who met him on 5 March 1658, brought an exact plan of the lion house with them, and permission to build a replica of it near the palace of Vincennes.

The envoys were sent to consult with Colbert, who entrusted the *Pianta del seraglio delli lioni* to Louis Le Vau, showing how the animals had cells and walkways and how their keepers approached them in safety to feed them and keep their accommodation clean. The circulation of visitors was shown, and the vantage points for watching the combats.

The Florentines were kept waiting for a response for several weeks – Mazarin told them that the delay was caused by Queen Christina of Sweden's visit – and then they were sent to Colbert once more amid rumours that the whole project was proving too costly and that the animals themselves had been neglected and were in a sorry state of health. But on 26 April, as he was about to leave Paris to follow the French army on campaign, Mazarin told the Tuscan resident, Pietro Bonsi, that he had that morning given the orders to start building the *seraglio* and to release the funds for it. Colbert seemed in no hurry to get on with it, and Le Vau was not available to start work. We can note in passing that Fouquet was building a house at Saint-Mandé at the same time, which may have encouraged close co-operation with Le Vau, who was designing his great house at Vaux-le-Vicomte.

But then, on 20 July, the project took off: Colbert signed the contract with the usual masons, Claude Dublet and Charles Thoison, 'for the construction of several small lodges, vaults and separate yards suitable for housing several animals in the form of a *serail*.'

* * *

Le Vau took over at this point, consulting closely with Ricci and Guiloni about details. He was going to build the *Seraglio* in a rural setting near the village of Saint-Mandé, whereas the Florentine building was right in the centre of the city. Le Vau saw that he had a simpler challenge in a construction that did not have to take buildings that were already in place into account, so he opted for a much more spacious version of the required structure. His predilection for oval spaces is well known, and he wanted to make the place where the animal fights would take place to be oval in shape, perhaps with the many classical Roman models of arenas in mind. But Guiloni, the experienced combat master, pointed out that that the oval proposed by Le Vau was too large to allow the tamers to keep what the lions were doing under their control and the oval was abandoned in favour of the Florentine rectangular combat area. Le Vau's version has thirty-one cages for different animals, with twelve exercise yards attached to them with grilles to let them out and in. The edifice has a yard for the combats directly accessible from nineteen of the cages. Stairs are indicated by which the spectators went to the galleries above to watch in total security.[33]

Construction began in July 1658, but things moved slowly. The Tuscan resident Bonsi attributed this to the Court not coming to Vincennes until after All Saints at the beginning of November, deciding to remain at Fontainebleau until after then. But the contract for roofing the building was signed on 6 November, by which time Mazarin had agreed to Ricci's returning home, leaving Guiloni to advise Le Vau. Then Mazarin was absent for the peace negotiations with Spain, the King's marriage and the subsequent journey of the court in the south and the Midi delayed the return to residence at Vincennes until the summer of 1660, where there were hopes of having the first event in the *seraglio* in August, at the same time as the King and Queen were to have their solemn entry into Paris. Guiloni was given a retainer by Mazarin in October to put the building in working order. Nothing happened, however, and Mazarin died on 9 March 1661 without having been able to offer the King the treat of seeing animals kill each other. Guiloni died in April.

There was a new Tuscan resident at the French court in September to replace the abbé Bonsi, and he brought a lion tamer called Birzi to take the place left vacant by Guiloni. Louis XIV was becoming more and more interested in his ideas for Versailles and losing interest in Vincennes as a way of not living in the Louvre. Mazarin's crackpot nephew-in-law, the Duke of Mazarini, had inherited the governorship of Vincennes, and Birzi was placed under his eccentric direction. There were few animal fights arranged, and the only ones that seem to have attracted attention were in March and July 1665 for the Prince of Denmark and for the Queen, as we have seen. They provided an attraction for ambassadors from Siam who took up residence for a while in the Queen's neglected pavilion in 1682, but there was little use for it after that.

Alexandre Cojannot, in his intricately sourced article that is the eloquent basis of most of this information,[34] points out that the plan of Le Vau's building by Desgodetz (which Cordey had printed in his 1933 article) shows that there remained only one tiger, one leopard, one wolf, an eagle and several mastiffs in 1694. In 1706 the few animals that were still there were transferred to the menagerie at the King's garden in Paris, while the building itself was used by the captain of the Vincennes hunt. It was all over.

* * *

What Le Vau learned in constructing this useless edifice did have its uses as a precedent, a previous learning curve, for what he was asked to do for the King at the menagerie in the park at Versailles five years later, where he revived the plan he first offered for the Vincennes *seraglio*. If what he was constrained to build at Saint-Mandé was a Colosseum in miniature on the Florentine model, meant to proclaim the more ferocious aspects of royal magnificence, the building in the park to the south of what would soon be the Grand Canal at Versailles would display other aspects of that magnificence in terms of the scientific curiosity that it would come to foster. He was to create a royal zoo where curious exotic animals and birds could be viewed in safety, not an arena where bloody and useless conflicts could be watched. This evoked a desire to do likewise on the next Grand Duke of Tuscany, Cosimo III, who established a zoo for exotic animals in the Boboli gardens.[35]

Le Vau's menagerie would have an attractive appearance that reverberates with Vaux-le-Vicomte rather than a utilitarian place of slaughter. Le Vau was a creative artist as well as an innovative technician.

Chapter 4

Mazarin's Louvre

The Fronde had been overcome by October 1652, and the royal family returned to Paris after its wanderings in the kingdom in search of provincial loyalty.

The Palais-Royal, Cardinal Richelieu's legacy to the King, where they had lived before the troubles, was too open to intruders to be safe for the young King to return to, so it was decided that the Louvre should be the royal residence in Paris from then on, though the court would remain itinerant between Paris, Saint-Germain-en-Laye and Fontainebleau.

The Grand Design for completing the Louvre Palace had been left unfinished by Anne of Austria as regent almost nine years before to the day, but in 1652 it still had its protective dry moat and a drawbridge, and the portfolio of plans was reopened and entrusted to Jacques Lemercier, First Architect to the King. Despite all existing financial restraints, it was decided between 1652 and 1654 that apartments for the King, the Queen Mother and the Council should be created or improved.[1] Lemercier had been the Louvre's architect since 1627 and Louis Le Vau, on the basis of the reputation he had established among financiers and royal officials for the mansions he had designed for them, now began working as his associate.[2]

Anne of Austria and her two sons were joined by Mazarin in February 1653. The unfinished Louvre was surrounded by and intruded upon by private mansions, which impeded its development. Two buildings constructed by Pierre Lescot occupied two sides of the paved court. The southern wing was unfinished, and the northern one had been demolished in 1639. A rubble stone wall hid a building site reached through the former palace garden. A large pavilion had been in course of construction by Lemercier between 1639 and 1642 through which the kitchen yard was approached, and a new wing was planned in keeping with the sixteenth-century constructions. Lemercier's project had been abandoned with only the ground level complete at the death of Louis XIII in 1643, when Mazarin removed François Sublet de Noyers from the post of Superintendent of the King's Buildings.

The condition of the building after the Fronde was far from that desired for a royal palace. The King and his mother were installed in rooms designed by Pierre Lescot in an outdated style. The Queen Mother's apartment of eight rooms was the first project to be taken up under Lemercier's direction. A sum of 12,000 livres was spent on her accommodation alongside the great picture gallery. Claude Mollet began work on the garden. That work was begun on Cardinal Mazarin's apartment on the second floor of the west wing is confirmed by previously unpublished documents in the National Library of Manuscripts.[3] Lemercier had the confidence of Anne of Austria after his work at her church of Val de Grâce,[4] the Palais Royal after Richelieu's bequest, and at Fontainebleau. His work at the Louvre consisted of the redistribution of the rooms available for her occupation, giving them extra natural light and adding her novel, marble-lined bathroom with its equally novel plumbing, all on the ground floor in the south wing of the Louvre's Square Yard.

The baton of the First Architect passed to Louis Le Vau when Lemercier died in his house in the rue d'Arbre-Sec on 13 January 1654 after an illness that had begun to incapacitate him the previous September. Le Vau took over the project and, from then on, his drawing office was the sole source of finished designs.[5] He was forty-two years old and was to remain in office for the next sixteen years until his own death in 1670. He was paid 3,112 livres 10 sous for the July quarter.[6] Le Vau's work at the Louvre after Lemercier's death is well documented, and several projects finished between 1655 and 1660 are retouched versions of Lemercier's, such as the Beauvais pavilion and the western half of the of the north wing of the Square Yard.

The first of the designs preserved at the Louvre archives is for the room intended for meetings of the King's Council, meant as a permanent construction for a purpose that had never existed before. In previous reigns, the meetings of the council in its different guises for its different purposes had been held wherever it had been convenient in the several royal apartments as and when required. A Council decree of 1 September 1653 changed all that and entrusted the responsibility for the design to Louis Le Vau.

The space earmarked was situated in the west wing of the Square Yard on the north side of the clock pavilion. The walls from where Lemercier left off in 1643 were still there and the roof space had been covered except for being left open to the elements at the north end since the Beauvais pavilion had reached completion only to the height of the first-floor ceiling, as an engraving by Israël Silvestre shows.[7] Le Vau's estimate for masonry submitted in 1653 was intended to deal with this situation, incorporating a chapel into the northwest corner of the Yard. Charles Le Brun was asked to furnish preparatory drawings for painting the vault of the council chamber,[8] but they were never used. A contract for wooden flooring and decorative carving was drawn up with Claude Bergerat and Étienne le Hongre.

In 1654, Le Vau turned his attention to the King's apartments, for which a good deal of documentation is extant,[9] in particular the contracts approved by Étienne Le Camus, then superintendent, for decorative design with Jean Cotelle,[10] for woodcarving with Louis and Claude Barrois and with Gilles Guérin, for sculpture with Pierre Bourdon, and for paintings with Eustache Le Sueur, who had also worked previously with Le Vau on mansions in the Île Saint-Louis and at one time was his tenant there. Cotelle's work incorporates a theme that had been initiated in France by Le Vau himself: the alcove bedroom. Le Vau submitted his own designs for chimney pieces, wall panels and a ceiling, evidently entrusted for their final form in detail to Cotelle.

When it came to the King's small office, the next room along the *enfilade*, Le Sueur was commissioned to provide an allegory on the theme of Magnificence for it. But Le Sueur died in 1655 and Charles Le Brun took over the intended decorations in collaboration with the architect. Contracts for this work bear, on their reverse sides, the signature of Antoine Ratabon, now Superintendent of the King's Buildings, dated 24 June 1654. But since there was no contractor's signature on the document, it seems that the final form of the room was still under discussion. A small oratory was added to this office, with decorations by Charles Errard and Noël Coypel.

Previously unpublished designs that Le Vau drew with his own hand once he was working for the King were brought together in the early 2000s in a collection that contrasts with the lack of extant designs from the first twenty years of his career. In his mature years, he built up an agency under his pupil François d'Orbay that produced a great deal of well-finished work in a distinctive style but, at this stage, his designs on paper lack polish and contain nothing like the detailed ornamentation found in François Mansart's work. Le Vau's particular interest is to be seen in the interplay of volumes, and he didn't restrict the talents of the artists and craftsmen who would carry out his designs. He expected them to show their own flair in implementing the overall pattern that he gave them. One of his noticeable skills was as a team leader, like a theatre director assigning tasks to men with other skills to achieve a scheme that he himself had devised. He seems to have recognised his own limitations in those other skills and, as is said nowadays, he knew how to delegate to good effect.

Prominent painters like Charles Le Brun, Eustache Le Sueur and Gilles Guérin, and sculptors like François Girardon, Laurent Magnier and Thomas Regnaudin had independence from any architect, since they were confirmed in their privileges as members of the newly formed Royal Academy of Painters and Sculptors, whereas there was no academy for architects until a year after Louis Le Vau's death. Such independently creative spirits would not have co-operated with him in his schemes so often if they had not had respect for his abilities. Le Vau's problems at the Louvre were not with his artistic associates, but with the King's appointees, as the rest of this chapter will show.

*   *   *

From the initial project in the reign of François I to turn the fortress that Philippe Auguste began in 1190[11] into a renaissance palace in the second quarter of the sixteenth century, the Great Design for the Louvre was to be a matter for the initiative of the monarch alone. But, after Henry IV's appointment of Sully to the superintendency of the King's buildings in 1602,[12] the development of the Louvre site was the concern of successive ministers in the persons of François Sublet de Noyers – who was also minister of war – in Louis XIII's reign, and Jean-Baptiste Colbert in that of Louis XIV. These officials 'saw the principal purpose and the most noble means of achieving all royal policy in artistic matters in the completion of the Great Design of the Louvre'.[13] However, this is to ignore the part played by Mazarin in the way the Louvre's design evolved and how it came to be constructed after his victory over the Fronde.

Mazarin had occupied the post of superintendent in 1646, the year in which the court abandoned the Louvre in favour of living in the Palais-Royal. Mazarin had succeeded in ousting Sublet de Noyers and, when this latter died in 1645, took the post himself until he yielded it to Étienne Le Camus in 1648.[14] At the time of his return after the Fronde, he did not seem to have made the Louvre a priority, being more concerned with the military future of the kingdom in terms of the new policy of royal grandeur. If, previously, he had shown only sporadic interest in the palace, from 1657 onwards he assumed responsibility for all new building at the site. This would continue for the four years that remained to him. Louis Le Vau, as the King's First Architect, had to work under Mazarin's direction, only finding greater freedom to take initiatives in the final year of the cardinal's life.

A study of Mazarin's correspondence, contracts for new work, and decrees of the King's council are the basis of recent conclusions about the development of the Louvre while the cardinal-minister lived. The Great Design for the Louvre, relaunched from 1657 onwards on Mazarin's initiative, was forcefully implemented by Antoine Ratabon, the Superintendent of the King's Buildings, supported by the cardinal's right-hand man, the young Jean-Baptiste Colbert. The architect ranked lower in the pecking order at first, but he emerged as time went on as a real force for the completion of the complex of buildings that constituted the Louvre palace.

The return of the sovereign to the Louvre on 21 October 1652 was the first sign of the reimposition of order in the kingdom as a whole. The young King (he was 14 and legally of an age to be recognised as the monarch) was aware of the way in which the members of the new financial class had begun to house themselves in the concluding years of his father's reign and had decided it was not for him. The installation of the court in the unfinished apartments of the Louvre served to assert the King's authority over all those who had recently tried to restrict it. The new tendency towards absolutism, elevating the monarchy above the nobility, was Mazarin's creation, even if he was still absent in the province of Bouillon when Anne of Austria and her son returned to Paris – her only motivation throughout the Fronde had been to preserve the monarchy undiminished for Louis to take it over himself when the time came.

The King and his ministers settled into old rooms in the south-west corner of the Louvre provided by Pierre Lescot. Courtiers who were not ministers were put up in the medieval buildings of the old Louvre and in rooms around Francis I's kitchen yard. Once lodged in the Louvre, the King himself, by his decree of 26 October, called for Mazarin to have an apartment near him where he could be called upon to offer advice. When the cardinal returned from exile, it was not to his own lavishly appointed palace, but into specially constructed rooms that would increase his availability to the King. So the decision was made to adapt the attic storey above the King's apartments in the royal pavilion and in the principal building of the west wing. The first recorded payments were for no more than repairs to existing structures, but the sums of money involved were large enough to cover 'considerable embellishments'.[15] Records show that this solution was followed up by taking over extra rooms as time went on.

Louis Le Vau found himself in charge of this process in 1653 and 1654. He inserted an alcove bedroom with a ceiling lavishly provided with a *voussure*, and added an oratory and small office, encroaching on a place earmarked to be left to lodge any future Queen. A masonry contract was signed in September 1653 for constructing an apartment for the King's Council, which was to occupy the whole of the ground floor of the building, consisting of a summer room, an office and a chapel. This was the first of the plans drawn by Le Vau for the King in the Louvre while Jacques Lemercier was in the throes of his final illness.

Until 1653, the end of the attic had been left open to the elements, but now a wall was raised to complete the building. A corridor was created in the clock pavilion connecting the first floor with the King's apartment, for which there is a contract dated 15 October 1655. Rooms here were to be occupied from 1655 by the Marshal de Villeroy, the King's tutor, and, two years later, by the Prince de Conti.[16] Above this apartment, rooms were made available for the King's First Physician, Antoine Vallot – the man responsible for the enlargement of the Jardin de Plantes for scientific and particularly medicinal purposes analogous to the Physick Garden at Chelsea – who had to give up his previous lodging to Mazarin in the main building of the same wing. Two contracts were involved in this, one for woodwork in the doctor's new rooms in the attic, signed on 1 September 1655 with Claude Dublet, and the other dated 18 October with Nicolas Messier and André Mazières for masonry.[17]

The Square Yard in embryo was limited to three principal buildings and two pavilions. The Little Gallery was being refurbished early in 1653. A payment of 1,245 livres was made to Claude Mollet for the design and planting of gardens outside the King's apartment windows. Other payments were made out of royal funds for buying sand and manure for the plants and bushes, and containers for orange and jasmine trees, though this seems to be a project that was soon abandoned.[18] An external balcony with iron railings was being constructed along the front of the building, but this too was to be no more than temporary.[19]

These arrangements proved to be too limiting for activity appropriate in a royal court. The Queen Mother decided after only a year to commission Le Vau to design a way of taking over the lower part of the small gallery to provide a new apartment suite and he drew up a plan for a building with three bays, copies of the first two levels of the south wing of the Louvre that looked out over the Seine. He added a pavilion at the northern end of the small gallery, containing oval rooms on each floor to provide an extension of the King's apartment. The work was decided upon in 1654 and carried out between 1655 and 1658 (at the same time as he was working on Fouquet's project at Vaux-le-Vicomte). The Italian artist, Giovanni Francesco Romanelli, brought to France to provide the decorations for his own palace by Mazarin, and Jean Valdor were made responsible for the wall and ceiling paintings.

What courtiers and contemporary Parisians could see was the royal palace threading its way among the houses of nobles that had grown up on the site. These would be bought up and demolished entirely as the Louvre palace expanded, but not for several years to come. Le Vau's projects at this time were still expected to conform to the Grand Design set by his predecessors in earlier reigns. Limitations on his freedom to innovate were also imposed by a dispute over administration between the superintendent, Étienne de Camus, and one of his subordinates, Antoine Ratabon, until the former's replacement by the latter in 1656.

* * *

Once Cardinal Mazarin had returned from exile, he imposed a guiding principle upon the continuing construction work at the Louvre, with Louis Le Vau still being First Architect. But until that happened, Anne of Austria was still in charge of piecemeal developments: her bathroom and the decoration of the King's alcove bedroom by Eustache Le Sueur. Her programme was very restrained. The painting of the story of Juno represented the happy end of her regency, but there was 'hardly any mention of the emergent glory of the King or to the role played by the principal minister'.[20] Furthermore, and more significantly, the project for a separate meeting room for the King in council would not be in keeping with the principle, inscribed in the French language for all to read on Le Brun's ceiling in the Hall of Mirrors at Versailles twenty years later, that 'The King rules by himself'. This room, decided upon in Paris in September 1653 by Chancellor Séguier while the cardinal was still in Picardy, was intended to be decorated by Charles Le Brun with the figure of Justice – rather than the King in person – providing good government. This was abandoned after Mazarin began to take an interest.[21]

The minister was on his way home with the court from the King's coronation at Reims when he received a letter from Colbert in Paris on 9 June 1654 that was redolent of their exchanges a little earlier about the works at Vincennes. It contained the first reference to the decoration of the King's alcove bedroom and his small office, which was still an idea in the mind of Le Vau. Contracts would be signed for these works on 23 June, and the undertaking was begun at the beginning of July but could not be completed until the end of October, by which time the court was meant to be back in Paris. In Mazarin's reply to the 9 June letter, he said that the project would not be paid for out of the King's funds, but by himself from his own copious fortune.

The completion of the apartment for the King was a personal concern for Mazarin, especially since it was being planned at the same time as his coronation. Power and authority was henceforth to be personal to the King, The décor set in place in his apartment was to be in keeping with this programme. Charles Le Brun was now commissioned to provide an allegory of Louis XIV governing the state for the ceiling of the small office.[22] A *Te Deum* was sung in Notre-Dame cathedral and a statue of Louis XIV was put up at the Hôtel de Ville at the same time as the coronation. There had been a shift in the way the monarchy was to be perceived.[23]

All this decoration was conceived and born in a hurry and Colbert was deeply critical of it, saying that the rooms were too little and badly lit, 'holes unworthy of the king's majesty and of the grandeur and beauty of the Louvre's design'.[24] When the court was in occupation of the Louvre in the autumn it was resolved to do what Colbert had suggested and enlarge the King's apartments in the direction of the Small Gallery as well as the Queen Mother's summer apartments, and this was planned for 1654.

From 1657, the rumour ran in Paris that the intensive enlargement of the royal apartments was a prelude to a vast project to complete the Great Design for the eastern entrance to the Louvre. It soon appeared that the origin of this rumour was in the complaints being made by Gaston d'Orleans about the King's intention to buy up all the private mansions that stood among and in front of the space required for the completion of the Louvre, namely those belonging to the families of Longueville, Choisy, and the Chevalier de Guet, but especially properties of the Bourbon family: their mansion, great hall and chapel. The rumour was confirmed from March onwards by the acquisition by letters patent of the Hôtel de Choisy and, in May, Antoine Ratabon was negotiating the takeover of the Longueville mansion in the space between the eastern limit of the Louvre and the church of Saint-Germain-l'Auxerrois.[25]

Gaston of Orleans rightly pointed out that the circumstances of the continued war against Spain would not allow for the expenses of building a palace on this scale. Besides, expanding the royal apartments was not necessary because the King was not yet married. But he did not know that there was a canny proposition to finance the acquisition of the Choisy and Longueville mansions by means of an exchange of forest land in the royal domain in Normandy. However, the taking over of the latter *hôtel* was subject to delays, as was its destruction to provide an open space between the Louvre's eastern facade and the buildings on the same line as the church of Saint-Germain l'Auxerrois: it was still standing in Louis Le Vau's final years, when he was lodged in a spacious apartment within it rather than in his own house in the rue Roi de Sicile, for the better performance of his duties.[26]

The King's long-term intentions were now in the public domain, especially when, as part of a decree made in Council on 23 March 1658, he ordered the Souvré mansion to be acquired by means of settling the debts of the heir to the property, who was still a minor. This building was in the rue Frémenteau, opposite Lemercier's north wing of the Louvre, and for the time being it would be used to house the King's and the Queen Mother's offices, allowing for the destruction of the old offices where it was intended to provide new kitchens.

This was the time when national circumstances changed for the better: a ceasefire with Spain was proclaimed on 7 May 1659, on which hopes of a permanent peace were based. So Antoine Ratabon wasted no time, once the peace preliminaries were signed on 2 June, over holding the meeting of heads of building firms (*entrepreneurs*) for adjudication of the masonry works that were going to take off into self-sustained growth very soon. The King, in reopening the Louvre site, was acting on advice given him by the cardinal-minister. The work was to continue on lines laid down in Lemercier's time – five years before – and Le Vau was not mentioned.

There is a little incident that emerges from the transactions carried out at this time that earths them in the interaction of the personalities involved in a way that is somewhat less than royal or ecclesiastical. The first lady-in-waiting to Anne d'Autriche was Catherine Henriette Bellier, and she was married to Pierre de Beauvais, who was having an *hôtel particulier* built to the design of Antoine Le Pautre in 1654–55 at 68 rue François Miron (at the time called rue Saint-Antoine). Loménie de Brienne relates in his memoirs that the Queen Mother had done her friend a favour by letting her take away a valuable stock of dressed stone being kept ready for use on the Louvre. Brienne says that when Mazarin heard about it he angrily shouted that the Queen Mother must have lost her wits to have made such a free gift and adds that the cardinal was motivated by avarice, but it was more likely that he saw the loss of the stone as a slight towards the royal palace. The cardinal concluded his intemperate outburst by adding: 'In all justice we ought to knock down the Hôtel de Beauvais, if there is such an hôtel, so as to give back to the Louvre what belongs to it!'[27]

When Antoine Ratabon had made his adjudication and the contractors had been chosen for the work, some money was needed up front for materials. The contract was signed on 20 June 1659 and required a payment of 12,000 livres to be paid on 1 July: the sum was paid from Mazarin's fortune, with Colbert acting as intermediary.

Louis Le Vau was to have little room for initiatives of his own for this next phase of the completion of the Louvre. Mazarin decided the programme in a way that was both imprecise and constraining for Le Vau. The contract signed in June 1659 was for the buildings to be begun while Sublet de Noyers was superintendent and stipulated that everything had to be in conformity with Jacques Lemercier's designs. But there was to be progress after the war with Spain was ended by the treaty of the Pyrenees. On 20 August 1659, a decree was issued that said all the houses from the Hôtel de Souvré along the rue de Frémenteau to the rue de Beauvais and the corner of the Louvre were to be bought up and knocked down. This would allow the building of a new kitchen block, but still following an old design that dated from the beginning of Henri IV's reign.[28] Another decree of 12 October 1660, promulgated by the King on Mazarin's advice, said that the Louvre was to be joined to the Tuileries and be just as large, adding to the Grand Design.

Furthermore, when it was decided to depart somewhat from the old plan to provide a theatre for events (*spectacles*) in the Italian style to celebrate Louis XIV's marriage, Mazarin employed Gaspare Vigarani from Modena, whom he had originally called to France to work on the first idea for the theatre in his own palace in the rue des Petit-Champs in July 1659. But there was no room for it there, and the *salle des Machines* was to be put up at the extreme north-western end of the Tuileries palace, constructed at first in wood and then clad in stone to make it permanent 'taking care that ... it should not spoil the Louvre's design' in the cardinal's words. Ratabon signed the contract for its foundations on 23 August 1659, envisaging that it would serve for the 1660 carnival. All this was involved in the cardinal's political decision intended to celebrate the military and diplomatic success achieved in the King's name with the completion of a plan that could be regarded as ancestral.[29]

Le Vau was faced with producing a design that lacked any architectural ambition. The only novelty in it was enlarging the Tuileries, but even that was to take the form of a mirror image of what was already there. He had been in charge of all new buildings since Lemercier fell ill in 1653, seven years before, and he had been the King's First Architect since 1654. His salary had been reduced twice since then and he was required at the Louvre to reproduce his predecessor's designs with nothing added of his own, besides having to cede his position at the Tuileries to Vigarani. While the peace was being negotiated, however, he worked – on his own initiative – on a plan for the whole building complex, which included a bridge over the Seine to celebrate the eventual peace. Such a bridge (the present Pont des Arts) had to wait for the First Empire.

He also worked on an alternative solution for the Square Yard despite the decisions already taken by the cardinal-minister, but even that was in accordance with the conservative principles already in force. Some of this was later realised in line with the incorporation of the Louvre into the urbanisation of the capital in the adjacent streets. No new work was being undertaken while the King, his new Queen and the court – including Mazarin – took so long in returning from the Spanish border. All that Ratabon could authorise in the cardinal's continued absence was work on Vigarani's theatre, on the Pavilion de Marsan, both in the Tuileries, and work on the roofs of Lemercier's unfinished parts of the Louvre in summer 1660. Le Vau was no more than a supervisor of these works. The logjam did not move before the court returned to the Île de France in July 1660 and the King and Queen had been installed in the new buildings at Vincennes, from which they made their triumphal entry into the capital.[30]

It was then that Mazarin, now in poor health, did not hold back from expressing his impatience with the delays at the whole Louvre site. He issued a declaration on 12 October 1660 to announce exceptional measures 'for the prompt perfection' of the Tuileries and the Louvre. No more delay in knocking down the Hôtel de Bourbon and several other houses in the way of the development was to be allowed so that foundations could be laid. Necessary materials were to be gathered: hard stone from the quarries at Saint-Cloud, Meudon, Vaugirard, Arceuil, Gentilly, and the Faubourg Saint-Germain, soft stones from Saint-Leu, Trossy, Tineray, timber for roof beams and carpentry. Four large royal workshops were to be set up so that work could start on 1 March 1661 or as soon as the weather permitted. No one else was allowed to undertake any building works any closer than ten leagues from central Paris, since all available workmen were to be taken on to work on the palaces of the Louvre and Vincennes, at the Val-de-Grâce or other royal building sites, and to be paid at the current rates.[31] From autumn 1660, designs had been ordered and the first contracts signed for the completion of the south wing of the Square Yard on the river front, the new kitchens and the doubling of the Little Gallery on its western side.[32]

Ratabon carried out his instructions. Le Vau drew up a complicated plan showing the lines of the Square Yard and the actual positions of the houses that were in the way of its being constructed.[33] On 3 January a contract was signed with André Mazières and Antoine Bergeron for the Queen Mother's apartment and the building next to it and a facade 28,000ft long with 'sixteen columns to enrich the facade ... along the waterfront.'[34]

But this happy situation for Le Vau would not last long. Ratabon suffered a stroke and his death came soon afterwards. Who would replace him as Superintendent of the King's Buildings? The answer in the King's mind was a foregone conclusion since, for him, 'culture was an instrument of power'.[35] Colbert was the only candidate for the post, which amounted to being minister for the Beaux-Arts. He would be the means whereby the King could express his own intentions, even if there were abrasive moments such as when Colbert would resist the attention his master was paying to the development of Versailles over and above the Louvre.

The King made the appointment as a Christmas bonus to Colbert – worth 40,000 livres in rents[36] – when he designated him as 'superintendent and co-ordinator-general of buildings, arts, tapestries and manufactures of France ... along with the direction of the artists lodged in the Grand Gallery of our Louvre Chateau'. as well as oversight of works at Fontainebleau, with effect from New Year's Day 1664.[37] This was in accordance with the King's design for absolutist, administrative monarchy, in which his decisions were implemented in detail by Colbert as his second self, as much for his buildings as for his commercial, economic, fiscal and industrial policy for the next nineteen years.

Can we be permitted to imagine Le Vau's fist scattering writing materials about his work table at home in his office in the rue du Roi de Sicile and his exasperated shouts when he heard this news?

Chapter 5

Vaux-le-Vicomte: Fouquet

Once more, we start with Le Vau's client. Nicolas Fouquet was a descendant of a rich commercial family who traded in silk and wool in Angers and were known to have provided a beadle for the University of Angers in 1559. The family was upwardly mobile because of the success of their business, their opportunistic marriages and their education in the law as well as the influential positions held by one or two of them in the Church with the passing of the decades.

The family was represented in the reign of Louis XIII by François Fouquet, a judge who presided over the tribunal at Nantes in 1635 that condemned Chalais for his conspiracy against Louis XIII and Cardinal Richelieu, intending to raise Gaston d'Orleans to the throne. Richelieu's patronage brought him into grandiose projects for overseas trade as well as into the orbit of the Counter-Reformation and the Jesuit Fathers. He married Marie de Maupeou, whose family were prominent *parlementaires* and also devout Catholics. Through Marie, they were associated with the Catholic priest Vincent de Paul, who was canonized in 1737 at the Visitation Convent in Paris, whose emphasis was on charitable works. François and Marie had twelve surviving children. At first, the family was more prominent in religion than politics. One of their sons became an Archbishop, another the Bishop of Agde, and one more remained a priest, but an influential one, known as the Abbé Basile. It was intended that Nicolas should be ordained, being the second son, but he felt no vocation and remained a layman. Their sisters entered convents that cost expensive dowries. The youngest brother, Louis, also in priest's orders, spent time in Rome buying up collectors' items for Nicolas.

They did acquire a political interest, however. When François was admitted into the nobility of the gown – the administrative nobility as opposed to the military (*robins*, with a long o) – he adopted the rampant squirrel as his heraldic emblem since *fouquet* was the word for squirrel in the dialect spoken in Anjou. He added the device *Quo non ascendet* (How far won't he climb?).[1] He was appointed as a councillor of state, due to Richelieu's influence, which brought him into Louis XIII's court, where he maintained his diligent trader's habits and added a love of learning and culture.[2] All these characteristics in the father were inherited by Nicolas.

His career was a rapid progression though the grades of *parlementaire* officialdom culminating in ministerial rank. He had been at the Jesuits' Clermont College, where he was recognised as a brilliant pupil with an abundance of self-confidence, despite his precarious health. When he was twenty, his father obtained the post of master of the requests for him. Five years afterwards, he married Louise Fourché, the only daughter of a councillor at the *Parlement* of Rennes, who brought him a rich dowry. However, she died a year later in childbirth, and his father soon after, leaving him with responsibility for his younger siblings as well as his monetary inheritance. It was then that he decided to purchase lands carrying ennoblement with them rather than making loans to the Hôtel de Ville or the royal treasury, which would have made him a *rentier* with interest on his loans providing him with an income. He met Lorin de Charny at a session of the *Parlement*, and decided to buy Vaux-le-Vicomte from him on 1 February 1641. Since noble status depended upon titled land owned, this purchase made him a member of the landed nobility in a prime location halfway between Paris and Fontainebleau and you could get there in a day from Paris.[3]

The chateau on the land was an old moated one with a drawbridge, a large courtyard and a keep built for defence against the English in the Hundred Years War. It had *dépendances*: a dovecote, barns and a sheepfold along with a park and garden, woodland, tillage and pasture, with as many as four watermills. Fouquet soon added half the manor of nearby Melun to his acquisitions, giving him another landed title.

For ten years he left his purchases as they were and, during the years of the Fronde, he was, like Colbert, faithful to Mazarin, accepting offices that took all his attention: intendant of the army in Picardy, then intendant, in succession, of Dauphiné, Catalonia, and Flanders, and the generality of Paris. Next, in 1650, he bought the office of procurator-general of the *Parlement* of Paris. For this last post he paid 100,000 écus and relinquished in exchange his post as master of the requests. All his energies had gone into his acquisitions until this point, but then he began to see himself as a patron of the arts and literature.

Fouquet was married again in February 1651 to Marie-Madeleine de Castille, daughter of another wealthy personality in the *Parlement*, with another hefty dowry worth 1,200,000 livres.[4] The final move was to become Superintendent of Finance, conjointly with Abel Servien, who had been instrumental as a diplomat in the conclusion of the Peace of Westphalia that ended the Thirty Years War in 1648, and was the proprietor of the chateau at Meudon, which Louis Le Vau had lavishly remodelled for him. The division of labour between the two superintendents was that Fouquet should raise money, which was seen by the taxpayers as 'fiscal terrorism',[5] and Servien would decide how it should be disbursed. When Servien died in 1658, Fouquet was rewarded by

Mazarin for his loyalty to him during the Fronde by being appointed the sole superintendent. He would have liked to have been Chancellor, but the squirrel had climbed far enough up the tree of state to make his fall remarkable enough when it came.

He tried not to draw too much attention to himself when he bought buildings and united them under one roof to enlarge as his mansion at Saint-Mandé, a stone's throw from the royal palace of Vincennes that Mazarin was developing – with Le Vau as architect – for the King, the Queen Mother, and, eventually, the new Queen Marie-Thérèse. Saint-Mandé was where he built up his library of rare books and his collections of art and curiosities, surrounding himself with artistic and literary personalities. Rumours that he would descend a staircase into his garden for more sensual pleasures were, it seems, exaggerated by the growing number of his enemies but he was building up a network of attractive women as his spies.[6]

By this time remarkably wealthy and rated highly as a creditable risk, his mercantile shipping business was flourishing, and to accommodate his fleet he developed fortified harbour facilities on his own property on Belle-Île, off the Breton coast, and elsewhere on the Atlantic seaboard, even using frigates as corsairs against the Dutch. In other words, he was building up a private navy.

Soon, enough, Fouquet wanted a palace to represent the high position he now held and the even higher one he was waiting to be given. He was in high favour at court. He could now become a Maecenas, surrounded by artists, poets, and lively spirits: his library and collections were enriched, and he gathered his own troop of attendants around him. Saint-Mandé had become overcrowded, but his lands at Vaux would accommodate a building and dependencies large enough for what his entourage had become and he set about realising their potential.

His colleague, Abel Servien, had already set him an example of how to go about it in his chateau at Meudon (demolished in the Franco-Prussian War) with immense works and redevelopments, even to the extent of an orangery, and Jacques Bordier, a mere intendant of finances, inferior in rank to Fouquet, had his superb establishment designed for him by Le Vau at Le Raincy, to the north-east of Paris.[7] Le Vau's creations and developments were now inciting envy in governmental circles. His designs had become what we would call a 'must-have' for those who were providing the monarchy with its resources, and cash was sticking to their hands as they completed their transactions. In any case, there had not been a superintendent of finances since François I who had not had a palace, either in Paris or in the provinces: 'often (the fact is certain for several of them) to the detriment of the finances of the state. The unfortunate thing was that Fouquet … went too far.'[8]

He made the decision to develop Vaux as quickly as he could in 1656. He began increasing his lands, adding a lake, vines, arable fields and meadows, by a purchase made on 14 January from Mme de Lionne, widow of his close associate Hugues de Lionne, in exchange for certain substantial debts owed to him, and a capital sum amounting to 42,000 livres.[9] He had already destroyed Vaux village and its church, where all his godchildren were growing up and their forbears were buried, together with the hamlets of Maison-Rouge and Jumeaux and even the watermills, so as to make room for his extravagantly grandiose scheme.[10] Those deprived of their families' homes went to live in other villages on either side of the projected development: Maincy to the west and Moisenay to the east of it. That these people still asked him to stand godfather to their children suggests that resentment was avoided by means of providing them with adequate housing in their new locations. This process of 'improving' land was becoming usual, comparable to the enclosure movement carried out by English squires a century later. Servien had destroyed part of his village to make way for his terrace at Meudon. The King himself would do something similar at Trianon and then at Versailles itself,[11] ordering the replacement elsewhere of the parish church of Saint-Julian to build the Grand Commun in a few years' time.

* * *

The decision to build the new chateau and garden on the lands at Vaux was taken while the Fronde was still taking its course in 1650–51, so Fouquet was ready to start the works in 1653, with hydraulic undertakings for the garden fountains and extended levelling of the terrain complete within a year. 'It was Mazarin who had taught Fouquet to dip into the public funds to finance his personal expenses, but it was his natural taste for the arts that created Vaux-le-Vicomte from these funds.'[12]

The aspiring architect Daniel Gittard, who later completed the church of Saint-Sulpice in Paris when Le Vau found himself over-committed ten years later, had at least a supervisory role if, indeed, he was not the original choice for designer. Gittard came from Blandy, not far from Vaux, and he would work for Fouquet on his defensive works at Belle-Île, and then the Prince of Condé brought him to Chantilly to work with Le Nôtre there. This was the time when Fouquet sent his brother, the Abbé Louis, to Rome to collect art for him, who suggested that whatever plans he had ready should be sent for the scrutiny of the master architects there. But then Fouquet decided that the forty-three-year-old Louis Le Vau, since 1654 First Architect to the King engaged on the royal projects at Vincennes and the Louvre, would be a better choice than

Gittard. Besides, Gittard's estimate was too expensive, even for Fouquet, at nearly 1.5 million livres. If Le Nôtre was not there already, he was brought in at this moment to collaborate with Le Vau on a combined scheme.[13]

As has been seen, the transformation of grazing land into a built landscape on the Île Saint-Louis had owed much to Le Vau. His reputation among the class of financiers and royal officials who were apt to order their town mansions and country chateaux from him was already well established and he was working for the King through the intermediary of Mazarin. His brother, François, was fifteen years younger than he, but it could reasonably be concluded that they had already pooled their ideas while François was remodelling the interior facades and the entrance to the chapel at Saint-Fargeau near Cosne-sur-Loire for the Duchess of Montpensier – the *Grande Mademoiselle* – when she had been exiled from Paris for her part in the Fronde. There are striking resemblances between the entrance to the chapel at Saint-Fargeau and the garden front at Vaux.

Mazarin had set the tone for bringing Italian architecture to bear on Parisian buildings. Although Le Vau's only foreign visit ever was to Saxony to inform himself about tinplate production to provide a cheaper solution for roof joints than lead, the inventory of his library after his death showed that he was well-versed in Palladio from sixteenth-century Venice and Vitruvius from the first-century BC in Rome. He had books about other classical architects too and illustrations of their ground plans and elevations. He owned works by and about nearly contemporary Italian architects like Sebastian Serlio, Leone Battista Alberti, and Vincenzo Scamotti.[14]

When Mazarin brought Giovanni Francesco Romanelli to Paris to work on his own palace in what is now the *Bibliothèque nationale*, he insisted that he used the principles and techniques of Roman Baroque style with discretion so as not to offend current French taste. Le Vau also heeded his warning at the Louvre, but all the same:

> ... the art in favour on the far side of the Alps, and especially in Rome, had seduced him, and he became one of the great protagonists of Italianism in France.
>
> [...] The mode was then towards ultramontain art. Rich patrons wanted to have, as the Roman cardinals did, galleries with painted and gilded vaults to show off their collections or the books in their libraries, domes, vast empty spaces, salons beneath cupolas: gardens with terraces; statues and balustrades seemed indispensable in decorating the lives of many art-lovers.[15]

But with regard to architecture, there were few severe breaks with French tradition and an indigenous taste remained in good heart.

Le Vau himself, as he had shown ten years before in what he built for Jean-Baptiste and Nicolas Lambert and for Louis Hesselin, brought a certain subtlety to bear on his work for his clients, as well as his qualities as an innovator in design. 'He knew how to bend himself to the exigences of his clients, even a little over-scrupulously, to give them what they wanted.'[16] This tendency in his work towards a careful sense of innovation was what appealed to Fouquet, who only had to go outdoors and look across the fields at Saint-Mandé to see what Le Vau had achieved at Vincennes, and he paid a visit to Bordier's establishment at Le Raincy to see how happily Le Vau had combined French tradition with Roman style.

This was what Fouquet wanted for Vaux-le-Vicomte. He and his family had already made use of his services in Paris: a house in the rue du Temple for François Fouquet, and an adaptation of his own house at Saint-Mandé in 1654 at the same time as Le Vau was working on the arena for wild beast fights nearby.[17] He made up his mind to put the construction of his palace into Louis Le Vau's capable hands, though he did not like his initial project because the treatment of the roof space made the building too top heavy, but, in general, he wanted that design developed. Le Vau accepted the dimensions of Gittard's foundations. Subsequent plans were accepted in August 1656 on an estimate of 600,000 livres[18] and Michel Villedo's name appears as the entrepreneur taken on to arrange for the works.

Villedo had made a less conspicuous, but nonetheless significant, career for himself since the early days on the Île Saint-Louis. He had been responsible for works to enlarge the Jesuits' Clermont Collage, where Fouquet went to school, became master mason to the King's buildings in 1636, and a speculative builder in the new *quartiers* that were springing up in Paris in the 1640s and '50s. He had been promoted to the post of master-general of masonry on the King's buildings in 1641 and of the French bridges and highways; since 1646 he had been one of the councillors and architects to the King. Villedo's brother-in-law, Antoine Bergeron, was also drawn into the massive organisation as site manager because Villedo himself was so often absent on other works.

* * *

Once started, the building rose from the ground very quickly as the impatient Fouquet wanted it to, and it was soon seen how quickly the costs also rose, especially when Fouquet decided that the main chateau should be built entirely in ashlar stone quarried at Creteil.

Work went ahead, with the money being found in the same way as Fouquet raised it for the King – by means of greatly increased indebtedness. So Le Vau made his design more lavish still. Above all the ground-floor windows he put bas-reliefs bearing his patron's emblems, and replaced plain Doric columns with rusticated ones. 'Behind the change ... stand an architect who was tinkering with his design while construction was under way and a patron whose taste for magnificence overcame his earlier budgetary limits.'[19]

It only took a year to have all the masonry and the roof timbers in place: from August 1656 to September 1657. The carpenters arrived to put the wainscots (known in the French texts as *lambris*) and mantelpieces in place, and to position the new-fangled alcoves in the bedrooms – this last was an Italian touch to which Le Vau was particularly devoted.[20] By the end of 1658 the finials were in place on the high roofs and the cupola, and the interior door frames were ready.

For the courtyard façade, Le Vau's triple arcade provides the entrance with four pillars imitated from what he had found and duplicated at the Louvre from Philippe de l'Orme, surmounted with a pediment of which the decoration is the work of Michel d'Anguier with the theme of children playing with lions representing love overcoming brute strength: the symbol is reinforced by one of the children counting how many teeth the lion has. These sculptures flank the left-facing rampant squirrel surmounted by the viscount's coronet, Fouquet's own escutcheon – not the King's – giving him the place of honour. Above the pediment, Anguier placed two seated statues representing Apollo and Rhéa, respectively gods of heaven and earth.[21]

Hilary Ballon pointed out the innovative quality of the facade:

Le Vau attempted to build a classical French chateau – not as Mansart did by adapting the orders to traditional French forms but by using antique fragments, like the temple front, in wholly new ways and contexts ... Le Vau rethought the chateau in order to fulfil the promise of his patron's classical interests: at Vaux he reinvented the chateau plan and, with Le Nôtre, merged house and garden so that the rotunda imaginatively restages ... the architectural sundial. The Farnese *Hercules* at the end of the garden paid homage to Fouquet's heroic labours at Vaux. The labours referred not only to the radical restructuring of the landscape and the minister's service to the state: surely they also referred to the search for a classical French idiom, a key to Le Vau's ambition at Vaux-le-Vicomte.[22]

* * *

Fouquet was becoming aware of the risks that he was taking and, despite his intentions to remain on good terms with Colbert, began working on what is called the plan of Saint-Mandé, whereby he alerted his Breton supporters to the need for him to defend himself should he ever lose the confidence that the King still had in him as a provider of funds for the conflict with Spain. This conflict was becoming more acute because Condé, French prince of the blood royal and former leader of the Fronde of the nobility, was in command of a Spanish army in association with Juan of Austria. The war against Spain was threatening to ruin France financially. Mazarin made an alliance with Oliver Cromwell, paying the hard price of yielding Dunkirk to the English.

There seemed every likelihood that the Fronde would re-establish itself, with frequent revolts by the nobility of the sword and opposition to new taxes from the provincial *parlementaires*. Hope in eventual victory was restored by Turenne's victory over Condé and Juan at the battle of the Dunes on 14 June 1658. But anxiety reasserted itself when the nineteen-year-old King fell gravely ill until mid-July. It was in this context that the plan of Saint-Mandé was completed, certain allegiances were signed and secret acquisitions were made. Despite what Le Vau and Le Nôtre were accomplishing for him at Vaux-le-Vicomte, he knew he was skating on thin ice. Nevertheless, he commissioned Jean de La Fontaine to write a poem in celebration of the building that was coming into being: the famous *Songe de Vaux*.[23]

* * *

During 1659 banisters (*rampes*) were provided for the staircases and Le Brun's painted ceilings were in an advanced state of readiness. It was possible for people to start living on the ground floor of the main building – Le Vau had two rooms at his disposition when he was working there[24] – and to the west of the building site in the village of Maincy they were re-measuring, making good and making sure of everything being ready, minimising the risks before the great public unveiling planned for three years' time. Literary figures moved there too from Saint-Mandé: Jean de La Fontaine, Madeleine de Scudéry and Jean Pellisson. The unfinished chateau for a short time became the artistic powerhouse that Nicolas Fouquet intended it to be.[25]

Le Vau constructed the service buildings: two blocks of them, one on either side of the courtyard in front of the principal entrance ranged in parallel. Long wings lead away from the centre, and their walls have panels in brick framed with *chainage* of cut stone. The slate roofs have a bluish tinge not as dark as those on the palace. This gives depth of colour and contrast with the view of the main building at a distance. The two different types of building complement each other: a stunning effect allowing for Fouquet's extravaganza to be appreciated. Pillars in white marble accentuate the three-dimensional effect. At each end of these service buildings there are pavilions with steep roofs separate from the centre of the roof space.

We go into the palace forecourt from the central door in the high wall of the right-hand *dependance* and advance through the *grille* to the façade. What might be taken for five independent high roofs surmount two stone storeys with pavilions at the corners. Up the steps, and we are inside the square vestibule; in 1661, we would have gone straight ahead into the astonishing oval salon, but at present we are directed to the left and experience it from the side. Our first encounter with it there is an unavoidable shock.

The size impresses. The oval extends upwards for 18m to take in both storeys, the windows on the upper level open half to the garden side, and half to the upstairs interior. The dome covers all, and its dimensions inside are fully visible. Le Brun had no time before the royal visit to do any more than design his painting for it. Other ceilings by him are to be seen in the apartments intended for the King should he have accepted Fouquet's offering to celebrate his *Gloire*.

Decorations in the salon include antique busts of Roman personalities with their faces positioned just above our heads so that we have to look up at them, implying our reverence to their authority analogous to the King's, recently established after Mazarin died in March 1661. These were among the ancient treasures sent home from Rome by Nicolas's brother, Louis, in January 1656 and subsequently.[26] The masonry is surmounted by a frieze and floral swags among the first achievements of the young sculptor François Girardon, underneath which are representations of the signs of the Zodiac on roundels held by caryatids set on supports called *termes* sculpted by his associate, Nicolas Legendre.[27]

Nature itself is pressed into service: half the interior of the structure is in shade and this allows the almost square upper windows and the lower full-centred arches separated by pilasters topped off with Corinthian capitals to provide an intriguing interplay of light and dark reflected in the marble floor. There was even a suggestion that there had been a sundial in the middle of that floor. This was to be a setting for monarchical grandeur, but Louis XIV decided that he would provide it for himself on his own terms and elsewhere. After all, Le Vau was *his* First Architect, not Fouquet's.

The eminent art historian Jean Cordey had an appreciation of Vaux-le-Vicomte published on the basis of a close association with the Sommier family of industrialists, who had made themselves responsible for its restoration:

... the façades as well as the plans, [had] no faults or calculation errors; the proportions are precise, the divisions logical and successful, the numerous open spaces well positioned ... Le Vau was really able to put everything he had into Vaux, because he did not have to reckon – as he did at Vincennes and Versailles – with the conservation of a building already in place.[28]

All this is one in the eye for Bernini's criticisms ten years later of his work at the Square Yard in the Louvre.[29]

* * *

We go through the triple arcade with the vista of gardens in front of us, descend the triumphal steps and turn round to see the garden façade with glaring masonry on a sunny day, surmounted with the slate roofs leading inwards and upwards to the cupola. In descending sequence, our eyes meet the cupola, a pediment supported by four pilasters between three windows with marble statues in front of them. Then at ground-floor level, the triple-arched exit or entrance with four rustic pillars borrowed from those used by Philippe de l'Orme at the Tuileries.[30]

Then we blink ... and on second viewing we see the extravagance that the young King saw on the famous night of 17 August 1661, just after dark when the fireworks went off, leaving the whole edifice in silhouette. That moment transferred everything, orange trees and all, to a marshy, forested terrain on the other side of the capital, where Louis-le-Grand built for himself what Fouquet had wanted to build for him. And he did it with the architect, the artist and the designer of gardens that his superintendent of finances had temporarily filched from him. And then he set out to erase Fouquet and his name from the whole enterprise.[31]

'It was not the wealth on display that would have impressed the King, but rather the taste that directed and transformed it. The rich Italianate baroque luxury that had cossetted the court of his mother and Mazarin and that to him had signified royal grandeur was replaced by an aesthetic of lightness, clarity and balance, and the example of Fouquet's achievement would exert an abiding influence on all that Louis XIV would later strive to embody and perfect.'[32]

Yet for the purpose of this study, it is Le Vau's building that counts more than the tragic story of Fouquet's arrest, condemnation to exile and the King's decision to imprison him in solitary confinement for life at Pignerol fortress in Savoy.

At the time that the chateau of Vaux-le-Vicomte was being designed, the high point of this type of construction was Maisons, built by François Mansart between 1640 and 1646 for a councillor of the *Cour des Aides*, René de Longueil. In some ways Maisons was a model for what Le Vau did at Vaux-le-Vicomte, in relating the main house to the service courtyards. But if it was a model for him, Le Vau used it very critically. At Le Raincy, built *ex nihilo* for Jacques Bordier, he used a quadrangular plan within a court of honour enclosed in a screen, but at Vaux he jettisoned that in order to provide a free-standing main chateau block with corner pavilions, a modification of what Mansart had done at Maisons. He did not provide for the service functions – principally the kitchens – in the wings he built on either side of the space before the house, but in a large basement, lit by windows between the footings of the pilasters of the house itself. Le Vau, who was fifteen years younger than Mansart:

> did not imitate Maisons: rather, he recast it in a classical manner ... he opted for a Palladian solution on the court façade: a temple front with Fouquet's coat of arms lodged in the pediment ... the executed design achieves a greater degree of integration by reiterating the tripartite rhythm of the arcade [what, elsewhere, we have called Le Vau's trademark]; instead of one segmental pediment, the clock forms a discrete unit flanked by lower balustrades ... Le Vau's plan fuses Vaux with its setting. A master planner, he exploded the conventions of chateau design by abandoning the stair, the showpiece of baroque design, and bringing the *piano nobile* down to the ground, all to serve Le Nôtre's art – just as Le Nôtre conspired to make the entire garden a platform for the building, such that, wherever you stand, the chateau rises majestically from measured planes of water, glass and stone.[33]

Charles le Brun was working on the *salon d'Hercule* for Nicolas Lambert de Thorigny in the *hôtel particulier* that Louis Le Vau was building for him on the Île Saint-Louis in 1656. There was a kind of freemasonry in the financial world that enabled Nicolas Fouquet, the Superintendent of National Finance, to take him off Lambert's project to let him work on his own, more lavish, programme at Vaux-le-Vicomte. Fouquet had already employed him at Saint-Mandé and he recognised his qualities. He also knew that he was accustomed to collaborating on good terms with Le Vau. Fouquet was in a hurry to have his new chateau up and running, being well aware of the hostility of Mazarin's other agent, Jean-Baptiste Colbert. Le Brun provided for him 'one of the glories of French decorative painting of the middle years of the century'.[34] For as long as it took to complete the work, Le Vau would have the supervision of an army of stonecutters, masons, carpenters, roofers, Le Brun's assistant artists, sculptors, stucco workers, commemorative medallion engravers, experts in weaving tapestries who came from Flanders, experts in hydraulics for the construction of fountains in the gardens, and the labourers needed for scaffolding and other ancillary tasks. On 8 February 1657, a gentleman from the neighbourhood told the Queen Mother that he had counted nine hundred men working on the construction site at Vaux, and on 21 November 1660, Fouquet himself recorded that he had double that number.[35] Fouquet realised that he would have to keep quiet about it, at least until all had been completed. There was to be a certain secrecy about the pharaonic works going on not far from the little town of Melun in the next five years with the labourers being taken off to work in the vines or the fields whenever someone prominent at court – like Mazarin or even Colbert – showed up on their way from Fontainebleau to Paris, Vincennes, or Saint-Germaine-en-Laye to express an unwelcome interest. This 'elicited borderline paranoia' in Fouquet, who stepped up his security arragements.[36]

But when the building and the garden were in a more advanced state of preparedness, Fouquet turned on a publicity mechanism. Israël Silvestre, born in Nancy in 1621, son of an artist, an orphan whose father died of the plague when he was ten, was brought to live in Paris with his godfather, an artist called Israël Henriet. This man, although not yet married, brought him up as his own son. The boy acquired his skill in drawing from him, went several times to study in Rome, and became one of the most celebrated *dessinateurs* and engravers in France when he returned. He concentrated on theatre projects and views of the changing cityscape of Paris, and entered royal service, providing views of the royal residences and being granted royal permission to publish his own engravings. It was only natural that his next career move was under the patronage of Nicolas Fouquet between 1658 and 1661 and he made several drawings at Vaux-le-Vicomte before the grand opening: a series of large and small prints in his distinctive and original style.[37]

His preparatory drawings were completed before 1661 and the prints were published afterwards. He was encouraged to roam round the whole terrain, when nothing had been completed, to look at Le Vau's and Le Nôtre's designs and to anticipate what the finished work would look like in the interests of subsequent publicity. Hilary Ballon suggested that Fouquet commissioned the prints himself: 'Market demand would not have justified a series of twelve prints devoted to a single building; no other private structure in France was portrayed in such great detail.'[38]

Charles Le Brun and his wife Suzanne were brought to live at Maincy[39] from 1658 onwards after having occupied an apartment in the unfinished chateau for a few months as Le Vau's neighbours.[40] Le Brun and his team of *artiste-peintres* were to be responsible for the ceilings in the chateau and for the many decorative panels on doors and interior window embrasures, but most of the walls throughout the house, except for the oval salon, were to be decorated with tapestries, which were not to be brought from elsewhere but woven within a short distance of where they were to be hung from cartoons designed by Le Brun at Fouquet's own tapestry factory close at hand.

In autumn 1658, he acquired the buildings of the old Carmelite monastery at Maincy and set it up there. As many as two hundred and fifty people could have worked there. Flemish experts were enticed and they were provided with their own brewery for the national drink that they could not work without. Fouquet took endless trouble to make this enterprise exclusive to him by following Mazarin south to Bordeaux on his journey to Saint-Jean de Luz for the treaty of the Pyrenees and the King's wedding to Maria-Teresa, Infanta of Spain, which was where the patent for high-warp tapestries was signed by the King in May 1660.

The carpenter in residence, Jacques Prou, built Fouquet a copy of the recently invented high-warp loom, but all the tapestries woven at Maincy were of the low-warp variety, which was cheaper, and, more importantly in this context, quicker to produce. The Flemish craftsman put in charge later became expert in high-warp weaving at the Gobelins, but for the moment he agreed to cut the costs and work rapidly. Charles Le Brun's assistants worked up his detailed cartoons, leaving no room for any other creativity than the technicalities of weaving to the *tapissiers*. Themes like Fortitude and Fidelity were among the preferred emblems used in the work, accompanied by lions and dogs to represent them. The King was to be flattered with images. representing Victory and Fame. Otherwise the usual biblical and classical mythology themes predominated. The work in hand was all confiscated, along with the artists and weavers, to be incorporated into the Gobelins factory in Paris. The memory of Fouquet was obliterated from the designs and Louis XIV's emblems replaced any remaining squirrels.[41]

Attention has been drawn to the double standards – if not blatant hypocritical dissimulation – in the wording of the patent Fouquet was granted for the works at Maincy.[42] At first appearance, the patent looks like many others granted for the same purpose by Henri IV. No one must imitate what shall be manufactured. Twenty apprentices shall be taught their trade and after six years shall be qualified to open their own workshops, and documents issued by Henri IV are evoked to announce that the directors, workmen and apprentices should enjoy privileges and exemptions from tax.

As already noticed, the time of the issue of the contract was the eve of Louis XIV's marriage at Saint-Jean-de-Luz. Mazarin was there with the court while Fouquet had come back to Paris, where he was at the height of his period in favour. He was protector of writers and artists, and he was looking forward to the completion of his chateau – where he was going to receive the King and his bride, together with the Queen Mother and the whole court.

In these letters patent, the King pays tribute to the services rendered to him every day by Fouquet with devotion and invariable fidelity in carrying out the great functions for which he is appointed. 'But all this was no more than brilliant appearance and deception (*trompe-l'oeil*)' and meant to give Fouquet a sense of security, although Fouquet was sensitive to the menacing tone concealed in it. Colbert was working to ruin him in the eyes of the King and the Cardinal.[43] Mazarin was playing his usual double game. The King was keeping up the pretence of favouring Fouquet, speaking in the document of his faithful service as if he knew nothing of the financial wastage in the kingdom and of the way in which the superintendent knew how to take advantage of it.

Fouquet's factory had only a year and a half of existence in front of it. It continued to operate after Fouquet's arrest but only because Colbert wanted it to. It was in full production and he intended to transfer the whole operation to Paris for the King's use. A year later, Le Brun, his assistant artists and the weavers settled in at the Gobelins and continued in their usual work 'to celebrate the glory of the King in coloured wool and gold and silver threads' for the Louvre and the Tuileries and, in a little while, for Versailles. The royal patent was meant for an eventual royal factory, but it would do no harm in Colbert's eyes to let Fouquet spend some of his presumedly embezzled national revenue on setting it up in advance. It has been pointed out how important that tapestries – and the control of their manufacture – were in the narrative of Vaux/Versailles.[44] Henri IV had encouraged their manufacture and use in a purely French context, establishing a style suited to the period of stability he had given to the French state to allow for the urbanisation of Paris. Nicolas Fouquet, having cornered the finance creation machinery of the state, used his tapestry factory at Maincy to create emblems for himself in the hands of his artistic agent Charles le Brun, who took the design of the tapestries out of the hands of specialist artisans. This better served Fouquet's intentions as patron. Fouquet privatised the manufacture of the images that suited his purposes at Vaux.

He had no ancestral portraits for his walls, but the heraldic squirrels were to be seen in abundance in the tapestries that Le Brun designed. The King and Colbert – as the discussion of the letters patent given above was meant to show – took the manufacture back for the nation and thus for the monarchy at the Gobelins to be used at Versailles. This meant that the pedagogical element involved in tapestry was entirely in the hands of the royal publicity machine. Tapestry and marble, as luxury items, were the best-suited media for the promulgation of the new style of the complexities of absolutist monarchy for which the King intended Versailles to be the showcase. Tapestries could have details unwoven from them: the squirrels disappeared in transit.

* * *

The context of Le Vau's life is the interaction of three forceful personalities, Mazarin, Colbert and Fouquet, along with the embodiment of absolute power in the person of the fledgeling Louis XIV. Accounts of Fouquet's disgrace mostly depend upon the account of how it came about in the *Mémoires* of Louis-Henri de Loménie de Brienne, whose father, Henri-Auguste, was secretary of state for foreign affairs under Mazarin. Brienne *fils* was at the heart of the action at court at Fontainebleau and Nantes in the months after Mazarin's death in 1661,[45] and what he had said was given a more literary form some sixty-five years later by abbé François-Timoléon Choisy, member of the *Académie française*, whose father was in the service of the Duke of Orleans under Louis XV.[46] Nevertheless, it has been pointed out that both of these chroniclers wrote from memory at some time after the events, Brienne being constrained to live removed from the court, and Choisy not a courtier at all.[47]

When Mazarin died in March 1661, few on a national scale regretted his passing. Everyone knew about his colossal fortune and how it had been amassed: 'These first days were spent only in discussing the immense riches left by the cardinal.'[48] Everyone remembered the *Mazarinades*, pamphlets that protested against Mazarin's undue influence, and there was a certain transference of these to Fouquet on a popular level. The twenty-two-year-old King declared that he was to be his own prime minister from henceforth. The declaration was welcome in the country because a certain legitimacy and royal charisma had been lacking since the assassination of Henri IV in 1610. When the court arrived at Fontainebleau for Easter, and the parties began, Louis XIV was seen as impassioned and tireless. Mme de Motteville commented, 'From every point of view, things seemed more like the way in which we used to live in the golden century rather than how things are in the one where we are.'[49]

The King had been embarrassed by the enormous sums spent at Saint-Mandé and Vaux while the expenses for repairs of dilapidation on the royal houses had been left unpaid, by pensions granted in secret by the superintendent to his own family and friends, by the fortifications he had carried out at Belle-Île as if he had plans for warfare, by his negligence of affairs of state and the delays in raising necessary loans. Fouquet paid unwelcome attentions to Mlle de La Vallière before she was openly known to be the King's mistress, trying to bribe her to gain her support, which she reported to the King. 'The King had therefore resolved to get rid of Fouquet.'[50]

However, the fact that Fouquet possessed the office of Procurator-General of the Paris *Parlement* gave him a certain immunity. Only eight years after the suppression of the Fronde, it would have been dangerous for the King to act against one of the leading officers of the *Parlement*. So he decided to persuade the naïve Fouquet to sell the office to someone else while remaining superintendent of the finances. Colbert set about trying to cause embarrassment to his rival by belittling his credit among the financiers.

Fouquet had his network of spies reporting on Colbert's activity – notably Mme de Plessis-Bellière, and decided to go south to join the Cardinal while he was on his way to negotiate peace with Spain and arrange the King's marriage. On the way he stopped at Bordeaux, where he learned that Colbert had sent a long memorandum denouncing him to Mazarin on 1 October and arranged to have it intercepted. He and his collaborator Jean de Gourville sat up all night and copied out the twenty pages of the document with their quill pens by candlelight. Gourville did not get to know the entire content of it, because he copied only every other page while Fouquet himself copied the rest, so, of the two, only Fouquet read it all and knew exactly what Colbert had levelled against him before letting the document go on to its intended recipient.

He caught up with Mazarin at Saint-Jean-de-Luz and took the offensive, complaining against Colbert's accusations, saying that what he had criticised had actually been done by others, without – of course – betraying any knowledge of the memorandum, and paid lip service to Colbert's talents and his loyalty to Mazarin. Mazarin – also of course – had read the memorandum by this time, but did not admit that it existed. Mazarin would not give up Colbert since he was too well acquainted with the way he had acquired his own fortune, and insisted that Fouquet had misunderstood Colbert's attitude toward him.

Meanwhile, Colbert had a setback of his own that affected his good standing with the Cardinal. His cousin, Colbert de Terron, had blundered into being the intermediary between Louis XIV and one of Mazarin's nieces, Marie Mancini, with whom he had fallen in love, the love being returned. Mazarin was determined to quash this love match in order to facilitate the marriage with the Spanish Infanta and secure the peace. When he heard that Terron was continuing as the letter box between the two *amoureux*, Colbert was furious and, because he knew what his cousin was up to, his future with the King was momentarily in the balance.[51] Eventually, the only toad that Mazarin forced him to swallow was that he should seem reconciled to Fouquet so as to gather more evidence against him. The taste was not too bad.

Mazarin's usual tactics of dissimulation were also brought into play towards Fouquet, since he knew the ins and outs of his fortunes just as well as Colbert, and he was asked to go on working in tandem with his rival. Fouquet agreed, having learned his master's preferred tactics from long years of association with him. Mazarin concealed any animosity he might have felt towards him. When Fouquet was back at Saint-Mandé in December, Colbert came to see him and they both contrived to tell Mazarin that they were reconciled.[52]

The King also resorted to giving Fouquet a false security, always asking for his advice in preference to that of others, and advancing his brother, the Bishop of Agde, to the influential position of Master of the Oratory. In the end, with false confidence in his own safety, Fouquet agreed to sell his office of procurator to Achille de Harlay. Fouquet ordered a million livres of the proceeds of the sale to be deposited at Vincennes for the King's own secret use, not realising his intentions against him. Colbert did not keep up the pretence of being Fouquet's ally, and kept his distance from then on.

Fouquet tried to defend himself by approaches to the Queen Mother, and attempted to win Colbert over, but seeing the impossibility of it, he developed his Saint-Mandé plan. A naval officer called Guinan was to raise Belle-Île in his name, arming his commercial fleet with the addition of fireships and corsairs at Le Havre and up the Seine to Rouen. There was even a plan to take war minister Le Tellier hostage in case of Fouquet's expected arrest.[53] Fouquet took the risk of having all this written down and hiding the papers behind a mirror in his library at Saint-Mandé, where they were found by Colbert's investigators after his arrest.[54]

Colbert pointed out that Fouquet ought to be dismissed before the 1661 harvest, so as not to lose any more taxation to the system that he had created. It ought to be done in Brittany, where Fouquet had a great deal of influence.[55] The King made his final decision to remove Fouquet from office on 4 May 1661, two months into his personal rule, but also decided to wait for the right moment to do it.

Meanwhile, in April, Colbert set his cousin Terron to look into what was going on in Fouquet's *seigneurie* at Belle-Île. His report left Colbert in no doubt about Fouquet's plan to escape arrest. He was maintaining a garrison of two hundred men there. They were armed with four hundred artillery pieces, with ample ammunition and explosives, mostly brought there from Holland, and enough weapons for six thousand men. There were three hundred barrels of wine and a proportionate amount of flour. People who lived in the vicinity would provide a guard for the island and for the town.

The letter Colbert received from Terron on 28 July as a supplement to his report was conclusive. It told him that Fouquet's secret trade in the Caribbean, where he had naval officers in his pay, was aimed at making himself ruler of Martinique: he had fifteen ships at his disposal there to the exclusion of commerce being carried on by anyone else. Belle-Île was to be the port for all this trade, well provisioned to sustain its occupants against attack. Moreover, munitions for arming ships were stocked there ready to be used in defence of the place. Commerce between Martinique and Belle-Île had been planned in detail and it was 'a good cover for having warships and all sorts of munitions in abundance'.[56] Colbert became even more determined to ensure Fouquet's deprivation. Only then could he begin his own rearrangement of the way the country was financed and the King would be able to assert his unique authority.

* * *

At the end of the extravagant fête given him by Fouquet at Vaux on 17 August 1661, the King would have had Fouquet arrested then and there to humiliate him on his own turf. 'The scale and quantity of the entire design, and the specific motif of the dome, were royal, not ministerial, gestures and thereby Fouquet over-stepped prudent bounds.'[57] However, Anne of Austria dissuaded him, and the dissimulation was kept up for nearly three weeks longer by means of keeping to the plan to hold the Brittany Estates-General at Nantes.

Jean de La Fontaine, one of Fouquet's cultural coterie and the only one who remained loyal to his memory afterwards, wrote an account of the fête for a friend five days afterwards, describing the great fountains like walls of water, the banquet, the new *comédie-ballet* organised by Molière, the fireworks, the final lavish collation. The letter concluded on an augural note. The King, La Fontaine recalled, did not want to stay the night at Vaux, and all was ready for the royal party to leave for Fontainebleau, with the Queen Mother's carriage parked in front of the garden facade. There was a final burst of fireworks from the lantern above the dome (or was it a sudden meteorological event – it is not clear from his account): 'We thought that all the stars, large and small, had descended to the earth, so as to render homage to Madame; but when the storm had ceased we saw them all in their places. The catastrophe of this enormous noise was the loss of two horses.' They shied, broke from their traces and fell into the moat, breaking their necks. La Fontaine could not forego putting their fate into verse:

> These horses which once pulled a carriage
> And now tow Charon's barge
> Fell into the moats of Vaux
> And then from there into the Acheron.

'I did not believe,' he adds, 'that this story would have had such a tragic and pitiful end.'[58]

* * *

Before the move to Nantes, a council meeting was held at Fontainebleau, during which the King issued decrees preventing the superintendent from maintaining secret funds. While this was being discussed by the ministers, Fouquet lost control of himself and blurted out, *Je ne suis donc plus rien?*' ('So, I count for nothing from now on?') He tried to recover himself – Choisy says 'he tried to replaster it'[59] – by saying that he would have to find other means of hiding the state's secret expenses. The young Loménie de Brienne, who was in the room, told Choisy later that the minister of state Le Tellier, no friend to Fouquet, knowingly nudged him with his elbow at Fouquet's outburst. This was the moment of truth.

Then they all moved to Nantes, the King by road, and others by boats – *cabanes* – well provided for passengers complete with galleys for preparing them meals and propelled rapidly downstream by oarsmen on the Loire from Orleans, amid speculation as to whether it would be Fouquet or Colbert who would be drowned, as it were, on arrival.

Brienne was appointed as the King's go-between from the King in the castle at Nantes to where Fouquet took lodgings at a good distance, for a time racked with fever. Captain d'Artagnan with his hundred musketeers was ordered to be ready to make the arrest, but to do it outside the castle precincts so as not to impugn the authority of its governor. The task was entrusted to the musketeers because the captain of the King's bodyguard, the Marquis de Gresves, was Fouquet's friend.

The King invited Brienne to have his supper at his table and ordered him to go and fetch Fouquet at six in the morning of the following day, 5 September, coinciding with the King's twenty-third birthday. Brienne slept in his clothes and set off for Fouquet's lodging at five, taking time only to put on a clean shirt. He arrived before six and found Fouquet's door guarded by six musketeers and an officer who told him that Fouquet was already at the castle while his papers were being seized for the King to look over. Brienne left a message with the official who was gathering the papers to tell the King that he had arrived to carry out his orders, and left quickly in his carriage, ordering his coachman to hurry, only to find d'Artagnan with Fouquet already arrested outside the castle in a carriage enclosed 'by cages or iron trellises' at a quarter past seven by his watch.

When he encountered the King, Brienne was told that the arrest of Fouquet applied only to him, and none of his friends were implicated. It was arranged with the King for a large sum of money to be lent to Mme Fouquet.[60] Fouquet himself was taken, first, to Angers, then to the donjon at Vincennes, and subsequently to the Bastille. D'Artagnan provided information about Fouquet's unpopularity: as he was being taken from Tours to Amboise during the days of Christmas, it was difficult to clear a way through crowds of people not at work, hostile to Fouquet, who jeered him, and assured the musketeers that if he were to escape from their custody, they would immediately lynch him. D'Artagnan also reported that Fouquet responded to the threat with courage and resolution.[61]

Many believed that Fouquet would be condemned to death. A commission sent to Saint-Mandé found the papers hidden behind the mirror in the library. All actions taken against Fouquet and any new discoveries about him were regarded as extremely newsworthy and were rapidly circulated. Inventories of papers were seized from Fouquet's associate, Paul Pellisson, and extreme measures were taken to find more evidence, even to the extent of asking for plans of Saint-Mandé from masons who had worked there to look for secret cupboards built into walls. A hate campaign was in full swing.

A specific chamber of justice was to examine abuses and malpractices committed in the national finances since 1635. The first meeting on 3 December 1661 evoked a massive popular response against Fouquet. However, as the trial took its long course up until 1664, the public mood changed in Fouquet's favour. The devout Catholics in the capital, in the midst of whom the Fouquet family found itself, became sympathetic towards him as a victim of his destiny, although without claiming vindictiveness on the part of the King or Colbert. Fouquet's mother, an extreme adherent to the *devôt* party in the Church, was even pleased at what was happening to him because, she said, the loss of earthly glory would bring about his eternal salvation. All the documentation of his trial was gathered and published in sixteen duodecimo volumes and there were enormous sales when it was published in 1668 and there was a reprint in 1696, sixteen years after his death.[62]

Brienne had nothing to say about the trial because he was no longer at court while it was going on, but he learned later from Olivier d'Ormesson, who had been present at it as recorder, that Fouquet had been condemned to exile from the kingdom in spite of six of the special *chambre de justice* organised by Colbert and presided over by Chancellor Seguier demanding the death penalty. It was the King himself who commuted the sentence of exile into life imprisonment, 'which,' said Brienne 'was a strange favour'.

On the day of Fouquet's sentencing, Louis XIV said to Louise de La Vallière, according to the playwright Racine, that had he been condemned to death, he would have let him die. Instead, he had invoked *raison d'état* to commute the sentence of banishment to one of life imprisonment with no reprieve to be allowed. 'This was the only time that a head of state used his right to grant a pardon to make the punishment worse.'[63]

From the Bastille, Fouquet was taken to the Alpine fortress of Pignerol, 'where he finished his days in Christian resignation, after nineteen years of imprisonment. He was about to be set free, it was said, when he died of surprise and joy at having the consolation at last of seeing his wife.'

Brienne concluded his account by quoting a political testament attributed to Colbert, Fouquet's insatiable enemy:

> It was in this year ... that M. Fouquet, whom Your Majesty condemned to perpetual imprisonment instead of the banishment which he ought to have suffered after his arrest, died at Pignerol. He accepted his disgrace with a fortitude that was not to be expected from a man softened by luxury and by pleasure, and who mixed every kind of distraction with the important matters entrusted to him ...[64]

Fouquet defended himself before his judges and gained increasing public sympathy from the street. But the King was even more implacable than his factotum. The treasure and the creators of Fouquet's luxurious lifestyle went eventually to Versailles, but everything about Fouquet himself had to be – and was – eradicated.

There is a psychological element in all this. It was, without doubt a *coup d'état* on the part of the King – then timid in making decisions, unsure of himself, resentful of his own and his mother's domination by Mazarin – who had transferred what he objected to in Mazarin to Fouquet. There was a moment at Nantes in September 1661, just before Fouquet's arrest, when the King stopped calling the superintendent Monsieur, referring to him to others behind his back by his undecorated surname. The King, disliking Mazarin for his attributes – he called him 'Le Grand Turc' – had nevertheless adopted the absolutist principles that he had learned from him. When he had become convinced by Colbert that the ambitious Fouquet 'had become too visible'[65] he persuaded himself that what he had long contemplated must actually be done, and done as a public event.

Colbert in contrast presented, neither then nor later, no challenge to the absolutist principle. Colbert was a functionary, and an efficient one at that with an eye for meticulous detail. He would develop colonies, emphasise the role of the *Marine royale*, make industry predominant over agriculture, adopt what some might call a policy of 'France first', but he would do it as the King's right-hand man. The King might have need of a First Architect, but he would no longer tolerate a first minister, and that was what the ambitious Fouquet gave every appearance of wanting to be.

Le Vau's building at Vaux-le-Vicomte remains with its statement about French classical style, and the architect's ambition to make that statement was not a threat to the monarchy. It is ironical that much of what he built for the King at Versailles has greater resemblance to the brick and stone dependencies at Vaux-le-Vicomte than to Fouquet's *corps de logis*.

Chapter 6

Colbert: A Difficult Taskmaster

Le Vau designed the *Salle des Machines*, at the northern end of the western facade of the Tuileries, and developed the southern end of the same facade between the Pavilions de Bullant and de Flore. (The whole western facade between the pavilions was destroyed in 1871.) Then, besides rebuilding the Little Gallery after the 1661 fire and adding the rooms surrounding the Sphinx courtyard in the Tuileries, he finished the northern side of the Louvre's Square Yard, begun by Lemercier, from the central pavilion to the north-east corner, and the interiors of the eastern facade and the western half of the south side. All the exterior of the eastern facade and of the southern facade as far as the King's Pavilion is taken to be the work of the committee of three set up by Colbert.[1]

These achievements were modified during later periods, particularly during the two Napoleonic Empires and the conservative Third Republic, and during the presidency of François Mitterand.

* * *

While Cardinal Mazarin was still alive and in power, he represented the complexities of an era in which, from the point of view of the financiers, the State had ceased to exist. When more money was borrowed from them for the war against Spain, Anne of Austria, as regent for her son Louis XIV, acted not as head of state. but as a *seigneur* among other *seigneurs*. The State did not borrow money from the financiers, but the monarch, as an individual, did.

The King, as an individual, was not rich. There was no question if his 'living of his own' in the phrase used about the more successful English monarchs in the Middle Ages. His own lands would certainly not be enough to finance his projects, particularly the warfare he was so keen to prosecute as time went on. The head of state could not call directly upon those who controlled funds since they had no confidence in a monarch who was not creditworthy, and they would have bankrupted themselves if they had. Mazarin, as first minister, seemed to accept this subjection of the State to a group of private individuals

– a situation dating back to Louis XIII and Richelieu – and muddled through on the basis of it.

As soon as Mazarin, his godfather and mentor, had gone to his eternal rest on 9 March 1661, Louis XIV called his ministers together and declared that he would keep the ministers appointed by Mazarin – Le Tellier and Lionne – but that there would be no first minister from then on. After the destitution of Fouquet within six months, he would be his own finance minister too. There would be political continuity, but the King would be the absolute master, reigning and ruling alike. When the Archbishop of Rouen asked him to whom he should address himself from now on, he replied 'To me, Monsieur l'archeveque.'[2] Neither the Paris *Parlement* nor the regional ones had any sort of autonomy. The King's decrees did not have the force of law unless and until they were recorded and published by them, and they did have the right to complain about such decrees as they might consider to be unjust or oppressive, but they could not oppose any of them if the King imposed his right to have them recorded by means of a formal, special session known as a *lit de justice*. The ministers meeting in Council were present as the heads of their departments in an advisory capacity. They would offer their informed opinions as to policy, but then the King would decide upon action to be taken, overriding any of their objections if he saw fit, and they accepted the situation.

Colbert, smoothly passing from being Mazarin's second self to being the King's, persuaded him, once he had assumed personal authority, to take measures against the financiers, branding this means of raising state revenue as unacceptable, but, even so, they would remain as an inevitable feature of the kingdom, tolerated but controlled.

'Overall, Colbert conceived a system which showed the continued predominance of the financiers. Far from chasing the merchants from the Temple, he kept them in place. Colbert had nothing about him of the reformer, especially in the sphere of state finance: he multiplied extraordinary measures *into peacetime*.'[3]

As early as 1648, Colbert had allied himself by his marriage with Marie Charron to one of the families who occupied many different places simultaneously or successively in the state financial system[4] and knew that the members of these families were deeply embedded in the functioning of the State. In order to control them, the King would have to adopt their methods. This was to become the basis of the order of things that, in retrospect, was to be known as absolutism. State revenue was '*volerie*' – continual theft – and Colbert proposed a Chamber of Justice as the way to curtail its worst effects. It was a Chamber of Justice, meeting over a period of four years, that led to Fouquet's manipulated disgrace and imprisonment for life and allowed

Colbert to coalesce power into his own hands as the King's alter ego, speaking in his name as the instigator of the policies that he – Colbert – had devised.[5]

* * *

It was evident that the King had a mind of his own in respect to his buildings, and a creative mind at that. A taste for buildings was in the Bourbon genes, and good taste too. Three months after Mazarin's death, he decided to develop the northern end of the western wing of the Tuileries Palace (destroyed in 1871) to accommodate a theatre, known as the *Salle des Machines* because of the elaborate apparatus devised for shifting scenery. It was meant to be the work of the First Architect, but Mazarin brought in Carlo Vigarini to do the main work as he was experienced in theatre construction. The building was wooden and clad in stone so as not to clash with existing structures. It was hardly used and then abandoned by the King, perhaps on account of inadequate acoustics.[6]

Once Colbert was in charge of the King's buildings, three years later, construction at the Tuileries was renewed with Le Vau still as First Architect. The building work then undertaken was complete in two years, and Le Brun and his artist colleagues finished its embellishment by 1671, when Le Vau was no more. The Tuileries was to be the royal residence while the extensive work at the Louvre was still incomplete. The royal family was to live in the south range facing the Seine, and the north side was to be for government offices. Le Vau was still constrained by works devised in the past, but he did make one original contribution in the form of the replacement of Philibert de l'Orme's spiral staircase by one flight of stairs that doubled back into two more flights within a unified space. This showed the King's interest in stairs for ceremonies later developed in the Ambassadors' Staircase – outlined by Le Vau and implemented in detail by d'Orbay – at Versailles.[7]

There was also an Ambassadors' Gallery made available under Le Vau's supervision as a place to exhibit the royal collection of Italian easel paintings as well as for diplomatic receptions, with the ceiling covered with copies from the Farnese Gallery in Rome. Its primary purpose was as a study facility for the Royal Academy of Painting and Sculpture, which Colbert had recently established. This adjoined the King's own apartment, and he made private use of it.[8]

* * *

Colbert's measures at a political level were gathering momentum at the same time as foundations at the Louvre were being laid according to Le Vau's plan for the eastern facade opposite the church of Saint-Germain-l'Auxerrois. For Colbert, the Louvre was to be the primary expression of the King's *grandeur* in equal measure as triumphant warfare would come to be. Ways and means were being found to take over the mansions of the *noblesse* that were in the way. The King had exchanged Géneviève de Bourbon's Hôtel de Longueville for the Hôtel d'Épergnon, which he had recently bought, near the church of Saint-Thomas du Louvre on the north side of the Square Yard.

It was claimed, after the excavations in front of the Colonnade in 1964, that Le Vau began his work on this side of the Square Yard earlier than generally thought: that is, in 1661 – as soon as Mazarin's restraint was lifted from him. By March 1662, the greater part of the work below ground level had been completed. A wooden and stucco model was made in 1664 respecting the ground plan of Le Vau's construction at the same time as Colbert sent plans by Le Vau to the Abbé Elpidio Benedetti in Italy as part of his scheme to open the design of the eastern facade to free competition. Colbert decided that the foundations already made should be put out of sight and out of mind in 1665 and he held the authority to act accordingly.[9]

Successive plans drawn up in Le Vau's agency on his instructions by François d'Orbay show how his ideas were developing. His suggestions were changing all the time, and the whole situation seems to have been fluid in his mind, although a constant was the idea of an eastern facade ornamented with columns and a central pavilion containing an oval vestibule with the doubling of the room space. What Le Vau intended has been identified from what he added in outline in red chalk on twelve ground plans for the same building drawn up by François Mansart. It has been concluded that these red chalk outlines of walls with columns represent the foundations begun just before Colbert was made superintendent of the buildings on the first day of 1664, when the basement walls of the eastern facade were 3m (8–10ft) high.[10] These indications of intended columns added to Mansart's ground plan let it be seen that Le Vau had ideas of adding free-standing columns to the facade (as opposed to colossal order pilasters as at the Hôtel Lambert) long before the King accepted the idea. That such an idea was being discussed among his colleagues while work was going on at Vaux-le-Vicomte is shown in the drawing made by Le Brun for the decoration – never achieved – for the inside of the dome in the oval salon there, which has such pillars rising from one side towards the centre of it.[11]

Charles Perrault, who was acting as Colbert's assistant, reported in his *Mémoires* that Colbert did not like Le Vau's submitted plan and invited all the architects of Paris to look at it – along with the wooden model – and nearly all of them made hostile comments. Colbert himself thought it was not worthy of the King, whose grandeur the building was meant to celebrate. A competition was opened to find a better solution, and the one most to the King's own liking would be constructed.

Colbert's dislike for Le Vau and his work was plain to see in this decision. Not only had Le Vau inadequately supervised the foundations of the Hôtel Bautru, which Colbert had bought and intended to occupy – though it has been pointed out that Colbert did not acquire the house until a year after he had turned down Le Vau's design for the eastern façade[12] – but Colbert suspected him of speculation with the funds from Mazarin's fortune that had been made available to him for the College of the Four Nations to use them at Versailles where, in his view, the expenses incurred were too great. It does not seem to have been remarked upon by commentators that, since it was Colbert who engineered Nicolas Fouquet's downfall, and Le Vau had been working for Fouquet at Vaux-le-Vicomte since 1656, Colbert's hostility towards the one might have been reflected in his dislike of the other (a sentiment not shared by the King). Hautecœur suggested that it was Charles Perrault, Colbert's assistant at the time, who mounted the coup to deprive Le Vau of the direction of the work at the Louvre since the hostile comments about his plans were by no means unanimous.

Other architects had been submitting plans to rival those of the King's First Architect ever since Mazarin's death. Colbert consulted François Mansart. His exaggerated expenses at the Val de Grâce for the Queen Mother led her to replace him there with Gabriel Leduc, but Mansart was responsible for so many buildings in and around Paris, and for Gaston d'Orleans at Blois, that Colbert decided that he could not ignore him. However, Mansart, nearing the end of his life, did not want the exertion of masterminding such a major project and submitted a plethora of designs without choosing any of them for serious submission. He had them engraved by Marot,[13] and they served as models for his great-nephew Jules Hardouin-Mansart when he came to design the Church at the Invalides later on. Some of the details on Mansart's plans were very close to what Le Vau offered for the Louvre, such as free-standing columns and the ornate lead roofs that he (Le Vau) would use afterwards at Versailles. Mansart presented a conservative solution in the spirit of Pierre Lescot, and he even wanted to keep the old moats around the palace.

Colbert persuaded Louis Le Vau's younger brother, François, to submit plans, against his better judgement. Despite the ten years difference in their ages, the Le Vau brothers had worked together at Saint-Germain-en-Laye and Versailles, and what he submitted resembled his brother's work at the Hôtel Lambert, as well as the chateaux at Meudon for Abel Servien and Saint-Sépulchre for Jacques Cordier. Jean Marot is perhaps more celebrated nowadays as an engraver of other people's work, but he was also an architect in his own right and was close to Colbert's family – he had built a chateau for his uncle ten years before – and he was included in the invitation. Others were also invited, or even pressed, to make submissions. Charles Perrault's physician brother, Claude, an amateur architect and, later on, the translator of Vitruvius into French, made a bid.

But, in the end, Colbert decided to open the competition to the great Italian architects, and this led to Gian Lorenzo Bernini being invited to Paris for six months by Louis XIV in 1665.

* * *

Mazarin had already brought Giovanni Francesco Romanelli to Paris, and he had worked, not only on his own palace, but also on the Louvre. Antonio Maurizio Valperga had been brought from Turin for Mazarin's palace too (though his long years as a prisoner of war in Naples prevented his accomplishing much[14]). Carlo Vigarani was commissioned, as we have already noticed, by Colbert to provide a *salle des machines* in the Tuileries for when the King made his entry into the capital after his marriage.

Colbert made his own obeisance to Italian culture. He wanted an Academy in Rome for French artists. He used Mazarin's Roman contact, Elpidio Benedetti, an architect himself as well as being in Holy Orders, to pass on flattering letters to established artists: Pietro da Cortona, Carlo Rainaldi, and Giovanni Lorenzo Bernini. Rich presents were placed in the hands of the French ambassador, the Duke of Créquy, to pass on as sweeteners to these worthies and they were invited to submit plans.

Bernini was at the time the most conspicuous of Italian artists. Now in his sixty-seventh year, he was at the height of his achievement as a sculptor and as an architect. His works included the Ecstasy of Saint Theresa, Apollo and Daphne, fountains in the Piazza Navona,[15] altars and the elaborate *baldaccino* in Saint Peter's along with the papal throne behind it. He was finishing the colonnade in Saint Peter's Square and had just built the church at Castel Gondolfo for Alexander VII. He had provided plans for the Chigi Palace.

Bernini was no stranger to French patrons. He had made statues with his father for Cardinal de Sourdis at Bordeaux, and had worked for Mazarin, whom he had known personally in Rome. From 1664 onwards, he was being enticed to work in Paris. He had made decorations in Rome at the French ambassador's house when Louis XIV's Dauphin was born. He sent his first submission for the Louvre's eastern facade to Colbert on 25 June 1664, and Benedetti supported its monumentality.

This design would not fit easily alongside what was in place already. Louis Hautecœur's comment was that it was 'a design by an artist full of imagination but not the project of an architect mindful of realities'.[16] Colbert raised objections: the royal apartments were badly placed for the King's safety in the event of a revolt; the climate in Paris would not permit roof terraces and sombre rooms. Bernini replied angrily that he would have made no submission had he known that other Italians were being asked for theirs. Cardinal Chigi and the French ambassador calmed him down. He did not waste his plan but used it later for a Roman church, and submitted another to Colbert in February 1665, only to be greeted with Colbert's worries about the extravagant costs that would be involved if it were to be realised. Bernini suggested raising the walls from 23 to 32m and inserting little courts that Colbert saw as inevitable potential rubbish dumps. The doors were too small. Yet the King himself was pleased with the facade that he proposed.

The King thought that further postal correspondence would take too long and that it would be better if Bernini were to come in person to Paris. Pope Alexander VII was persuaded to allow such a visit, and Bernini was paid 30,000 livres to make his journey in company with his son, two of his pupils, and their domestics. He left Rome at the end of April 1665 and was presented to Louis XIV at Saint-Germain-en-Laye on 4 June.

Bernini was offered sumptuous accommodation, and the King had him accompanied by Paul Fréart de Chantelou, who had visited Rome twice and was well acquainted with the Roman artistic milieu. He was nephew to François Sublet de Noyers, Minister of War and Superintendent of the Buildings until Mazarin ousted him, and he had counted Nicolas Poussin among his friends. What is more, he spoke good Italian and was noble enough to keep the great man company. He kept a detailed diary of the visit, recounting all the opinionated comments that Bernini made about the people he encountered.

Being aware of the enhancements to the splendour that Bernini had brought to papal Rome, the King wanted him to design similar changes in Paris to the east of the finished Louvre. From the outset, he accorded him rare access to himself, which was adequately anticipated in their first meeting when Colbert took Bernini and his pupils Paolo and Mattia, as well at the abbé Buti and Chantelou, in his carriage to Saint-Germain-en-Laye at nine in the morning. The King was still at his *levée* so they waited until he was dressed, going into his cabinet and making the acquaintance of several high-ranking courtiers such as the Marshals de Gramont and du Plessis. Once the King was dressed, Colbert took Bernini into his chamber and had him make his obeisance to His Majesty.

Bernini saw no problem in being the first to speak. He told the King, 'Sire, I have seen emperors' and popes' palaces and those of sovereign princes which are found on the way from Rome to Paris, but one must be constructed for a King of France, a king of today, something more grand and magnificent than all those.' Then he turned to face those who made a circle around the King to add that he was not there to engage in small talk. Thereupon, it was the King's turn to speak, and he said that he had some desire to keep what his predecessors had done [at the Louvre] but if, for all that, nothing great could be done without destroying their work, he would abandon it; as for money, he would not spare it. His Majesty made Bernini very welcome.[17]

Annexe IV of Milovan Stanić's 2001 edition of Chantelou's *Journal* presents later letters from Mattei de' Rossi, Bernini's pupil, to Bernini's eldest son, Pietro Filippo. One of them gives an eyewitness account of the considerable personal liberty accorded to Bernini by the King. Rossi related that on the eve of Saint-Jean, Bernini went back to Saint-Germain to make sketches for the King's portrait bust. He took Rossi and the abbé Buti with him. When they arrived, the King was playing tennis and he greeted Bernini with a smile. When the game was finished, the King took Bernini to his apartment. The English ambassador came in for an audience, which was held with Bernini standing by. When it had finished, Colbert, de Lionne, de Trigli and the Marshal de Turenne stayed in the King's apartment while Bernini called for Rossi to give him his drawing board and began sketching while the courtiers read letters to the King. But first he asked the King to take up a position standing with his elbow on a small table without his hat. 'His Majesty's hair was not to his liking, and the cavalier asked for a comb and arranged his hair with his hands as he wanted it.'

The four courtiers were astonished to see the facility with which Bernini captured the King's features and his expression, and wondered at it.

'Instead of keeping still, the King often looked in the direction of the drawing, so impatient he was to see it, and, while he talked with the others, moved his head so much that the cavalier had to carry on as if in flight. When the drawing was nearly finished, the cavalier stopped for a while; everyone admired the sketch, above all the King, who said: "*For biene*, that's the most beautiful and the truest likeness that anyone has ever made of me!" After having finished the full-face portrait, the cavalier made one in profile, and, when he saw it, His Majesty immediately cried out: "It's me, and I recognise myself!" The two drawings took the cavalier an hour and a half, no more. That was what was so much admired: having created such a resemblance in so little time.'[18]

This was the origin of the bust commissioned by the King that was first exhibited in the Queen's summer apartment at the Louvre and now graces the Diana salon at Versailles. Was that his own hair?

Other members of the royal family and the court commissioned works from Bernini. Anne of Austria, displeased with the altar designed by Leduc for her church at the Val de Grâce, asked Bernini to design another, though Leduc had a hand in the provision of it – a more modest version of the *baldaccino* in Saint-Peter's Rome. For Monsieur, the King's brother, Bernini made a design for the park at Saint-Cloud and a project for a fountain. He designed an altar for M. de Souvré, prior of the Temple, and a project for a staircase for the Duke of Aumont.

Bernini had established his acceptability to the King himself and within the King's immediate circle. But when it came to presenting his ideas for the future development of the capital to the east of the Louvre, Colbert bridled at the costs that would be involved if his elaborate plans were ever to be adopted. In a memorandum to Colbert, Bernini observed that if he were going to raise a monument worthy of the King, then a good deal of Paris would have to be knocked down first. But then he remembered what the monarch had said at first about wanting to respect his ancestors' buildings, and he wrote a letter to the Duke of Modena to say that he had drawn up a plan for which it would not be necessary to knock down anything at all and that the King seemed satisfied with it.

Colbert was not. Both Fréart de Chantelou in his *Journal* and Colbert's then right-hand man, Charles Perrault, in his *Mémoires* written much later, understood and reported on the antagonism between Bernini's theatrical approach to what the King wanted for his palace and its surroundings and Colbert's requirements for precise details about the accommodation of courtiers, guards and office holders, kitchens, wine cellars, effective drains, and the King's security, besides any aesthetic considerations. Colbert wanted a reservoir in case of fire and the provision of firefighting equipment.[19] In the matter of the King's safety, Colbert reproached Bernini for putting His Majesty's apartment too close to Saint-Germain-l'Auxerrois. Besides that, he had again provided too many places where would-be assassins could conceal themselves. Perrault defended Colbert against Bernini, and Bernini told Perrault, 'You are not worthy to clean the soles of my shoes!'[20]

Bernini's vision for the open square in front of the eastern facade of the Louvre included dismantling the church of Saint-Germain-l'Auxerrois and rebuilding it further to the east. He wanted to raise a rock structure in the middle of the square, reaching a height of 100ft and decorated with marine deities and tritons in cascades of water that ended up in a marble-lined basin.

The whole piece would be surmounted by a gigantic statue of the King. He had provided something like it in the Piazza Navona in Rome. He also thought of putting up columns resembling his solution for Saint Peter's Square as well. Statues of Hercules would enhance the main entrance to the Louvre. The King of France would be housed in splendour similar to the palaces Bernini had designed for the Pamphili and Chigi families in Rome. Louis Le Vau, Charles Le Brun and Claude Perrault found it all too extravagantly imitative and, above all, too Italian.

Bernini had a good supply of invective against this three-man faction that took a stand against him. His own projects, he claimed, were inspired by God, whereas Le Vau was incapable of observing basic rules of construction or taking accurate measurements, remarking that his staircase at the Meudon chateau would not be worthy of a village hotel in Italy.

When he looked at Le Vau's foundations for the Louvre's eastern facade laid the year before, Bernini said the mortar was too chalky so that it would soon crumble, making it easy for rats to nest in it. However, his Italian builders did not know about the intensity of the frost in Paris, and the wall they built collapsed after a year. There is no record of Bernini being taken to visit Le Vau's masterpiece at Vaux-le-Vicomte, but Paul Fréart de Chantelou reports that on Sunday, 11 October Bernini came back to his lodgings after Mass to find the drawing for the painting Le Brun proposed to execute on the inside of the dome above the great oval salon there, which he said was full of confusion.[21] By implication, however, he also criticised Le Vau's design for the salon. Chantelou reports:

> As it is an oval, he said, if the palace of the sun, which is represented by it, had been of the same shape, or even round, perhaps it would have been better suited to the site and to the sun itself. It was the four seasons and the four elements, which were represented in this drawing. As it is for the vault of a dome, the work is very constrained, all in the foreground related to a single point and foreshortened, being seen upwards from below. I (Chantelou) said that Raphaël had made this sort of representation. The *Cavaliere* turned the drawing in all directions to look at it more closely, and afterwards said that M. Colbert ought to have had it completed somewhere or other, and that it was a pity that he had not.

All of this seems to damn with faint praise and assent with civil leer, and found fault with Le Vau, who had chosen the oval at Vaux as well as elsewhere as a valuable form. He regarded what Le Vau did as shoddy, and insulted the Perrault brothers as we have seen.[22] Towards the end of July, Le Vau submitted fresh plans to Colbert. The question of the King's safety was a prior consideration, obviously, and even Bernini had changed the location of the royal apartments.

Another visitor from Italy had been in Paris a little while before. Sebastiano Locatelli was a young Catholic priest from Modena, making a voyage through France with two aristocratic friends. He kept a journal every bit as detailed as Chantelou's and everything he saw and heard is meticulously recorded.[23] He and his friends stayed in a boarding house kept by an aristocratic widow in a Henry IV building in the Faubourg Saint-Germain, which he and his companions found comfortable. On 11 November 1664, he visited the Île de la Cité on his own, enjoying Notre-Dame and the shops around it. Towards the end of the morning, thinking he might catch sight of the King, he came to the Louvre.[24]

He walked there at his ease, going past several guard posts, and came to an entrance – he does not say which, but his later observations make it certain that it was on the eastern side of the palace. He said the door 'opened at a touch, no need to knock on it, just scratch! The King would like all his subjects to enter freely, so that he can be informed, if need be, of all important events, such as rebellions, treasonable acts, threats of revolt and everything of that kind.' Seeing the guards getting on parade, he thought rightly that the King was going to come out to hear Mass 'in a beautiful church nearby called Saint-Germain which they were going to knock down if the Louvre were ever finished on that side'.

Locatelli went into the church and knelt down to wait for the courtiers to enter with His Majesty. He even found himself in eye contact with the King, and did not dare to look up any more in case it happened again in spite of his 'insatiable curiosity'.[25] He did, however, meet the King later and exchanged a few words with him, and the monarch was not very complimentary about Modena. This gives the impression that security at the Louvre before its completion was not very tight, but this probably belies a discreet watchfulness that was sufficient fourteen years after the Fronde had been overcome.

Chantelou reported hearing about Le Vau's new plans in his *Journal* for 30 July. The setting for the beginning of a meeting was Colbert's house – can we assume it was the Hôtel Bautru? – and, while Chantelou was waiting for Colbert to come downstairs, an intendant of the buildings, whose name was de la Motte, informed him about what Le Vau had prepared.

It appeared that he proposed that the King would be housed outside the Louvre court, where *grand seigneurs* would be lodged. The conversation was cut short by the arrival of Colbert and Le Vau together. Also present were Colbert's brother-in-law, Desmarets, and one of the Perraults, though he does not say which one. They all got into a carriage together to go to the Hôtel de Frontenac, which had not yet been knocked down, where they were to meet Bernini. Le Vau had taken his hat off, and was silent, with his face showing despondency for part of the short journey. But then he said to Chantelou: 'I don't know whether M. le cavalier Bernini has taken his measurements for the Square Yard of the Louvre. It ought to be of sufficient grandeur to carry out [military] exercises in it.' Chantelou says that he made no reply to this, and then, after a little, Le Vau added: 'We shall have some embarrassment for the houses which we must take down to the foundations, and we can only have them by going through the formalities.'

They arrived at Bernini's lodgings at that moment, and they went in to find him working on the King's bust – arranging his marble hair this time. Le Vau had to listen to Bernini explaining to Colbert that he had not been able to take the measurements of the foundations of the Louvre court, although his pupil, Mattei de' Rossi, had been occupied with them incessantly and had found that they did not indicate a true square but had a discrepancy of a span and a half. This was not much, but enough to put the whole building out of alignment.

Colbert expressed displeasure that things were no further forward, since the high summer was the best time to make foundations when the water table was low. But Bernini resisted attempts to make him work quicker. He showed himself to be more a sculptor than an architect when he basked in the lavish praise that Mme de Lionne heaped upon the King's bust, begging him not to change anything. Colbert ended the encounter and left. Chantelou does not say who left with him, but we can speculate on Le Vau's continuing despondency.[26] Bernini would be in Paris for nearly another three months.

After only one month had passed, however, it was becoming more and more evident that Bernini's designs would not prove to be acceptable, and that Le Vau was receiving the support of other French architects, while Colbert was becoming more exasperated and less willing to tolerate Bernini playing the international celebrity all the time. So disagreements gathered momentum, and on 31 August, the papal nuncio found Bernini to tell him that his plan was not going to be carried out and that Le Vau, Le Brun and Mansart had been called together to draw up a new one.[27] The nuncio quoted from the gospels: 'and the same day Herod and Pilate were made friends together'.[28]

Discussions continued all through September, however, between the intendants of the buildings, Madiot and de la Motte, the builders Mazières and Bergeson, and the intendant of furniture de Metz, in Bernini's workshop. Colbert sometimes joined in these meetings. The disagreements became worse, and then, at the beginning of October, in the King's Council, Colbert declared himself opposed to Bernini's project altogether.

There was to be a face-saving exercise nevertheless. The King wanted to let Bernini go home, but a foundation-laying ceremony was arranged for 17 October. A commemorative medallion by Jean Varin, who had designed the Louis d'Or, was placed in the foundations in the presence of the King and Bernini together. Bernini received royal gifts and pensions for himself and his son. His pupil, Mattei de' Rossi, was also assured one so long as he worked at the Louvre. He came back to France after six months in May 1666, bringing additional designs and a model made of wood and stucco. Apart from the royal bust, Bernini's influence in France otherwise was 'next to nothing'.[29]

This seemed to shut the door on any further contemplation of Bernini's solution for the completion of the Louvre, but there were other discussions, especially as it seemed to have been decided that the King's apartments would be in the Tuileries. This brings us to March 1666 and then, in April of that year, Vigarani let it be known that Bernini's plans were no longer being talked about. On 15 July, Colbert informed Bernini that the expenses of the War of Devolution required that the execution of his design be postponed to a later date. He was still attempting to save face – this time the French one – by adding somewhat dubious sentiments:

> His Majesty, having need of being lodged, is seen in the necessity to have the design which was begun by his ancestors continued, and which could be completed in the course of two or three years, keeping in reserve having your design carried out one day and choosing for it some situation advantageous and proportionate with his grandeur and his magnificence, of which he does not despair of your coming to reconnoitre and even take over the conduct of it, once more giving him the joy of seeing you work.

We can trust Hautecœur's judgement to a certain extent:

> There was opposition between Italian concepts and French ones. Bernini's voyage, far from marking the coming of an ultramontane mode on French soil, was doubtless one of the causes of this reaction. Academic rationalism in France was opposed to the picturesque fantasy of Italian decoration.[30]

The last of Louis XIV's royal academies to be established was that of architecture, in 1671, a year after Louis Le Vau's death, and one of its purposes was to establish and maintain what French style was – as well as what was not.

Mazarin had been right. The extravagances of the Baroque style could only be brought to Paris in discreet doses. Le Vau understood this and used the realisation to good effect at the College of the Four Nations, where he was essentially working for the King.

Le Vau's 1663 foundations had been replaced by the ones that were begun in October 1665, and were entirely different from them. After Bernini's departure, Le Vau found a greater liberty to create a new design for the eastern facade. His next designs have to do with the emergence of the idea of the colonnade and lead to new suggestions about who had the idea first.

* * *

Jean-Aymar Piganiol de la Force, a century after the decisions about the Louvre were being made, in his capacity as tutor at Versailles to the Count of Toulouse's[31] pages – in other words, a privileged schoolmaster – became a historian with access to documents and wrote an account of what happened after Bernini had left. A new and augmented edition of Piganiol's principal work was published two years after his death, and it gives indications of his sources, particularly relevant in this case.[32]

An authentic document with a note in the margin in Colbert's own hand: *vu et approuvé au camp de Charleroy le 7 juin 1667*, is an extract from the Register or Journal of deliberations and resolutions touching the King's buildings. It relates that Colbert had decided that none of the plans submitted for the completion of the Louvre by French or Italian architects had succeeded in fulfilling his expectations and that he had turned his attention to Messieurs Louis Le Vau, Charles Le Brun and Claude Perrault. He had ordered them to come to his house on April 1667, where he would explain to them what he had decided to do.

The completion of the Louvre was to be the King's project, and the King's alone (despite his determination known to Colbert of abandoning it for Versailles). In direct denial of the saying that a camel is a horse produced by a committee, Colbert's solution was to make Le Vau, Le Brun and Claude Perrault 'unanimously and conjointly' responsible for a new design that would 'be regarded as the work of all three of them equally'. Further: 'in order to keep unity and good understanding, no one of them would be able to say of himself that he was the particular author of it to the prejudice of the other two. They were to work incessantly in common to draw up a ground plan and an elevation of the facade of the entrance looking towards Saint-Germain [l'Auxerrois].'

Colbert showed the two plans that they produced to the King at Saint-Germain-en-Laye, and he chose 'the one that was ornamented with an order of columns forming a peristyle'. Then the officers of the King's buildings were summoned to meet with the members of the committee in Colbert's outer office to look at this plan. Large copies of plans and elevations were to be made, signed by Colbert and sent to the King. A week afterwards, work began on the Square Yard to raise it to just above the first cornice, after the east wing's foundations had been dug out a second time.[33] Le Brun was made responsible for the statues to decorate the various facades, and the committee would meet every Thursday and Saturday between six and eight in the evening to supervise the work's progress. Le Vau's drawing office – with François d'Orbay in charge – was to produce two identical copies of the detailed plan for the facade that the King had approved, one each for Le Brun and Perrault, so that they should all have the same plan from which to work.

Le Brun had provided a number of architectural plans previously, being not only what is called in French an *artiste-peintre*. Le Vau had modified his style in 1667–68, influenced by the Italian engravings that he had been studying assiduously, and construction of the inside of the eastern range of the Square Yard was going on during these negotiations. Claude Perrault was occupying himself at the same time with his translation of Vitruvius, fascinated by peristyles and facades. Colbert ordered them 'to regard the admirable colonnade as the work of the three of them equally'.[34]

However, analysis published by Mary Whiteley and Allan Braham in 1964[35] allowed for a different conclusion. They underlined the importance of what Piganiol de la Force had said on the basis of the document with Colbert's autograph in the margin of 7 June 1667 about the committee and the two documents submitted to the King, with his choice of the colonnade acted upon. When Le Vau died in 1670 under the cloud of his failure as a speculator, Claude Perrault made his claim for authorship, backed up later by his brother Charles's *Mémoires*, and the rival claims have persisted. Parisians of a certain age were taught when they were young that it was Perrault's design that the King enthused about.[36]

Whiteley and Braham reminded their readers that the idea of a colonnade had been in the atmosphere for some time and concluded that the detailed evidence about who was responsible for putting it down on paper in the form of a plan and elevations 'points unmistakably to Le Vau', and they add a few pages later that 'there is every indication that the Colonnade of 1667 was developed together with a general design for the whole of the Louvre from his [Le Vau's] earlier scheme of 1665'.[37] The scheme remained fluid, subject to alteration on the basis of drawings that Le Vau had provided before he was withdrawn to work at Versailles in 1668. He left many matters of detail to d'Orbay 'with the seemingly ineffectual intervention of Perrault'.

Whiteley and Braham claimed to have identified a drawing of the east facade elevation of the Louvre, kept in the *Cabinet des dessins* at the Louvre itself, as the design for the Colonnade chosen and approved by the King in April 1667. They suggested that, in its present condition, it is what remains of a larger document 'cut where the design stops awkwardly along the present margin three-quarters of the way through the central pavilion'. They attributed it to Le Vau, while acknowledging that there are similarities between it and one submitted by Le Brun (also in the Louvre's *Cabinet*) that the King did not accept.

It is important to note that the drawings made by architects for the completion of the Louvre came to be divided between three collections: those in the *Archives nationales* and the *Bibliothèque nationale* differ in kind from those in the *Cabinet des dessins* in the Louvre. These latter were all presented to the King in person and include all the projects known to have been sent from Rome. 'It may well be that, like the Italian projects, the colonnade drawing and the Le Brun elevation were those directly requested by the King and remained finally in his possession.'[38]

The conclusion of the whole matter seems to be that, even if he were preoccupied with his work at Versailles, Le Vau kept his eye on his Paris drawing office directed by d'Orbay, and that the winning drawing was his own, despite any opposition put up by Colbert. After his death, when he had been disgraced for financial malpractice,[39] there were few to defend his reputation at the same time as the credibility of Claude Perrault's authorship was increasing, aided by the tradition created by his brother Charles, who was famous – regardless of all else that he was – as a collector of fairy tales that tell of events that are nearly, but not quite, true![40]

Chapter 7

The King in All His Glory

If you came to the garden facade of the Palace of Versailles directly after a visit to Vaux-le-Vicomte, you would not conclude by simple observation that they were both created by the same architect. Vaux-le-Vicomte is extravagant, unrestrained, baroque: high roofs and a central dome. Versailles looks back towards Italian villas of the Renaissance: a concealed roofline: displaying the King's grandeur in a different style from that which Fouquet wanted to offer him. Louis XIV profited from Louis Le Vau's versatility. Versailles was the King's own creation, as was its later establishment as the seat of French government.[1]

War against the House of Habsburg, the women whom Louis XIV loved, and developments in French artistic taste were the determining factors in the stages of the complex building works for transforming Louis XIII's modest, moated hunting lodge into a solar palace with satellites at Clagny and Marly. The timescale for this was between the treaty of the Pyrenees in 1659 and Colbert's death in 1683,[2] although the claim could be made that Versailles never ceased to be a building site during the King's long lifetime and even afterwards.[3]

The King, who saw the palace of Versailles as the outward and visible sign of the nation's glory (and therefore of his own), was never satisfied with the architectural developments over which he presided and upon which he overspent that nation's resources. He slept for the last time in the Louvre in 1666 and, once Anne of Austria had died, the Louvre and the Tuileries were finished as the principal royal residence until Louis XVI was brought there as hostage for the Revolution by the market women of Paris in October 1789.

However, in 1659 when 'the Pyrenees were no more' after Mazarin's conclusion of the peace treaty with Philip IV's Spain, the sun was shining in all its radiance. A surge of building at Versailles was signalled after the King and Queen made their triumphal entry into Paris in 1661. Thereafter, the peripatetic court no longer included Vincennes in its itinerary.

The '*château de Papa*' had already been enlarged between 1631 and 1634 to provide a building in brick and stone surrounded with moats on a U plan with pavilions at each corner and high, typically French, roof spaces. Saint-

Simon later described it as a 'house of playing cards' – not on account of any fragility, but for its colours. The architectural tutor Henri Sauval, in charge of the Academy of Architecture after 1671, used the same term to describe it. Once Louis XIV had been freed from the scaffolding of the regency, he ordered new alterations there. From 1661, Charles Errard and Noël Coypel were commissioned to recompose the interior decoration, and a balcony going right round the building was added at first floor level.[4]

* * *

Louis Le Vau's first engagement at Versailles was his commission from the King to build the *Ménagerie* there on a site bought in November 1662 from the brothers Nicolas and Toussaint Molin consisting of their two lordships of Vivier and La Boissière along the road that leads to Saint-Cyr (where later on Mme de Maintenon would have her convent and school for girls), for which he paid 37,770 livres. This site was to the west of the old chateau, on which a certain amount of development had already begun. Eventually, when the first stage of the chateau's enlargement was complete, the menagerie would be to the left of the Grand Canal, balancing the corresponding position on the right of it where Le Vau would build the Trianon de Porcelain in 1669. It remained there until after 1789 on a site previously used for raising pheasants for shooting parties.

The proposal to develop it was influenced by the hunting park established not far away at Chaville in 1659 by Chancellor Le Tellier.[5] There were renaissance buildings that could have served as precedents for such constructions, but what Le Vau provided here bears some resemblance to the menagerie that Varro, a patrician in ancient Rome, had built between Rome and Naples at Casinum, then still visible as ruins and illustrated in a print by Antonio Lafreri after Pirro Ligorio's *Speculum Romanae Magnificentiae* of 1558, which, it is suggested, Le Vau found during his preparatory researches. He certainly did not copy it but accepted its main principles for keeping animals not usually domesticated. He also capitalised on his experience of the arena for animal fights that he had constructed for Mazarin at Vincennes.

Le Vau provided an octagonal pavilion as a visitors' centre from which the birds and animals kept in a series of enclosed yards with shelters fanning out from the octagon could be observed. Entertainments would be offered in the upstairs salon under the dome, and in the *corps de logis* behind it, such as concerts and small-scale banquets, though it was not proposed that anyone should live there until it was extended to become the Duchess of Burgundy's residence after 1697.

The King's First Architect, recalled to his service while Fouquet was standing trial before the special tribunal, designed a miniature version of Vaux-le-Vicomte 'to stand in a remote corner of Versailles great park' to proclaim the fact Fouquet had been rejected. The detailed symbolism of the *menagerie* was directed towards this vengeful purpose, a really Ovidian metamorphosis, where Fouquet/Actaeon is transformed into a stag and devoured by his own hounds.[6] If that is a crude image, then the phallic ground plan of the *menagerie* was even more crude.[7] The King was to be potent above all others, and Fouquet was condemned as a loser in the manner of a modern reality show.

* * *

Symbols proliferate in the Versailles menagerie. The basement of the octagon was a grotto from which an ascent was made by means of fifteen stairs to a dark landing and then into the full light of the octagon. A ritual purification and enlightenment is signified, since fifteen is Lucifer's number, and the grotto is the realm of the beasts, from which the ascent is made into the rectangular hall that represents a basilica, thence to the space under the vaulted, octagonal dome (in itself an upturned baptismal font) with its figuration – easily recognisable in the minds of contemporaries – of Christian perfection, where Louis XIV is the Most Christian King (*Rex Christianissimus* on his coinage), intermediary between God and his people, 'the ultimate source of peace and all good in his kingdom'.[8]

At the time of the construction of the menagerie the concept of divine right in an absolute monarchy had just been reasserted by the monarch in person. No more Richelieus, no more Mazarins during this reign. On the day after Mazarin's demise, Louis XIV had told his ministers and an archbishop that they were answerable to him and only to him. '*L'État, c'est moi*' was never said at any time but it was implied all the time after the defeat of the Fronde. There were, indeed, fundamental laws for governance of the state, but the idea that *parlements* stood for government by consent of the people was not sustainable any longer. They existed to pass the King's edicts into law. They had the right to remonstrate, but only until they had received fuller explanation on an innovative royal edict. Louis XIV would sustain this rupture introduced by him into the French governmental tradition for the rest of his reign.

The vaulted octagon is deliberate imagery for this interpretation of monarchy, since it stands for heaven in the Italian models that had such an influence upon Le Vau's work: Pietro di Cortone at the Pitti Palace and, nearer home, in what Romanelli had provided for Anne of Austria and in the Apollo Gallery at the Louvre under his own direction. In the King's cabinet at the Louvre,

Le Brun had used the octagon to signify heaven. For that epoque, which had inherited neo-platonic ideals, the octagon also stood for life itself, and its Resurrection: it was the shape adapted for baptistries attached to cathedrals. In the European seventeenth century it had come to represent the Sun in its glory, conveniently enveloping its rays in its shape. The salon of Daphne and Apollo, soon to be provided in the new chateau, would be an octagon, and it had been the centrepiece that Le Vau provided at Vaux-le-Vicomte to be the palace of the Sun, full of Zodiac imagery. The Swedish architect Tessin, for whom the collection of French drawings at Stockholm is named, wanted to provide such a salon for his own monarch.[9]

That these observations about the symbolism used at Versailles are made in relation to the menagerie rather than to the palace itself is because the menagerie was being constructed while Fouquet was still defending himself from the charges of treason being brought against him by Colbert on the King's behalf. The symbolism was part and parcel of the vindictiveness that induced the King to change Fouquet's eventual sentence from exile to perpetual imprisonment in isolation at the comfortless Pignerol. He could only do that if his monarchy was absolute and, from now on, it was and would be. The extent of allegory used in the menagerie was unprecedented in Le Vau's previous work. At Vaux-le-Vicomte it had appeared, but only in collaboration with Charles Le Brun. So the question has been raised for Versailles – both at the menagerie as a pipe-opener and in the new chateau – which of the two, the architect or the *artiste-peintre*, was the dominant partner. It seems that the answer was clear to Colbert after he took over the superintendency on 1 January 1664. Le Vau was 'barely tolerated within the royal buildings administration' and the foundations he had already begun at the Louvre were covered over. Le Brun, on the other hand, 'was offered a virtual monopoly over the visual arts in France and orchestrated the Ovidian programme permeating the first half of the King's reign'. Colbert clearly regarded Le Vau as subordinate to Le Brun in the hierarchy of design, 'indicating that he could only operate effectively in royal projects in conjunction with Le Brun'. Le Vau was to be 'a collaborating architect and construction supervisor under Colbert's oversight'.

'Le Brun was the wellspring of ideas, the allegorical conceptualiser, while Le Vau, a seasoned and innovative architect, but one disparaged for his baroque tendencies and his occasional design lapses, was charged with translating those ideas into viable architecture.'[10]

It is not surprising that Le Brun, Le Vau and Le Notre had been taken from Vaux to Versailles as an established triumvirate. The King and Colbert had seen what they had accomplished together and wanted their energies and abilities redirected to serve the new monarchy, not the old one that worked through prime ministers. Yet, his being part of the triumvirate that designed and interpreted the King's intentions for Versailles until 1670 does not detract from Le Vau's essential role as the First Architect. His contribution to the work was that he was well-known for paying attention to his patrons' requirements and gave them what they were paying for. He knew he was not Bernini. He knew that the King admired the Italian's genius. He knew he could not repeat Vaux at Versailles. Something in the spirit of Bernini but in a French body would be needed and he provided it, even if Colbert did consider him to be no more than 'the brightest light of an eclipsed generation [of architects] trained in an era when design, judged as a whole, was struggling for coherence: an admixture of vernacular forms commingling with classical elements derived from Italian models'.

Furthermore, 'from necessity born of a dearth of widely competent talent, the principle of collaborative design, implemented by Fouquet at Vaux to maximise the contribution of the design triumvirate of Le Vau, Le Brun and Le Nôtre, was adapted for the *Ménagerie*, and this system *would* become the standard practice for the reign until the death of Colbert and the rapid ascendancy of Jules Hardouin-Mansart'.[11] Colbert had the delegated authority to put the designs for Versailles into committee, as he had done previously in the case of the Colonnade at the Louvre. That meant that all building projects in a system of absolutism could and should be the King's own.

* * *

There were seven zoo enclosures, a resource for the recently established Academy of Sciences. The animals would be exotic, imported by the *Compagnie des Indes* and other relevant bodies, following instructions issued by Colbert, though some of the large birds would find their way to the kitchens in the newly built commons at the chateau for dinner parties. Madeleine de Scudéry relates that 'you see seven different yards from the corridor, full of all sorts of rare birds and animals; their pictures are in the cabinet so as to prepare you for what you are going to see, or to jog your memory afterwards'.[12]

It seems that Louis XIV was not often presented with exotic animals as ambassadors' presents, but there were two significant exceptions. One of these was given to him in Le Vau's lifetime: an elephant offered by the regent of Portugal, the future King Peter II, in 1668, and the other was the tigress given by Moroccan ambassadors in 1682, which had been in unequal combat with a cow at Vincennes and was then retired to her new home. There were to have been crocodiles from Siam but they were dissected by members of the Academy before they could arrive.[13]

In the octagon itself, there were painted wainscots by Charles Errard and other artists, paid for in 1666, and other walls were covered with fabric hangings. Downstairs from the salon a grotto was established before 1670 with panels of decorative stones as would appear again in the Grotto of Thetis a little later, only they would be much more elaborate there. There was even a simple chapel with a crucifixion painting by Rabon, hung in July 1668, a copy of something similar by Le Brun that was done for the earliest chapel in the chateau in 1682. Another feature of the assemblage of buildings was a dairy for supplying the chateau. For everything at the menagerie, the King exhibited his usual hands-on attitude. 'The *Ménagerie* reveals the richness of its contents in such a way as to portray the particularly complex allegory of a young monarch still lacking in experience but armed with a supreme self-confidence. [The buildings] reflect the spiritual and intellectual interests of French society in this beginning of his reign.'[14]

The buildings played an important part in the festivals held in the gardens, and the pope's emissary, Cardinal Chigi, attended a concert of Italian music in the Octagon on 10 July 1664. The ensemble was not finished to the King's satisfaction until 1668, but, as with the gardens and other places put up for spectacles, there was a good deal of luxurious improvisation, some of it by Louis Le Vau.[15]

* * *

Once Louis XIV had asserted his own sole authority in the state he began making changes to the interior of his father's hunting lodge at Versailles. He replaced the central staircase with a more commodious one and remodelled the royal apartments upstairs. Downstairs, he installed a guardroom and a whole apartment space was reserved for occasional council meetings. In 1664 he had found room on the ground floor for a theatre and space for musicians, achieved by having features that could be put in and taken out at need. The following year saw the insertion of rooms signified by their names: an office for keeping watermarked papers, an office with mirrors, and another decorated with crystals, meant to surprise those who saw them with their magnificence. The first floor was also to include four rooms for the Queen, matching those of the King, while Monsieur, the King's brother, and Madame would have an apartment on the ground floor.[16] The royals would be accommodated in suitable grandeur so as to be impressive, and courtiers were being encouraged to have their own lodgings around the *place d'Armes*.

At this stage, according to his secretary Charles Perrault, Colbert was happy that a royal palace had been finished and he would only have to come there two or three times a year to maintain it in good order. Nevertheless, the King wanted further development there, and Le Vau was involved in keeping his resolution on the front burner. Colbert tried to dissuade the King from doing any more. If the King thought that what had been done was already enough, it was up to Le Vau to persuade him otherwise, and he seems to have done so.

* * *

The young King spent pleasant days in hunting and excursions into the countryside west of Paris in company with Louise de La Vallière, subsequent upon his triumphant return to the capital with his respected but neglected Spanish bride, Queen Marie-Thérèse. According to the Archbishop of Sens, who came to know the new Queen well, after two years of marriage 'she preferred to live retired among her dogs and Spanish dwarves rather than please him by taking part in the fêtes and other diversions with which he entertained the Court'.[17]

Louise de La Vallière was the ideal partner for the King's festivals, although she did not relish being the centre of attention at them. The principal royal chateau was still Saint-Germain-en-Laye, expanded by Henry IV nearly sixty years earlier, but his father's small-scale pleasure dome was nearby for his parties, especially when the famous *Plaisirs de l'île enchantée* took place from 9 to 14 May 1664, with the double purpose of effacing the memory of Nicolas Fouquet now that he had been condemned after his long trial, and of presenting La Vallière to the courtiers as something near to a royal *maîtresse en titre*.

Louis Le Vau had responsibility for setting up a temporary – but nevertheless elaborate – theatre space for a spectacle based upon *Orlando furioso*, with the King himself playing the part of Roger. Mazarin's protégé, Carlo Vigarani, was again responsible, as he had been at the Louvre, for all the scene-changing machinery. The gardens and fountains were being developed by André Le Nôtre as a permanent feature of Versailles, though their final form was by no means established yet.

The eastern facade was restyled with a balcony and columns and the buildings that advanced from either side of it for the stabling and the kitchens were now joined to the new chateau and the iron fences and gates were entirely remodelled without the two guardrooms. In 1662–64, Le Vau provided the two single-storeyed commons wings, not part of the U plan, but marking out a courtyard in front of the eastern facade, closed off by railings with a guardroom at each end. (This was confirmed by the excavations carried out on site in 2006[18]). The three colours style was continued on all these constructions. Le

Vau had already used it at Vaux-le-Vicomte for the dependencies and meant to use it for the palace itself there until Fouquet decided otherwise. That style was part of his repertoire by now. The roofs of the kitchens on the left and stables on the right were of the *combles brisés* style used at Vincennes, although the visual effect on a single-storeyed building was entirely different. The rounded shape of the front court, with its horseshoe-shaped access ramp, coincided with Le Vau's planning for the facade of the College of the Four Nations at present at its design stage.

The doubling of the chateau, the construction of the menagerie and the Grotto of Thetis (although that was meant originally to be no more than a reservoir for the fountains until Le Brun, the Perrault brothers and the hydrologists got to work on it), together with Le Vau's orangery on the western side of the old chateau, were the new enterprises that reflected what Fouquet had ordered for Vaux-le-Vicomte, used now to proclaim the glory of the Sun King on his own initiative.

Apollo was creating a home for himself. Grown trees were brought to be replanted from the forests of Artois and Normandy. The 'goose foot' in front of the *place d'Armes* gave on to three avenues, also lined with grown trees, leading eastwards towards Paris, where four pavilions on each side were built with the intention of housing the ministers of state.[19]

* * *

The American architectural historian Fiske Kimball interested himself in Le Vau's work at Versailles as early as 1940, but decided to keep his powder dry until certain political rearrangements had been achieved in France after seven years, when he could take up the project again with his friend Alfred Marie. Marie was making archaeological discoveries in the wake of building works on site and had found the ground plan proposed by Le Vau for Colbert's competition in the Tessin collection of French architectural drawings in the Swedish National Museum in Stockholm.[20]

On the basis of these finds, Kimball revised his article and doubted the assumptions that Pierre de Nolhac, the nineteenth and early twentieth-century conservationist who lived at Versailles, had drawn without question from Charles Perrault's reminiscences (published forty years afterwards) by which Colbert had been made the advocate of its destruction. Because Perrault had been Colbert's secretary, de Nolhac had given him the benefit of any doubt, although he had the humility to acknowledge that future revision on the basis of the architecture might be necessary.[21] Subsequently, another American historian, Robert W. Berger, has altered the conclusion by substantiating his claim that:

> In 1668 Louis XIV decided to enlarge Versailles by preserving his father's building ... by enclosing it in a new structure, Le Vau's *Enveloppe*. For a few months during the summer of 1669 the King changed his mind and wanted the old building torn down, but Colbert urged a return to the *Enveloppe* scheme. Louis accepted this advice, and work on the *Enveloppe* was resumed and brought to completion. The historical evidence thus essentially supports André Félibien and Charles Perrault, who insisted that the king wanted to retain the Petit Château for reasons of filial respect [Kimball, in contrast, had concluded in 1949 that Louis XIV at heart had always wanted his father's building to be razed]. The architect of the *Enveloppe* was Louis Le Vau ... who departed from his usual Italian Baroque sources to draw upon Italian High Renaissance for the first (and last) time in his career.[22]

The happy accident of excavations at the south-east corner of the pavilion on the *enveloppe* in 1947 (under Alfred Marie's architectural supervision) in order to insert a larger septic tank found the corner of the retaining wall (*fausse braye*) of the old chateau with 'its brickwork like new' since it was exposed only for a short time between work done in 1662–63 and the filling in of the moat in 1669. A photograph taken of it also shows a longer projection of the side of the *enveloppe* than was visible above ground.

It could be deduced, then, that Le Vau's earlier proposal to double the south wing had been taken in June 1668. Le Vau had already provided something similar for Jacques Bordier at Le Raincy. Nevertheless, Colbert asserted that the project was not royal enough.

* * *

The *Plaisirs de l'île enchantée* in 1664 had convinced the King that there was need for more accommodation to provide lodging for his family and the court on occasions like it by knocking down the old chateau and building everything anew. It was decided that the old rooms should not be demolished until the new ones had been completed. Since the new rooms were to the exterior of the old ones, this was perfectly practical. The north and south facades were to be placed as they still are, and on the garden front there were to be two large rectangular salons with a terrace open to the sky with a fountain at first-floor level. Works were begun on Le Vau's design, already labelled as the *enveloppe*.

The next major festival was that held in 1668, to celebrate the triumphant end of the War of Devolution against Spain to gain the payment of Queen Marie-Thérèse's delayed dowry.

The old chateau was too small to hold the festival in, so it was no more than a place for the guests to be served with refreshments after their arrival from Paris. The festival proper was held in three temporary structures among the wooded groves (*bosquets*) in the garden. Le Vau had built the largest of these for a ball, and to draw attention to the need for a permanent structure of the same size he did not take it down after the festival but kept it in place, so that the King would see it falling apart from the effects of wind and rain each time he went past it, as he was bound to during his walks outside. So, at the end of the summer, the King made the decision that Le Vau wanted from him. There would be enlargements to the old chateau, and any future plays, balls and banquets would take place in the spaces to be provided as soon as could be managed. He saw that in the long run it would be less expensive to have permanent structures than to keep on paying for ephemeral ones to be put up and taken down at regular intervals. Such enlargement would also involve more accommodation for the courtiers to prevent all the toing and froing from the capital that had caused them to be resentful in 1668 but, for the moment, the King and his First Architect kept these ideas under their broad-brimmed hats – but only for a year …

They had earlier regarded the refurbished old chateau as the pinnacle of magnificence, so it was not to be demolished: it would be kept as the heart of the new palace. The new building would rise in the space between the moats and the garden. The King's and Queen's apartments would be on the garden side. The ballroom would be on the northern side, an octagon surrounded with four large spaces for ancillary purposes, and the theatre on the southern, and further on from what was to be constructed as the Grotto of Thetis. These buildings would be separated from the main palace by small yards. This was known to be the intention, witness Madeleine de Scudéry saying to her visitors at the end of summer 1668 that when they came next time they would see that great changes had taken place.[23]

The King had conceived the construction as taking place in two stages: first the royal apartments, and then the theatre and the ballroom. On 20 October 1668, the contractors Viart and Maron were having their accounts settled for work on levelling the terraces. Their final settlement was paid on 4 November. It is not clear whether the building intended at that point was the one that actually arose a little later. The case is made for the King being disappointed with what he saw rising out of the ground. Probably in December, he ordered the work to be halted and the masonry already in place to be demolished. Le

Vau then presented the plan for the *enveloppe* and work began again on the revised formulation.

Once the King had decided to enlarge the building at Versailles by means of dispensing with the moats that surrounded it, the term *enveloppe* was in use to describe the form the new chateau was to take.[24] Coinciding with this festival, and justified by the Treaty of Aix-La-Chapelle, which added part of Flanders to France's territory, the King decided to enlarge Versailles to replace the palace at Saint-Germain, though its final form would take longer to decide upon. Charles Perrault gave the impression that the King had decided to keep the old chateau out of filial piety, saying firmly that if it were destroyed he would have it rebuilt with nothing changed,[25] but it is more likely that the King accepted Colbert's advice on the basis of economy. The surrounding of what was already there was quite advanced already, the solution being adopted of providing the King with his apartments on the southern side and the Queen with hers on the northern. Such a solution had been adopted in the past at Amboise and at Blois when Anne of Brittany had married Charles VIII of France. It was suggested that this duplication of apartments was dictated logically by Marie-Thérèse being sovereign in the Spanish Netherlands by the Treaty of Aix-la-Chapelle and Louis XIV's victory in the War of Devolution having rescinded the clause in their marriage treaty in which she had renounced the right to succeed to the Spanish throne. She would be Queen of Spain once the feeble and childless Carlos II was dead and a sort of double monarchy with France would come into being.[26] The idea has been dismissed as 'no more than feebly founded'.[27]

Two long *corps-de-logis* were to be built at either end of the old chateau on the garden side where the moat had been; the King's would look out over the garden at the north, and the Queen's to what is now the *parterre du Midi*. These royal rooms would be displayed as such by their columns and colossal pilasters in the Ionic order. Le Vau designed the garden facade with small entries that would make shadows. The whole building possesses an architectural simplicity with the roofline concealed that expresses royal dignity in stone, as Le Vau had already provided above the royal apartments at Vincennes: far removed from the theatrical spirit shown on the eastern facade. Perhaps all this expressed a lingering liking on the King's part for what Bernini had submitted for the Louvre, which Le Vau reinterpreted and re-expressed.

On the entrance side, a new *cour d'honneur* was proposed also reflecting the influence of Bernini that either the King or Le Vau remembered: to bring a carriageway right into the court for the King and Queen to be able to enter their apartments directly from their vehicles in intemperate weather, something that Colbert had criticised at the Louvre as offering places for would-be assassins to hide.

Work had begun on the *enveloppe* at the end of 1668, but the King was forever wanting modifications, which provoked from Colbert the remark that 'it is certain that incertitude, perpetually changing things, and the great expense doesn't coincide with the King's great actions'.[28] Because of the King's not wanting to be disturbed by noise from passing traffic, the arcades in the *Enveloppe* at ground-floor level were to be suppressed and windows were inserted into them under the royal apartments. This might have produced a rather monotonous design, but it was avoided by extra decorative elements; the wall was brought forward on each of the royal apartments to form an *avant-corps*, making a large bock of masonry on the ground floor and four ionic columns on the floor above. This presented 'a certain monumentality'. The front of the terrace thus seemed to be drawn backwards towards the wall of the old chateau.

Progress was being made steadily until 8 June 1669, when the controller of the buildings reported to Colbert that the walls of the *enveloppe* were more than 6m high and the beams to support the terrace were near to being assembled in place, when the King made a severe U-turn: he decided that all the important officials of the court must be housed at Versailles.

Two long wings would have to be added to what was planned. To make this possible, the old chateau would have to be demolished, and the King made a public declaration to that effect. The expense was naturally alarming to Colbert, who still preferred to display the King's glory at the Louvre, despite its change of use since the Queen Mother's demise, and set out to show the King that it was impossible to do what he wanted. There was just not enough space for it.

Colbert thought that the only design possible would produce something abhorrent: 'Anyone who has any taste for architecture, both in the present and for the future, will find that this chateau resembles a little man who had long arms and a great big head, that is to say, a monster of a building.'

This was his justification for knocking the new work down and starting again, while preserving Louis XIII's building. The King went along with Colbert's ideas, especially when he proposed a more viable solution than Le Vau's, which was to ask the architect to raise the *enveloppe* by at least an attic storey.[29] This would provide the courtiers with either two or four rooms each.[30] It would not be a complete solution, but Colbert hoped to persuade the King to act upon it. Furthermore, it would be senseless to incur unnecessary expense by demolishing the old chateau.

It was to be a practical compromise. Colbert had convinced the King that what had been proposed earlier was not only monstrous but too small and not royal enough. How much dislike for Le Vau did Colbert nurture after what he had designed for his real enemy at Vaux-le-Vicomte? Yet Le Vau had been the King's First Architect for fifteen years when the Versailles project was revived in the wake of the Treaty of Aix-la-Chapelle and, as with the decision to have him put in charge of Mazarin's College of the Four Nations in 1661, he was first in line when it came to this work. Nevertheless, for the second time in his career in royal service, Le Vau had to submit to the rigours – and the possible humiliations – of a public competition for the contract imposed by Colbert.

The King deprived Le Vau of responsibility for making new plans, although he was to be invited to take part in the contest with five other French architects. It is even possible that Bernini was invited – why not? – to submit an entry.[31] Colbert drew up his lengthy memorandum entitled 'What the king wants in his Building at Versailles'. This was issued to the candidates, who were given eight to ten days in which to present their submissions to Charles Perrault, Colbert's agent. Colbert would present them to Louis XIV along with his own comments.

The deadline was not met by any of the six contestants despite their working night and day at the project. By 1 July, none of them had responded to all the requirements for the building and the responses of Vigarani and Gabriel were 'of a ridiculous nullity'. Claude Perrault's fell short of meeting the criteria. Antoine de Paultre (the future builder of the palace of Saint-Cloud for Monsieur) could not complete his design in anything like the time required. Thomas Gobert had not met the deadline either. That left only the First Architect's design.[32] He was the only one who had understood what the King wanted.

Colbert rejected the round vestibules at the ends of the western facade as being too 'baroque and reminiscent of medieval survivals'. He approved the idea of a ceremonial staircase with a space in front of it. He thought that certain small courts would soon accumulate unsightly rubbish (he had said something similar of Bernini's Louvre proposals!), the Queen and the Dauphin would need more living space, the external ornamentation was banal, and the openings of the external arcades on the ground floor ought to be 7ft wide.

The main features of Le Vau's proposals are found in the plan that Alfred Marie discovered in Stockholm, and Kimball calls it 'the revised competitive plan'. Colbert foresaw a saving in cost if the old chateau were to be preserved. So for Colbert, Le Vau's plan offered 'a tolerable monster of an architectural composition' by which the Petit Château could be conserved but 'imprisoned between a large wall and a large *corps-de-logis*'. There would thus be no visible clashes between its out-of-date style that Philibert Le Roy had expressed in brick and stone and the present proposals.[33]

So what was resolved for the building was decided by autumn 1669. The drawings were issued from Le Vau's office, in charge of which we find François d'Orbay, his principal assistant and successor (not son-in-law, as Kimball thought), and it is possible that they both still pressed for the demolition of the old building. Le Vau died on 11 October 1670 and d'Orbay took over the direction, as he also did at the College of the Four Nations, though without the accolade of being the King's First Architect. It was not until 1672 that the final decision about the old chateau was taken. Part of it had already been taken down to facilitate the new one.

What was to be done with the eastern facade of the old chateau? The King had his own vision of what he wanted there if Louis XIII's building was going to be left at the centre of Le Vau's *enveloppe*. Once Colbert had agreed with him that he should keep it, despite his sudden decision to do otherwise in 1669, the King would be obstinate in maintaining his intentions against several attempts by Louis Le Vau to make him change his mind in the provision of something more grandiose. In this connection there are six undated elevations – probably from Le Vau's drawing office presided over by d'Orbay – found in the *Archives nationales*, which have been taken to represent the stages of the exchanges between the King and the architect over the design of the east facade back to back with the *enveloppe*.[34]

This elevation is the 'prisoner of the wings' of what had been constructed earlier as the stables and the kitchens to right and left. If greater grandeur was required, then there should be seven large windows on the first floor instead of five middling ones, and they should be full-centred to give them increased elegance. An extra storey was to be added since height also brings elegance and would bring the roof level upwards to correspond with what was being provided on the garden side. The slate roof was to be replaced with a dome and pierced with three *oculi* to represent a crown above a triangular pediment supported by Ionic pilasters. The King refused it, since the slate roof was an essential part of the facade as it was, and the dome was out of all proportion, more of a disfigurement.

So the second suggestion put the slate roof back pierced with four *oculi* above a pediment, raising the height of the roofs on the two enclosing wings as well, while keeping the dome with its three *oculi*. The King refused this also. The third elevation suggested changed the shape of the dome to a truncated pyramid with its point cut off, suitable, a couple of centuries later, for a particular type of cheese but lacking all elegance for a royal palace.

The next suggestion was to reinstate the old roofline with its decorations and the addition of a clock face – though there was a last cry for a timid little dome. A print of 1674 by Israël Silvestre showing a performance of Lully's *Alceste* in the Marble Court is the point of reference for what the King finally agreed upon, with statues inserted between the five first-floor windows, and five windows inserted into the slate roof for the attic, which is extended into the enclosing wings, preserving the brick and stone that had been provided for the service wings now part of the palace proper. None of the preliminary suggestions saw the light of day, but what we see taking place is lively exchanges between the King and Le Vau – and in all probability d'Orbay after him – before arriving at an agreed solution in accordance with the King's intention. His architects had the status of professional advisers. As Le Brun's ceiling for the Hall of Mirrors was to proclaim in French for all to read after another decade, as in politics, so in artistic matters, 'The King rules by himself'.

* * *

Colbert made notes of what had been undertaken for the coming year: marble had to be ordered, the fountains must be designed and put in place, and consideration given to what he called 'the water path' destined to become the grand canal leading westwards, not unlike what Le Nôtre had provided at Vaux. This was to be the same co-operative effort between architect and landscape gardener producing similar harmonious effects. By June, the walls on the garden side had reached a height of 13ft in the form of arcades and were ready to receive the timbers for the pavilions and floor above. The contractors Cliquin and Charpentier were to prepare pathways to bring in the heavy timbers for this first floor and there were 566 men at work on the site. By 1671, 350,000 livres had been spent on these works and they were far from complete. Between the pavilions, the great terrace took shape. Louis XIII's moats were filled in. On the inside, the new court was considerably larger than before, closed off with lengthy majestic railings after enormous work to terrace the yard. In the reordering of the chateau after the peace of Aix-la-Chapelle, all its proportions were increased.

The design being implemented was certainly Le Vau's, but the intention was from the King himself, having had the project in mind ever since he had taken over the reins of government at Mazarin's demise. Le Vau had transformed the King's vision of the embodiment of his grandeur into the constructions around what was already there in the taste of the new architecture developed by Lemercier and Le Vau himself. Nevertheless, 'Versailles as a whole – the gardens as well as the Chateau – was not carried forth in accordance with an

A Pavilion from the Place Royale (since 1800, place de Vosges).

Hotel Lambert, Façade on the Seine.

The Two Pavilions in Place Dauphine opposite Henri IV's statue.

The King's Apartments and Charles V's *Donjon*, Chateau de Vincennes.

The Queen's Apartments, Chateau de Vincennes.

The Service Buildings to the East of Vaux-le-Vicomte.

The Service Buildings to the West of Vaux-le-Vicomte.

The Main Entrance, Vaux-le-Vicomte.

The Oval Salon, Vaux-le-Vicomte.

The Garden Façade, Vaux-le-Vicomte.

A Bay from the *Cour Carrée*, Interior Façade, The Louvre, Paris.

The South-West Corner, The Versailles *Enveloppe*, from photo by Gerard Robaut.

The King's Apartments facing the *Cour de Marbre*, Versailles.

Courtiers' Apartments, Versailles, from photo by Gerard Robaut.

Cornice by Louis Le Vau behind Hall of Mirrors, from photo by Gerard Robaut.

Pyramide Fountain, Versailles.

Cupola and Dome, College of Four Nations (now the *Institut de France*), Paris.

Centre Court of College of Four Nations: Mazarin's Library.

Mazarin's Library, Site of Shops and Façade of Church, College of Four Nations.

Site of Louis Le Vau's *Manoir* at Beaumont-la-Ferrière from photo by Odile Whitaker.

unvarying master plan; indecision and changes of mind ... occurred throughout its growth and development ... because artistic decisions at Versailles were particularly subject to the press of contemporary political and military events; and because the taste of Louis XIV himself underwent change.'[35]

The interiors of the service wings were emptied of stabling, which was eventually to be replaced on the eastern side of the *place d'Armes*, and lodgings for courtiers were to take their place. The four secretaries of state were to have special treatment inasmuch as they were to be housed in four large pavilions where Hardouin-Mansart's ministers' wings are to be found now.[36]

* * *

Colbert's reports were minutely detailed: workshops had been set up for the rockery maker, and for the sculptors of the trophies and balustrades that would decorate the roofline, the mythological statues destined for the front court, and the two large balconies supported by colonnades for the east fronts of the two wings. After Louis Le Vau's death, much of the purely architectural, as opposed to the administrative, supervision would devolve upon the new Academy of Architecture, the last of the royal academies to be set up. Their first report was signed by the members – including François Le Vau and François d'Orbay – on 31 March 1672. André Félibien, also a member, wrote a description of the new chateau that was published in 1674.

Félibien had been secretary to the Marquis de Fontenay-Mareuil, French ambassador to Rome, from 1647. While in the Eternal City, he became acquainted with Nicolas Poussin, and maintained his contacts there afterwards. He writes with enthusiasm about Versailles with all the religious overtones of the word. He was a fanatic for the place: a true 'fan' for it. We can imagine him in hard hat and luminous yellow jacket, measuring stick in hand, carefully recording the dimensions of the rooms in toises (1 *toise* = 2.95m), pedantic but persuasive.[37]

In the sections of Félibien's document concerned with the *enveloppe* itself, his frequent mention of the types of marble used and their sources is the most striking feature. Marbles streaked with white and red from near Dinan and Liège are seen in rooms serving as a vestibules on the ground floor. The capitals on the columns are made from a different sort, a grey marble called Petit Brèche that comes from the Pyrenees. There are other pilasters in assorted colours, red, black, violet, blue, yellow, on a white base, also in marble from the Pyrenees. In an octagon room off the vestibules, frames for the doors and windows are of marble from Languedoc in fire colour and white. The bedroom and bathroom at the side of the octagon have columns in violet marble and the sunken bath is itself in marble; there are smaller marble baths serving to keep water ready.

Félibien points out that the King had these marbles brought from several places in France and they were every bit as good as those previously bought more expensively in Italy and Greece. 'The most rare ones were to be found near the King's person in the new chateau, and passing from one room to another greater riches were to be seen, whether in the marble itself or in the sculpture or in the paintings on the ceilings.' Upstairs, the use of marbles of all kinds extended to the wall coverings (*lambris*) and the door jambs and window surrounds were again in marble shot through with red and white: the provenance of this was Campan in the Pyrenees. The guardroom had marbles from the Bourbonnais region, a mixture of red, white, black and yellow, while some more from Brèche provided a white base for these pieces. In the royal bedroom, emerald-coloured marble was used, called Egyptian green by the masons, but which also came from the Pyrenees. In the King's large office there was black marble veined in yellow, a type known as Portòro, also Pyrenean.

There is a *Memorandum useful for the marbles* dating from 1662,[38] written in Louis Le Vau's own hand for his own use, which reflects upon how marble from Flanders was to be obtained and brought to Versailles. He notes that the best marble that he was using came from a town called Rancé in Hainault (now in Belgium) eight leagues from Mons and seven from Namur.

He notes that there are three means by which it can be brought to Versailles for the *enveloppe* and to Paris for use at the Louvre and the College of the Four Nations. The first is by road and that is not to be entertained because it was the fully finished product that emerged from the quarry as pillars, pilasters or components for window and door frames, beside large pieces for cladding walls indoors. The jolting of carts on uneven roads would be likely to break them. They must come either in sea-going ships from Rotterdam and then up the Seine to Rouen, where they would be transferred to barges for the last leg of the journey, or be brought all the way on barges by the river system via Pontavert near Laon. There was a trader in marble in Hainault called Le Grue who had been instructed to rent the quarry at Rancé for three years on the basis of samples he had provided for the works at Versailles. Lemercier had bought the marbles he used at the Sorbonne Chapel from this man, who became a regular supplier for Parisian architects.

The King's minute interest showed in the details of Colbert's reports on the subject, even when he was away from the Île de France or on campaign in Flanders. This one of 5 May 1670 is typical:

For Versailles, the cornice on the facade of the garden front is entirely in place.

They are continuing it with great care and have begun to prepare tie timbers for the roof beams. I had the number of men working on the pavilions on the front court increased. The roofs on the two wings and the pavilions joined to the Small Chateau are nearly completed, and the stucco work will be carried out on the interior in the coming week. We have found that raising the basins carried by the figures on the canal [*Allée d'eau*] by four inches has been a great success and even making the figures in the Dragon basin four feet longer; but it was extremely necessary to empty the water from the basin so that all these figures would not be ruined by the freezing conditions we have been experiencing. I recommended, and will take, the necessary precautions so that this doesn't happen again in the future.

This unifying classical cornice was above an open-air first-floor terrace that stood in between the two pavilions that held the King's and the Queen's separate apartments as presented in Félibien's 1674 *Description*. In it he says that the cornice was conceived in 1668, finished in 1671, embellished in 1674 and replaced in 1678 with Hardouin-Mansart's Hall of Mirrors. M. Robaut's photographs of the cornice, from which he most generously allowed me to make my drawing, also show the embrasures of the square-headed windows of the second floor that looked out over the terrace in Le Vau's building.

The terrace never gave the King complete satisfaction, especially since its floor leaked into the rooms below on rainy days, a problem that was made worse by the installation of a fountain, the middle of whose pipes were not watertight. There was a little-known project of 1673 to replace it with a '*somptueux vestibule*' with an ornate extension of the attic floor over it supported on pairs of red marble Ionic columns with white capitals and pedestals. This project is attributable, not to d'Orbay, but to one of the pupils in his agency, Antoine Desgodets, and it never saw the light of day outside the drawing office.[39]

* * *

Félibien's *Description* continues by recounting that the terrace was approached on either side by the staircases that went up to the royal apartments, and from the salons alongside those apartments you could look on to the terrace above the single-storeyed ground floor paved with white, black and red marble with a great fountain in the centre, as yet lacking any figures in gilded bronze.[40]

To return to Colbert's reports to the King, he says on 9 May 1670 that he was at Versailles and the Trianon, where all the works were going ahead, and he hoped that His Majesty would be satisfied with the progress being made. Half of the fountains of the little children (to be found on the gradient that leads down from the north of the *enveloppe* to the Dragon fountain) were in place. The figures of the Dragon and the boys riding on swans shooting arrows at it had been put back (evidently the frost had, indeed, damaged them) and the process of gilding them was about to start.

* * *

The *enveloppe* was to fulfil the King's own vision of the symbols of absolute monarchy. It was to be a representation of the Sun in all his glory as all the statues and decorations would indicate. The two wings in front of the marble court contained the services areas for the King's food and drink, so the four elements were represented above their entrance porticoes. Each element had three figures to represent it. Earth was represented by Ceres, Pomona and Flora on the left of the balcony. Neptune, Thetis and Galatea represented Water, also on the left balcony. On the one at the right were Juno, Iris and the Zephyr on one side for Air, and Vulcan and two cyclops, who stood for Fire. The Accounts of the King's Buildings provide the names of the sculptors of these figures, with the familiar names of Le Hongre and Tuby among them. The whole work appears in an engraving by Israël Silvestre of 1674. Of course, the building was developed under d'Orbay's direction after October 1670, so it is difficult to decide how much actually came from Le Vau's own designs and how much, in his characteristic fashion that we observed in the Louvre, he left to the initiative of the other artists involved.

Félibien's imagined visitor passes through the vestibule on the ground floor into the gardens on the western side (one of the few correspondences with Vaux-le-Vicomte) and, turning round, looks at all the bas-reliefs at first-floor level, finished in 1671. Later remodelling made all the windows full centred, which did away with the bas-reliefs, but the statues at the level of the attic that represented the twelve months were not taken away. On the right-hand pavilion there were March through to June, above the terrace and in the middle of the old building were July to October, and then above the left-hand pavilion, November to February since the year began in March. The accompanying bas-reliefs portrayed children engaged in the appropriate activity for the seasons represented by the statues. The masks of human faces presented all the ages of human life from adolescence to senility. The totality relates to the Sun's activity throughout the year.[41]

As with other projects – Hôtel Lambert, the Louvre, Vaux-le-Vicomte – Le Vau did not work on his own. The essential collaborator for the interiors was Charles Le Brun, First Painter to the King since 1658. The timescale of construction meant that Le Vau had died before Le Brun had really begun on the wall and ceiling paintings in the new chateau. This collaboration 'would best serve the interests of French art'.[42] Le Brun had just completed his paintings for the chateau of Saint-Germain-en-Laye, and he also had responsibility for the enlargement of the tapestry factory of the Gobelins in Paris.[43] His output was prolific, complemented at Versailles by the work of the naturalised Italian craftsman Domenico Cucci on the doors and window frames, as well as a complete team of other artists – all named by de Nolhac (p.120): the whole roll call of the Academy of Painters and Sculptors. They translated Le Brun's drawings into paintings under his direction. Other Italians also worked on details of the embellishment of the framework that Le Vau had established and d'Orbay was continuing from the plans of his teacher until the work was achieved.

Gaspard and Balthazar Marsy took on the stucco work of the interior as well as various features of the fountains in the gardens. Jean-Baptiste Tuby, who created the figures for the Bassin d'Apollo, was also involved in the decorations for Queen Marie-Thérèse's apartments. These artists did not particularly specialise in their works. In fact, their versatility, along with that of their collaborators, brought the Versailles *enveloppe* about, and Le Vau was, as it were, their enabler *d'outre-tombe*.

All this work conformed to contemporary taste and the preferences of Louis XIV, for whom the claim is rightly maintained that it was he who created the Sun's palace. The seven planets were the themes for the successive rooms in his royal apartments, each one showing the actions of the heroes of antiquity and the achievements of the King himself so far in his recently established reign. The marble baths in the octagon room on the ground floor, so much admired by Félibien in his 1674 description, begun in 1672, were not completed until 1677 when the accounts show that they had cost 100,000 livres altogether. There were still the painted ceilings, the bronze ornaments and Tuby's bas-reliefs over the chimney pieces and the door frames to be provided.

Since these apartments surpassed in magnificence all that had been seen in France before them, they needed a worthy entrance and Le Vau intended to achieve this by his Great Staircase at the right of the court of the Fountain (later called the Marble Court).

The monumental staircase at the Louvre from the time of Henri II followed the Renaissance scheme of inclined vaulted tunnels. It was a single flight with three runs around a central well that characterised the stairwells built under Henri IV, Louis XIII and Mazarin, whereas in Italy the baroque scheme was of paired flights riding around the walls in an open cage in two storeys: the one at San Georgio in Venice being the prime example. Le Vau used paired flights at the Hôtel Lambert but these did not surround a stairwell, they simply turned back on themselves. He repeated this at the Tuileries in 1665 and planned the same thing for the Louvre in 1667. When Colbert wanted something more monumental for the Louvre, Le Vau proposed extending a double staircase extending around all four sides of an enlarged space rising from left and right along the rear wall of the building at first-floor level.

He had intended a monumental staircase right from the start at Versailles, but, after his death, in October 1670, François d'Orbay carried out his own design[44] by doubling the staircase in his plan of 1671. There was space available across the Venus and Diana salons and so the staircase was surrounded by building masses and lit from above in the Italian manner: the first time this was done in France.

For a short time during the 1960s, the Versailles *enveloppe* was attributed, not to Le Vau, but to his pupil d'Orbay, since Le Vau was too much occupied in the Nivernais for the manufacture of tinplate with which Colbert had entrusted him – a claim that was soon discredited.[45]

Nevertheless, d'Orbay does have his place in these constructions and in the completion of Le Vau's undertakings for the College of the Four Nations on the left bank in Paris. He had been born in 1634 and had become Colbert's protégé so as to be appointed as an architect in ordinary for the King's buildings in 1664. Since he was the gifted draughtsman in charge of Le Vau's agency, it was only reasonable that he should assume responsibility for unfinished work on the *enveloppe* while Le Vau was preoccupied with tinplate and naval armaments at Beaumont-la-Férrière in November 1669.[46] He had many talents, seen in his work on plans for the gardens at Saint-Germain-en-Laye, and he provided the alignment for several towns in his capacity as a surveyor and often showed his capabilities as an urbanist and a landscape designer.

He demonstrated his abilities as an innovator on several occasions, not least in the lighting for the Ambassadors' Staircase for which Colbert, never lavish with his compliments, singled him out for praise. He had the good sense to work closely with an able head of a building firm, Jacques Gabriel. Yet he was modest and discreet, unlike his master, not bringing attention to himself with the skills acquired during his visit to Italy in 1660 where it most mattered – before the King, and he never received the 6,000 livres a year that he would have had he become the First Architect. That post was kept vacant after Le Vau's death until the wonder boy Jules Hardouin-Mansart made such a good impression by his work on the chateau at Clagny that was intended as the King's gift to Mme de Montespan before relations between the lovers went sour.[47]

Le Brun's additions to the décor on d'Orbay's staircase to celebrate Louis XIV's marshals' and admirals' victories in painting and tapestry made this the highest achievement of the First Painter's career. It was his triumph to commemorate their triumphs and, of course, the King's grandeur, whose greatest recognition from Heaven was seen in terms of successful warfare and monumental building. Later on Coysevox's bust of Louis XIV, a rival to the one by Bernini placed in Diana's salon, was positioned above the staircase suitably embellished with the legend, strangely in Latin,[48] *Nec pluribus impar*.

Construction work began in May 1672 with payments paid for masonry to the contractor Gabriel in September, and for roofing the staircase. The lower parts of the double flight of stairs were entirely encased in marble, with accounts settled in November 1672 and January 1673, when the *marbriers* were taken to work elsewhere, to be brought back after a year.

Le Brun decorated the great parallelogram on the first floor with his paintings, above which the light was admitted. A balustrade in gilded bronze was added on each flight of stairs. Metal trophies by Tuby and Coysevox were put in place, as were fleurs-de-lys on the capitals of the pilasters, an impressive place for foreign ambassadors to be received by the King in front of golden doors. All this work was finished before Hardouin-Mansart began his transformations in 1678.[49]

* * *

We have seen how a recent assessment of the *enveloppe* has taken Colbert's point of view in disparaging Le Vau's contribution to its design, and of his abilities overall as an architect, repeated in a final assessment of the building as 'a patchwork', even if 'an inspired one'.[50]

But this need not be the last word on the subject as it seems to claim to be, despite the historiographical chronology. The English art historian Anthony Blunt, in a book first published in 1953, saw what Le Vau achieved in the difficult circumstances of the *enveloppe*'s development history very much more positively.

Looking at the new building from the gardens, observing a 'vast block of twenty-five bays of which the middle eleven on the first floor were set back behind a terrace', Blunt commented that the composition of the building was in the tradition of Bramante (1444–1514), the ground floor had rusticated arcades, the first floor an order of Ionic pilasters and columns, above which came an attic forming a straight skyline broken by urns and triumphs. Blunt concludes by asserting that:

> more than any other building of Le Vau, Versailles [the garden facade] shows a real grasp of the principles of classical architecture and at the same time a feeling of grand scale. The blocks are clearly defined and conceived in cubical terms, the two side sections standing out from the recessed centre in the simplest manner, their surfaces being broken only by the projecting central frontispieces with coupled columns. It is hard for us to judge the real quality of the building because the effect of varied depth was destroyed by the filling in of the terrace in the middle of the facade when Jules Hardouin-Mansart made the Galerie des Glaces, and the scale ruined by the addition of Mansart's vast wings to north and south. But, as far as we can imagine it from engravings of its original state, it proves that Le Vau rose finely to an opportunity far beyond anything which had confronted him earlier in his career.[51]

Some comment on the nature of the changes that Hardouin-Mansart made to the garden and north and south facades of the *enveloppe* is necessary to explain this illustration. At the level of the first floor, Le Vau's elevation had square-headed windows surmounted by rectangular bas-reliefs, similar to the ones he had provided on the ground floor at Vaux-le-Vicomte. The bas-reliefs were never put in place – a Colbert economy, no doubt – and Hardouin-Mansart would replace the square window heads with full-centred ones as is apparent from the painting, *École française, vue du château sur le parterre d'eau, vers de 1673*, found at Sceaux in the musée de l'Île de France.[52]

* * *

The King in the meantime was mulling over ideas for developing the town of Versailles to correspond with what he intended for his own residence alongside it. 'Another Versailles was being born, and its enlargement would march in step with the creation of a town in the vast lands bought by the King and in the midst of which the three great avenues would converge upon the chateau.'[53] But for the present, when the King and the courtiers came to Versailles they found themselves too confined and could only stay for a day at a time. It was too small a town to accommodate them all, clustered round the parish church of St Julien, which had recently been refurbished in the area known subsequently as Vieux-Versailles.

On his journey home from Spain ten years before, the King had visited the palace that his father's prime minister, the Great Cardinal, had provided for himself at Richelieu in the Poitou (destroyed, with the building materials sold on by his inheritors, who could not afford to maintain it), and been impressed and influenced by it, together with its dependent town and church built in a uniform style to correspond with it (which is still to be seen, virtually unaltered). This became his model for the new town at Versailles. None of this, of course, was accomplished while Le Vau was still alive, but it was all part and parcel of the King's visionary project in which he remained involved while he lived, despite his frequent absences for another royal project in the Nivernais.

This would lead eventually to a *hôtel particulier* being built as the *Surintendance des Bâtiments* – that is, for Colbert – in 1671, quickly followed by another one for the *Chancellerie* (both buildings have just been beautifully restored). On 22 May 1671, being at Dunkirk to begin the war against Holland, the King issued a resolution in favour of Versailles town, which amounted to its royal charter. For the next ten years, land was to be made available – on very favourable terms – from the Versailles pump at the north of the new palace as far as the farm at Clagny for all who wished to build houses there. These houses were to be built and maintained in a uniform symmetry set by the *Surintendance des Bâtiments*. At the end of the year the first stone was laid of a new church dedicated to Saint Louis meant as the chapel of the convent to be established on the south side of the place d'Armes for the convent of the order of Recollets, who were to serve as army chaplains.

* * *

We have already noticed how much the *enveloppe* was a co-operative effort between the architect and other artists, and that Le Nôtre and Le Vau were used to working back to back with each other. This realisation can be extrapolated to the statuary in the gardens, most of which was accomplished while Le Vau was still living.

When the King stressed the urgency of the project, Colbert had to point out a certain delay on account of a fortnight of bad weather they had had at Versailles after the King left, and that the King was intending to come back a fortnight earlier than expected. Buildings superintendent and architect, together with Monsieur Petit, the official directly in charge of the site, were looking over their shoulders all the time, wondering where the King would intervene next – even when he was far away. Colbert sent Petit off to Fontainebleau, where he would not be so harassed, and replaced him with the more dynamic Philippe Le Fèvre. All the time the King was sending back

Colbert's reports with their margins full of notes in his own hand expressing encouragement or impatience: 'Make sure that there is no let up, and speak always to the workmen about my return!'[54]

Jean-Baptiste Tuby, another Italian naturalised as French, was the creator of the group of Apollo rising from the waters accompanied by the horses of the Sun and by his attendant tritons announcing the day with their conches, in the fountain placed at the western end of the end of the *allée royale* that leads away from the chateau. The horses are galloping towards the Latona Fountain, originally all on ground level without its present wedding cake appearance. The goddess Latona is presented in Marsy's statuary group as shielding her children, Apollo and Diana, from the people of Lycia who had muddied the water they wanted to drink and they are seen in the process of being turned into frogs, lizards and turtles by a vengeful Jupiter, another commemoration of Louis XIV's triumph over the Fronde, fifteen years before. Instead of Latona and her children, we are invited to see Anne of Austria, King Louis and his brother Philippe.

Apollo in the evening rests in the grotto of the sea deity Thetis and her nymphs attend to his bath, while he is unmoved by their allure – as he should be since he is so far elevated above them in rank. This group of statuary by François Girardon and others was placed in the Grotto of Thetis on the north side of the *enveloppe*, which can be dated as 1666–67, and Le Vau could have been the designer of the building whose practical purpose was as a reservoir for a head of water on its roof for the fountains in the gardens. Lilian Lange's definitive article on the grotto[55] says that he was its creator, and that he worked with Denys Joly, the engineer/hydrologist, and the Francini brothers on the project to raise water from the Clagny lake by means of the Great Pump to fill the reservoir on the roof and the others nearby. The grotto is fronted by Le Vau's trademark triple arcade with gates showing the Sun motif, sculpted roundels in between them, and surmounted with three bas-reliefs of mermaids and tritons, Apollo dozing in his chariot towards evening, and then more marine people with musical instruments. It is not Apollo who is commemorated but the King, who had recently crossed the Rhine in triumph.

The arrangement of the interior with its shells and coral is characteristically claimed as created by the Perrault brothers. The overall design was a drawing by Charles Le Brun. The statuary itself is by François Girardon, another of the team that worked together so often, who made the Apollo figure, and Thomas Regnaudin, responsible for three of the nymphs. The Apollo group was flanked in the grotto by sculptures of the Golden Horses of the Sun groomed by tritons, the creations of the Marsy brothers and of Gilles Guérin. The grotto was later broken up to make room for Hardouin-Mansart's extensions on the same site. Later still, the statuary was placed where it is now, in a bosquet on the north side of the Latona Fountain under the shelter of artificial caves created to a design from Hubert Robert in Louis XVI's reign.

* * *

In Chapter 5, we saw the significance of transferring the tapestry factory at Maincy to the Gobelins in Paris to supply the decorative needs of the palace of Versailles. Again, under Claire Goldstein's guidance, we need to see here how the hydraulics for the fountains and the respective grottoes symbolised the significance of international commercial activity, private in the case of Vaux, and national at Versailles:

> While both spectacular chateaux were created to draw in the gazes of French subjects (and those beyond the nation's borders), the aesthetic and social spaces Vaux and Versailles engineered also gestured *outward* to an ever-expanding global economy. Planting the foreign and the manufactured into the earth of the garden powerfully staged the incorporation of trade and technology into the domestic French marketplace, and printed descriptions, promenades and newspaper accounts and popular collectible prints widely circulated these naturalized plans for France. Garden water features and citrus groves demonstrate how in the seventeenth century, both of these new visions of France entailed looking beyond as well as within the country's borders. Fouquet reimagined the nation on the cusp of a rapidly changing, expanding world. His modern vision of France – and the garden he designed to showcase it – prepared for Louis XIV's reign both a newly outward-looking (we might even say imperial) sensibility and the means for domesticating political intention by literally grounding it in French soil.

As far as technological innovations in water management were concerned, Fouquet was installing them at Vaux several years before the King declared himself independent of his ministers. His complicated hydraulic systems were feeding the water jets and fountains that were enhancing Le Nôtre's gardens very early in the process of constructing his palace. After Fouquet's arrest, the pipes at Vaux and Saint-Mandé were pillaged to such an extent as to reduce the values of both properties.[56]

The Grotto of Thetis at Versailles was begun in 1666 to announce the King's absolutist reign as glorious. 'To contemporaries the resting sun god represented Louis, since the King's device was the sun, and Versailles was where he refreshed himself for his great actions.'[57] Madeleine de Scudéry emphasized this in her *Promenade à Versailles*. Furthermore, the grotto cast Louis as a god inviting a comparison with the dying Emperor Vespasian, who joked to his attendants during a serious crisis, 'Oh dear! I think I am becoming a god.' (*Vae, puto deus fio!*) Vespasian had come to Rome to claim his *imperium* in the year of the four emperors (AD 69), which, once achieved, gave him total power, as Louis XIV had also done *mutatis mutandis* in 1661.[58]

Jean de La Fontaine's *Songe de Vaux* and the last volume of de Scudéry's novel *Clélie* celebrated international trade and exploitation of new territories in the hands of a new wealthy and private sector working in the context of mercantilism, and descriptions of Versailles celebrate all wealth, and production, natural or manufactured, as if they had been created by the King of France, presenting his absolute domination over the natural world, art, trade and technology.[59]

Certain sections of the *Songe* go further and make explicit the idea of the fountains at Vaux as allegories of successful mercantile trading. Fouquet held stocks in the French global trading companies being set up in the wake of Cardinal Richelieu's enterprises. He even held the title of Viceroy of America, which gave him authority over all the French companies that traded with the West Indies.[60] Daniel Dessert even goes so far as to say that Vaux-le-Vicomte was paid for not by the embezzling of national revenues of which Fouquet was accused, but by fruitful enterprises in overseas trade.[61] In La Fontaine's poetic dream, a salmon and a sturgeon are two envoys sent by Neptune to offer Fouquet vast treasures of petrified rocks, coral, and sea shells to decorate the grotto at the end of the gardens at Vaux. The talking fish tell him of these riches, which are embodied in the hydraulic effects seen throughout the gardens. These exotic fish 'represent contact with faraway places and the ability to transcend the natural limits of Europe's climate'.[62]

The King, at a very early stage of his transcending Vaux with and at Versailles, had his Grotto of Thetis constructed to take over what Vaux had represented while effacing the success attributed to Fouquet. Just as he could not allow Fouquet any chance of becoming a centre of opposition to his own power — which is why he changed the tribunal's sentence of exile to one of imprisonment for life in the Piedmontese Alps — so he was not allowed to be remembered anywhere near where he had been glorious.

Any glory was to belong to the state and therefore to the King. So bas-reliefs on the outside wall of the grotto included decorations by Jean Le Pautre in the form of six maps of world regions where French trade was to be predominant, and de Scudéry treats the grotto as the starting point of her *Promenade* with 'all the vocabulary of astonishment and enchantment characteristic of Versailles'.[63] The grotto appealed to sensual delight: birdsong and the sounds of a hydraulic organ, and the sight of coral and sea shells, were all in place by 1666, with plaster precedents of the statuary by Girardon and Regnaudin, Tuby, Guerin and the Marsys in place until 1676, when they were replaced by the finished works in marble. The grotto was destroyed in 1684 to make way for Hardouin-Mansart's extensions, and the statuary dispersed, but it had been there long enough for its announcement of royal power to have been noticed by all who were brought – often by the King himself – to visit it. André Félibien was instrumental in the process of making what it stood for comprehended far and wide. Let him have the last word on the grotto:

> One can say that Versailles is a place where Art works alone, and that Nature seems to have been abandoned, in order to give the king the opportunity to make appear there, by a kind of creation, if I dare call it, several magnificent works and an infinity of extraordinary things; but there is no other site in all of this Royal Residence, where Art has more felicitously succeeded, than in the *Grotte de Thétis*.[64]

* * *

Girardon's Fountain of the Pyramid put up during the last year of Le Vau's life, while he was away so much in the Nivernais, stands on the northern side of the *enveloppe* before the *allée* leads down to the Dragon fountain through groups of children holding up little fountains, which caused Colbert such anxiety in the early stages.

This piece is amusing decoration in its entirety, with nothing allegorical about the King at all. Shaped like a chandelier, it rises above animals' legs and feet, while fully grown tritons – strange mythological hybrids with men's bodies and fishtails instead of legs – move around it. Younger tritons with their arms held up support the next level, then fish use their tails to hold up the plate upon which we see lobsters: all at play together. At the same time, as if it were a merry-go-round at a fun fair, everything seems to be moving in a clockwise manner while you watch it.

After a while, you might even hear the voice of Lewis Carroll, saying in your ear from another, very different, wonderland:

> See how eagerly the lobsters and the turtles all advance,
> They are waiting on the shingle – will you come and join the dance?
> Will you, won't you, will you, won't you, will you join the dance?

* * *

The King needed somewhere to put all the valuable orange trees that he had confiscated from Vaux-le-Vicomte. The orangery was one of the earliest contributions made by Le Vau to the transformation of Versailles after the arrest of Fouquet. He designed it in 1662, and it played a large part in the King's adoption of the Sun as his emblem. This, as Félibien pointed out, was something the King was doing even before he was claiming personal triumphs on the battlefield. Perhaps it has more to do with the vegetable and fruit grower Jean-Baptiste La Quintinie with his manure and bell jars than the King's effective influence, but the orangery that Le Vau set up under the terrace that would soon become the western foreground of the *enveloppe* was to be the winter shelter for these fruits. They grew well in the warm climate of south-west Spain and Portugal (had not Mazarin made presents of these to Anne of Austria?) but were rare in middle France with its chilly winter, with frost on the famous feasts of the 'ice saints' from 11 to 14 May of which gardeners in *France profonde* are still wary. These wonderful trees with their intriguing blossoms and glorious fruits erupted into the imagination of writers who were the cultural trophies from Vaux-le-Vicomte, Jean de La Fontaine and Madeleine de Scudéry, who compared these oranges to the golden apples of the Hesperides that Hercules had stolen in the story: was not Hercules a former image for the King?[65]

In Israël Silvestre's 1674 engraving, the orangery is directly behind the Latona Fountain where in our time we see the steps and the large urns, to be moved and developed anew by Jules Hardouin-Mansart in its present position facing south.

* * *

Having taken so much trouble to establish a principal residence on a grand scale for himself, the King was eager also to have a smaller retreat. He would later have the chateau at Marly, where he invited favoured courtiers to spend days of leisure with him, and Mme de Montespan would have Clagny, but in 1670 he took up the suggestion made by Mme de Montespan to build a quiet, secluded place for invited members of the court to relax at table. This was to be not far away, hence easily accessible, on the northern side of the Grand Canal to balance the menagerie on the southern side of it in the hamlet called Trianon that he had recently bought.

It was built as a group of pavilions around an oval yard, according to plans drawn up by Louis Le Vau, but it is unlikely that the concept for it came in the first instance from the architect himself. A translation into French of the German Jesuit Athanasius Kircher's *China Monuments* of 1667 was very influential upon taste in court circles at the time. The French version was dedicated to Louvois, Louis XIV's minister of war (subsequently Superintendent of the King's Buildings as well) and, once in circulation, influenced a passing phase at court of French taste in the exotic – a taste already fed by the foreign animals in the menagerie that the courtiers took to boats on the Grand Canal to go and see. 'The Porcelain Trianon contributed to the notion of Versailles as an amalgam of the rarities of the world.'[66] It was set in a garden created by Michel II Le Bouteaux (related to Le Nôtre by marriage to his great-niece), with orange trees and jasmines planted directly in the earth[67] rather than in urns or the square boxes on wheels known as *bacs*, and this was a notable first for horticulturalists. On 9 May 1670, Colbert had told the King that Le Bouteaux had been provided with all he needed and his work [on the Trianon] was coming on well. That it was surrounded by flower beds is important, since 'over and above war and architecture and his own personal glory, flowers were an unfailing passion for Louis XIV, to which he gave himself immeasurably', as the accounts show year after year. The pavilions were surrounded and interspersed with flower beds, so much so that when the tuberoses were in flower the courtiers avoided going there for fear of being overwhelmed by their scent.[68] To extend the time that the gardens were colourful, moveable greenhouses were included in the design to protect the southern plants from the more northerly winters. Trianon was meant to be a place for sensual pleasures, with two apartments ready for the royal *sieste* and four pavilions devoted to gastronomy – whether for preparation or consumption of exotic collations. The effect was heightened by the proximity of cages for exotic songbirds. There was, in fact, no porcelain in the pavilions, but a great deal of faience tiling, predominantly in blue and white, covering the interior walls. Le Vau and his assistant and continuator d'Orbay had never seen a Chinese building, so they made an admixture of classical French walls, surmounted by high roofs, tiled in slate and lavishly decorated with urns, wading birds and cherubs, known to French taste as *amours*, dangling their legs over the cornices. There was no attempt at a pagoda. It was all fantasy, without the elaborate symbolism of royalty that had predominated a few years before over at the menagerie. On this side of the canal, it was all 'pure scenography', constructed in a hurry to satisfy the demands of the impatient monarch.[69]

Le Vau had supervised the destruction of Trianon village in 1663, consigning the stones taken from the destroyed village church to the walls of a nearby cemetery, but, although the conception of the Porcelain Trianon is usually ascribed to him, it has been stated that his name is only mentioned once in the accounts relative to it. Most of the work was carried out by d'Orbay, but there is still no persuasive argument for saying that it was built to his own design.

Félibien accepted that there was something incredible about it, as though it had sprung up overnight after an April shower.

It was to serve as an 'architectural manifesto' against the domination of trade with the Orient by shipping from the United Provinces. By 1670, Colbert's intensive development of a commercial fleet to rival the Dutch East India Company, and a military one to assure its dominance, was yielding dividends and envy of Dutch supremacy was being replaced by French success. Colbert founded a North Sea Company in 1663, and the East and West Indies Companies in 1664, which successfully eroded the Dutch and English trade monopolies, also reflecting the failure of Dutch financiers to continue to regulate the prices being charged for imports of Chinese commodities to Europe, commodities that included porcelain tableware in blue and white. What was reflected in the porcelain Trianon was carried to its conclusion in the decorations at the palace of Marly, soon to be accomplished.

The Trianon was entirely theatrical, where the King could be the Emperor of the Orient, despite its architectural references to Palladio's Venetian style and to Renaissance descriptions of Pliny's villa being influential in the forms given to the pavilions. The most striking thing about the principal pavilion is the decoration applied to its roof, with the gilding on the tiles of the *enveloppe* replaced by the effects of blue and white paint. A bill settled in 1671 shows an expense of 40,000 livres worth of work paid for the painting of sculptures and the urns fashioned in lead for the roofs of the pavilions by Louis Le Hongre. The delicacy of these decorations demanded great additional expenditure on regular maintenance.

After sixteen years, it was all over. It was to be Le Vau's last creation. It did not weather well and was replaced with the Marble Trianon created by Hardouin-Mansart when the King wanted Mme de Montespan out of his system after she had tried to keep his affections by means of sorcery. There was not a little input from the King himself during a period when his new First Architect was not there.

Chapter 8

Mazarin's Memorial

We can pass briefly over the marriage of Louis XIV and Marie-Thérèse (as she was now known) at Saint-Jean-de-Luz on 9 June 1660 and their slow return to Paris through several French provincial centres until we come to their solemn entry into the capital in late August. The treaty and the marriage were the high point and conclusion of Mazarin's career as a French diplomat, but he was too ill to take part in the *entrée* as such, delegating the ceremonial part he should have played to his intendant Colbert.[1] He sat on the balcony of the Hôtel de Beauvais in the Tuileries with Anne of Austria, the Queen Mother as she now was, and Queen Henrietta-Maria of England at the end of the royal couple's progress from the Chateau de Vincennes to the Louvre under triumphal arches and past obelisks specially put up for the occasion.[2]

The hatred shown to Mazarin during the years of the Fronde had evaporated and he was regarded as a hero for his double achievement of the peace and the Bourbon–Habsburg marriage. He was even nominated for the papacy, and the Paris *Parlement*, the author of his exile a decade previously, publicly acknowledged his contribution to the well-being of the State. He was given 'a co-starring role in a ritual act of kingship'. Mercury had brought Hercules and Minerva together. He was well enough to be the host at a dinner party that ended the celebrations at his own residence (now the *Bibliothèque nationale* in the rue Richelieu), so that:

> dignitaries from courts across Europe ... [were given] an opportunity to admire their host's sumptuous palace and the unsurpassed library and art collection it contained. The summer of 1660 was the climax of a remarkable career. Nine months later Mazarin was dead. His timing was perfect; once an outcast, he had managed to die a hero. Without that precondition Mazarin's College would not have been built.[3]

While Mazarin was ill, he did not actually live in his palace but in a third-floor apartment in the Louvre not far from where the King sometimes laid his head at nights. His illness seems to have been a bundle of the symptoms of exhaustion after the drawn-out negotiations with Luis de Haro, who had not pulled any punches during them. During the night of 6 February 1661, fire broke out in the building and, helped by his captain of the guard, he made his way back to his palace, as it were to bid farewell to his collection of fine art objects. Then he was taken to another of his habitual residences, an apartment in the Queen's wing of the Chateau de Vincennes at the eastern edge of Paris, which Le Vau had remodelled for him three years before.

The King and the Queen Mother were currently at Saint-Germain-en-Laye, and they came to see him often during his last days. Louis XIV had lost his father at an early age and was Mazarin's dutiful godson, borne out by his leaving of Marie Mancini for the Queen he married. It does not seem that this sense of obligation to the Cardinal extended to more than duty on the King's part: the nickname he gave him while still a boy was 'the Grand Turk', and, although he put the absolutist principles imparted in the tutorials he had with Mazarin in 1660 into practice as soon as his mentor was deceased, neither he or his mother seemed to have missed him much, at least in public. As the educators of the young King and sometimes as his protectors, Anne and Mazarin were very close to each other, and, when they were apart, they used a secret code to communicate with each other in an intimate manner.[4] It was sometimes rumoured that Anne of Austria and Jules Mazarin had been married secretly, yet when courtiers wanted to continue talking about the late cardinal, the Queen Mother stopped them, adding the suggestion that 'they could find better use for their time than in listening to speeches which had become useless'.[5]

As he lay dying, Mazarin's confessor, Angelo Bissaro, a Théatine monk – from one of the counter-reformation orders the Cardinal favoured – had advised him to prepare his will and, beginning on 3 March 1660, he did so. There were plenty of goods to dispose of since Mazarin was the wealthiest man in France by then. The money that he left to his four nieces for their dowries amounted to 2,700,000 livres in cash. There was a gift of 100,000 livres to the general hospital to build an extension. There were investments including the 60,000 livres placed with the Madagascar Company that he had lost, and this may be true of other investments as well. His fortune could be estimated in total as approaching 39,000,000 livres and the debts and outstanding payments he owed were small in comparison. At his death, he was worth more than Richelieu, than Henri II of Condé, than Chancellor Séguier.[6] 'In fact, Mazarin's fortune had no equal throughout the history of the Old Regime, which is all the more astonishing because he amassed most of his riches in only nine years – between 1653, when he returned to France after the Fronde, and his death in 1661.[7]

As Mme Claude Dulong showed, any historian has a hard time discerning from Mazarin's documents and those of his agents what the sources of his revenues were with any precision. That was because he did not intend contemporaries to know what they were and took measures to conceal them.[8] When he returned from exile the sources do not lend themselves to any greater transparency. His collections of fine art and jewellery, tapestries and statues began again and he sent letters all over the place to give orders about where treasures were to be found and how much he was advancing to pay for them: 'I am told that the Ludovisis are selling some bronzes, see if they can be bought. I learn that the cavalier del Pozzo is dead; he had some Poussins that I would like to get my hands on ...'

In fact, 'so ample and fruitful was the harvest gathered in Italy in 1653–1654 that it needed a galley to transport it from Civitavecchia.' His nephew-in-law, the governor of Provence, ensured that it could be unloaded safely and the goods brought to Paris in the most secure conditions.[9] All of which implies secrecy.

So when the Cardinal came to dictate his will to his confessor, he had an embarrassing amount of this world's goods to dispose of and did not want the usual process of compiling an inventory to take place. Some of the assets had been gained legally but there were a good many dodgy deals behind what could be uncovered.[10] This would be embarrassing for the crown, and for the Mancini nieces and their spouses. Cardinal Richelieu had given his palace to the crown as the Palais-Royale. Mazarin wanted his to be for his family.[11]

The King did not agree to refuse an inventory as Mazarin asked him to but he entrusted it to Jean-Baptist Colbert, who at that time was Mazarin's secretary[12] – literally, the keeper of his secrets – and they were safe with him, especially as he was implicated in the way the fortune had been amassed. Despite the King's order, the inventory was no more than partial, but it satisfied the requirements of probate.

What has all this got to do with Louis Le Vau, who is the subject of this study? Let Hilary Ballon give the answer – after all, had she not died young, she would have written a continuous account of his life. She drew attention to the contrast between Mazarin's two ambitious subordinates:

> the charming, gregarious Fouquet, who was in charge of raising money for the crown, and Colbert, Mazarin's wily personal lieutenant who outflanked his rival, engineered Fouquet's downfall and consolidated his position at court ... while Fouquet was condemned to spend the rest of his unhappy life in prison. The events of 1661 involved two of the greatest monuments of seventeenth-century French architecture: the

chateau of Vaux-le-Vicomte and the Collège des Quatre-Nations, both designed by Le Vau ... The king had resolved to arrest Fouquet well before he laid eyes on the chateau, but Vaux was a useful distraction. So was the Collège des Quatre-Nations; it shifted attention away from Mazarin's ill-gotten fortune.[13]

As his predecessor Richelieu had done, Mazarin acknowledged that he would not have been rich had he not been the King's first minister, and a good deal of his bequest was by way of returning gifts to their origins: paintings, tapestries, furniture, diamonds, emeralds. But these were not a public monument to himself. For that, he devised the construction of a new college in the University of Paris. Richelieu had a similar idea in his embellishment of the Sorbonne. Mazarin's foundation would bear the title 'The Four Nations' so as to leave no doubt that he had created it, for he had brought four new 'nations' into France by his treaties of Westphalia and of the Pyrenees. There were to be sixty students – boys the age of fourteen to take a bachelor's degree, all with free places. There were to be twenty of them from Flanders, Artois, Hainault and Luxembourg, fifteen from Alsace and other former German states, ten from Roussillon, Cerdagne and Conflans, and another fifteen from Pignerol. There were to be a few from the Papal states included in this final fifteen. They were to be chosen from noble or higher bourgeois families and turned into Frenchmen loyal to the monarchy and speaking its language who, on their return home, would share their assimilation into French culture with their countrymen. Those from the north would include Protestants who were to be converted to the Catholic faith. Their re-education would provide cultural stability in the new territories. Hilary Ballon pointed out that there were not four nations that were included but 'discrete parts of ten different provinces. The term 'Four Nations' called to mind the University of Paris in the high Middle Ages when it had European status in which the teachers were separated out into four governing nations: French, Norman, Picard and English. In that epoch, the University had an international character. Mazarin's college was meant to take foreigners in and make sure they left as Frenchmen. This was part of a tendency that had begun under Henri IV and which later Bourbons would continue, turning the notional national groups into colleges with a new programme of humanist studies, symbols of the relation between education and the state.

Mazarin entrusted the teaching in his college to the rectors of the Sorbonne since there was no doubt of their counter-reformation orthodoxy. The aim was religious solidarity and nation building through a new kind of elite. There would also be an academy, where equitation, dancing, the practise of arms and mathematics were to be learned, since aristocratic life turned on the court and the battlefield. But this needed more space than was eventually available in Le Vau's design and, in any case, there were seven such academies in the Faubourg Saint-Germain alone during this period to perform the same function and, in the end, it was not provided.

Mazarin's design was completed with his plans for the library, his own library, partly dispersed during the Fronde, but regathered afterwards and incorporated into the college: the largest library in Paris with close on 38,000 books. By moving his precious collection from the Palais Mazarin to this new location attached to his college and allowing all *bona fide* researchers to use it, it went from being a luxurious privilege into a public resource. It was to be both part of Mazarin's monument and a symbol of royal patronage.[14] It is still open as such, and was kept in being by the men of 1789 because it was available to all who would put it to democratic use.

* * *

There was a body of executors responsible for setting up the college. They were Guillaume de Lamoignan, First President of the Paris *Parlement*; Nicolas Fouquet, who was Procurator General and still Superintendent of Finance; Jean-Baptiste Colbert, soon to become a minister; and Michel Le Tellier, future secretary of state and Chancellor. There was also Zongo Ondedei, bishop of Fréjus, who had been a close associate of Mazarin. Members of Mazarin's family were represented on the body by the Duke of Mazarini, his primary heir. They had at their disposal from Mazarin's estate 2 million livres in cash, 45,000 livres in *rentes* (bonds producing interest) from the Hôtel de Ville, and the income from the richest of Mazarin's twenty-eight church benefices, the Abbey of Saint-Michel-en-l'Herm in the Vendée, for the purposes of setting up the whole establishment. Their task was to produce a body of buildings on an acceptable site that would provide the sixty boarders with individual study bedrooms, classrooms, dining facilities, kitchens and other services, a worthy chapel that would also be Mazarin's burial place and monument, and suitable space for his library. They had to do all this as best they could without drawing public attention to Mazarin's fortune, which was at the same time providing lavish sums in dowries for his nieces.

In 'a little masterpiece of disinformation', as Mme Dulong calls it, Mazarin's foundation deed for the college offered the whole project to the King 'which could bring about great good for the kingdom'. The twenty-two year old King accepted the gift and gave it the status and the tax privileges of a royal foundation, seeing what Mazarin had done as a great gesture of loyalty. He said that it would mean that the new territories were not merely assumed into France, but that the hearts of the new subjects would be truly French as the cardinal, whom he called his cousin, intended.[15] Louis was a loyal godson in all that mattered.

By 1661, Louis Le Vau had been the King's First Architect for seven years, working on the Louvre after having remodelled the Château de Vincennes as apartments for Mazarin and for the Queen Mother. It would have been strange if he had not been put in charge of the construction of the college, for which Colbert chose an administrative committee. Jean de Gomont was trusted by Mazarin with administrative matters and he presided over the committee. He brokered the meetings between Colbert as controller and Le Vau who, naturally, would have preferred a free hand such as he had when working on the competition of the Louvre. They had weekly meetings and Gomont rigorously kept minutes of them 'so that posterity will be aware of the effort that led to the realisation of this great design'.[16]

Colbert was a dyed-in-the-wool administrator, ever seeking efficiency, and he saw an advantage in uniting the new college with the Théatine convent on what is now the quai Voltaire even while Mazarin was drawing up his will. This horrified the two monks of that order who had been at Mazarin's side as he was dying. Mazarin himself intended that the college should go after the standards of excellence set by the Sorbonne and that there should be association with the teaching body there. When the dying man heard that Colbert had changed his testament, he commanded him to remove the alteration.[17]

Colbert took no notice and, as soon as the cardinal was dead, started the procedure to buy land around the Théatine's church of Sainte-Anne-la-Royale so as to combine it with the college chapel. In his view the same building would serve for both institutions and limit any tendency towards lavish overspending. Gomont was put in charge of the project. The rectors of the Sorbonne agreed reluctantly to accept oversight of Mazarin's college provided that the Théatines were excluded from the small power Mazarin wanted to give them over the fifteen Italian scholars on the foundation. The monks lacked university qualifications. The Sorbonne rectors were resisting crown control together with any Jesuit influence there might be. It was a happy coincidence that the Théatines were content with what they had in their own set-up.

The Sorbonne rectors did not like the idea of the academy for aristocratic and courtly skills either and wanted it located apart from the college in the interests of academic discipline. They considered that Paris had too many temptations for the young gentlemen. Their experience told them that classroom rigour and military skills were best kept apart from each other. The executors tended to agree with this. The format eventually adopted included locking the boys (for that is what they were) in their individual rooms at night with a chamber pot and only allowing them out in tightly supervised groups.

The most important question that faced the executors was where to build the college. Since the college would be small it needed to be within the ambience of the university so that visiting teachers could be called upon and visiting students could help overcome introversion. Several suggestions were made, including replacing the newly established Jardin des Plantes. Objections to this quickly appeared, first from Antoine Vallot, first physician to the King, who presumably did not want to lose his facility for obtaining herbal medicines – the directors of the Chelsea Physick Garden would have thought the same. Vallot had bought his post as director for 30,000 livres (paid to Mazarin) and developed the garden. He died in office there in 1671. Then the rector of the university objected that the garden was too far away from the rest of the university to be administered properly.[18]

Another suggestion was to build on an empty site (urbanisation, begun under Henri IV, was not complete by 1661) behind Cardinal Lemoine's college, whose directors would only allow Mazarin's college to be built behind theirs if they had control of it, and that was not going to happen. Le Vau was present at the Christmas Eve meeting at which this was decided upon and he brought forward his own suggestion that the best place was on the site that included the Nesle Tower on the quay on the opposite side of the Seine to the Louvre's south façade, which was his creation. Colbert, now the King's unopposed minister and likely to be the superintendent of royal buildings after he had ensured Fouquet's downfall in the September before, told him to prepare plans. Le Vau had them ready on 21 January 1662.

'Gomont reported that Louis XIV found the drawing very beautiful and was delighted to have a majestic object to view from his apartment in the Louvre. On 11 March 1662 the building commission endorsed Le Vau's design.'[19]

As the minutes of their discussions records, the First Architect's proposal was to build the college near the Nesle gate opposite the Louvre, where a public square could be created that would certainly be an ornament for the Louvre.[20] However, one of the most influential personages in the life of Paris, the Provost of the Merchants, raised objections. To build a demi-lune embankment out into the river would impede the anchoring there of the boats that carried trade goods. When the river iced over in winter, they would be damaged. The south facade of the Louvre would also be inconvenienced. It was important that time should be allowed for public discussion of the project.[21] He had an argument: look at any engraving of the Seine and its banks made during this period and you see the river chock-a-block with boats of all kinds.

This public discussion was to take eighteen months and, in June 1662, Mazarin's heir, the Duke of Mazarini, who had changed his noble title when he married one of the cardinal's nieces,[22] had already behaved irrationally by damaging the classic nude statues he had inherited from his uncle-in-law and would later be abandoned by the niece, interjected that a better solution for the placement of the college would be to take over the Luxembourg Palace at the time occupied by the Orleans family but up for sale with an asking price of 1.1 million livres. The executors took the proposal seriously and submitted it to the King.[23] [The Luxembourg was taken over later by Gaston d'Orleans' daughter, the Duchess of Montpensier, 'La Grande Mademoiselle', authoritative chronicler of the period, who already had a part-interest in the property with its extensive gardens.]

Meanwhile, Le Vau had not wasted any time in drawing up a plan for the college to replace the Nesle buildings (familiar to enthusiasts of Maurice Druon's series of novels, *Les rois maudits*). The chapel was to rise up in the middle of a large, semicircular area, and its portal would be directly opposite the south facade of the Louvre. He was contemplating a bridge to join the two sites, but that did not arrive until the college became the Institute of France in 1805 on the orders of Napoleon I, with the construction of the Pont des Arts. Louis XIV appeared to have been all for this scheme, and against the acquisition of the Luxembourg since it was a *maison royale* built by his grandmother, Marie de' Medici. The change of use was too much of a consideration. He ordered the adoption of Colbert's project and Le Vau's plan, although he certainly did not agree to pay for it.[24] The executors set about gaining possession of the land and knocking down the Nesle tower.

* * *

In order to start acquiring the land, Le Vau negotiated with the Provost of the Merchants to buy the 3,800 *toises* needed at a going rate of 127 livres and 10 sols. This was no more than the price of the bare earth. The price of the buildings already there had to be negotiated one by one with the individual owners.

The first owner to deal with was the town of Paris. This was because the crown had granted the site of the Nesle moats to the town on condition that the former port, in a ruinous state, was quickly replaced and the quay extended up to the site. Colbert's offer of 120,000 livres was not enough for the provost, who was asking 170,000 for it. It was decided that the town did not have to pay for repairing the quay and in that way Colbert's offer was accepted and paid to the town receiver.[25] Thirteen thousand livres were paid to the Marquis of Coislin, who made no difficulties, but M. de Guénéguaud wanted 250 livres for every *toise* he owned in the moats. He also wanted an indemnity for having the Nesle tower destroyed and drew out the negotiations. The Benedictines of Saint-Germain-des-Près also created obstructions.[26] The King himself eventually had to intervene. Others who had vague claims in the former port of Nesle also received payments. The keeper of the keys of the former port, named as Estienne Leguay, was paid 800 livres for his lodging and the job he lost. The shops along the quay belonged to the town, but for forty years they had been let to Magdeleine Gruin, widow of Guillaume Sachet, *premier valet de chambre* to Queen Margot until her death in 1615. She sub-let them to small-scale artisans for 1,245 livres, and received an indemnity for the lost rent when she gave them up. The executors bought up the remaining small properties on the site for no great sum. Alfred Franklin listed the owners' names, including the agent of Loménie de Brienne, who was foreign minister for a while during the King's minority. There was also a coal depot in the quay and a payment was made to the coal merchant. There is a wealth of social detail in the list of property owners: a locksmith, a quartermaster in the Swiss regiment, a King's councillor and secretary who stood a good chance to be able to buy himself nobility in time, and an official at the Chatelet. All of these owned houses on the quai Malaquais, later quai Voltaire, near the Théatines. In all, 674,500 livres were paid out by Mazarin's executors for these purchases and indemnities. It may have been partly in ruins, but we have the economy of a little village here.

Le Vau and his two assistant architects, Lambert and Dorbay (note the absence of a nobiliary particle), could now get to work. His plans had been accepted, so Le Vau was in charge of the construction in return for a fee of 3,000 livres a year as long as the project lasted. The differentials were considerable since Lambert and Dorbay were to receive no more than 200 livres a year, as the college treasurer's accounts showed.[27]

* * *

Colbert would soon come to advise Louis XIV and try to redirect his enthusiasms, but the final word was always to be his, as was what Hilary Barron calls 'the controlling fact' of the design that his First Architect produced on 21 January 1662: 'the king had the only good view'.[28]

That was without the bridge, which Le Vau had decided was not worth pressing for at the time in view of the cost of building it. Nowadays we can stand in the centre of the Pont des Arts raised a few feet above the level of the quay, and obtain an even more satisfying view; afterwards, we can complete the aesthetic experience by going into the *Cour carée* of the Louvre and turning to look back through the entrance. Le Vau's use of the Baroque style for the college goes well towards completion of the classicism he had already used for the Louvre south wing:

> From the middle of the 1650s … Le Vau's art had not ceased to lurch between baroque and classicism as if two temperaments inhabited the creator, on one side the movement, the light and shade, illusion, theatricality, served by a certain liberty in using the orders of architecture, and on the other the calm balance between components, monumentality, repetitive structure. If we add the force of the French renaissance tradition which comes from Lescot and l'Orme and their follower Salomon de Brosse, we find the sources of the tradition which gave Mazarin's college its exceptional character and flavour.[29]

From the middle of the bridge we see the college facade with its three main elements: the pavilions at right and left, the central portico, pediment and the surmounting cupola and dome, the pavilions joined to the centre with curved wings topped with a balustrade to conceal a low roof, as opposed to the pitched roofs on the pavilions. The courses that support the balustrades are in turn supported by Corinthian orders, repeated at the level of the ground floor by more orders beneath more courses. There is a beautiful balance between the proportions of the centred arches above the ground floor and the square-headed windows on the first.

* * *

In August 1662, when the estimate for the construction of the college was prepared, Louis Le Vau and his family were still living at the house he had bought in the rue du Roi-de-Sicile in 1645. He was about to move into an apartment that went with his job while he was working on the Louvre in the Hôtel de Longueville, rue des Poulies, which the Duchess of Longueville had exchanged with the King for another mansion nearby in view of the fact that it was scheduled for demolition as soon as the east facade of the Louvre – the Colonnade – might be completed; it was intended that there should be uncluttered space between it and the church of Saint-Germain-l'Auxerrois, as there still is. She had made this agreement on the very same day that the meetings for the estimate were recorded in the minutes of the notary responsible: 13 August 1662.

So on 24, 25, 26 and 27 July the prospective site managers had gone to Le Vau's office in the tall house behind the Hôtel de Ville to look at the drawings

– principally by d'Orbay – that had been prepared by the draughtsmen in his agency that was also installed there. They came and went as they pleased during those days and Le Vau was there to answer any questions about details.[30] Six months later the work was set in hand.

The foundations began to be laid in February 1663. By January 1665, the east pavilion and a part of the chapel were built; in 1669, letters patent announced that 'the buildings are so far advanced that in a little while Mass could be celebrated in the church and the exercises in the college could begin. All books left and given could be put in the shelves of the new library.' When Le Vau died in October 1670, the decoration had been set in hand and d'Orbay finished it in 1672.

Le Vau's plan had to be ingenious to cope with the difficulties of the site, but he was no stranger to a difficult site since having to cope with the limitation of the ground available for the Hôtel Lambert on the Île Saint-Louis at the outset of his career. The main drain for the Faubourg Saint-Germain flowed into the Seine by means of a creek where there was frequent flooding. Le Vau followed its course in his plans, which had disadvantages: since it was inadequately canalised it could have poisoned the college wells if not dealt with. There was also an advantage inasmuch as the semicircular frontage imposed by following its course corresponded with a style already developed in Italy, which Le Vau knew about from ground plans and engravings, and in France by François Mansart's designs for Blois and the Minimes.

The church formed the central motif: the portico led to a vestibule, then to a space under the elliptical dome flanked on both sides by a chapel, with the high altar in another chapel. Side chapels were provided for the Mazarin family tombs. Le Vau used ideas from the Val-de-grâce church, which Lemercier built for Anne of Austria, and he knew about the ellipses often used on their churches in Rome by Borromini and Bernini from engravings.[31]

The first designs that Le Vau produced in his drawing office were burdened with too much ornamentation but he dispensed with the niches separating the orders and the channelling since they offered too much substance to the pilasters and the attic that surrounded the drum under the cupola. 'A care for economy doubtless,' says Hautecœur, 'but also for sobriety.'[32] His aim became to achieve a certain lightness and to give the whole ensemble a unity. Hilary Ballon points out that the French tradition of building separate bodies of masonry was preserved, with the pavilions almost free-standing and the portico projecting from the curved frontage.[33] The church floor was to be covered in a mosaic of Jaspé marble representing Mazarin's own taste.

The pavilions were to have ground and first floors united with colossal pillars, such as Le Vau had used at the Hôtel Lambert. The ground-floor arcades were fully centred and the bays between the columns were to be used as shops, in the tradition established by Henri IV's architects at the place Royale (Vosges) and the place Dauphine.

Le Vau showed his preference for solid regular forms. Behind this inviting facade, the college ground plan was set obliquely because it had to keep within the limitations of the existing road. In the first court, there are the peristyles on either side, one for the library and one for the chapel, approached in either direction from the exit from the quadrangle in which the study bedrooms, classrooms and dining areas were to be found, off the far end of which were the kitchens and other services, including the water supply. The river front was decorated with bas-reliefs and a balustrade seen in Israël Silvestre's engraving of about 1670 that the construction of the Pont des Arts caused to be modified.[34]

But the construction of something that was a royal project was not acceptable to everybody. We have already mentioned the Provost of the Merchants' objection to the quay in front of the chapel as a threat to navigation on the Seine. This was resolved by shaving the projection into the river back after a meeting of experts in July 1662, but the essential feature of the projected quay alignment with the south facade of the Louvre was respected. There was a complaint from an angry neighbour, who compared the new design for the quay as like the meandering of a medieval street – an objection to a reversion to times before Henry IV's urbanisation that did not understand Le Vau's intentions at all. When Bernini came on his visit in 1665, the courtier appointed to accompany him, Paul Fréart de Chantelou, observed to him that the college was badly planned in relation to the curvature of the riverbed, although he did not report the great man's reply in his memoir of the visit. Christopher Wren passed by in September of the same year and echoed the criticism: 'The College of the Four Nations is generally admir'd but the Artist hath purposely set it ill-favouredly that he might show his Wit in struggling with an inconvenient Situation.'[35] Le Vau did not have the same freedom that Sir Christopher would have in rebuilding a city after a fire, however.

When Gomont and his committee had heard that there were objections to the two new pavilions spoiling the view of the river front and suggested that the college be built further back from the river, Le Vau 'fought the suggestion tooth and nail'. The cost of such an action would be prohibitive, and what he was doing would enhance the view, especially from the Louvre, he said.[36]

Le Vau had taken care to provide a good solution for the buildings at the rear of the college to blend in with what was there already. As early as 1657 he had the idea of a large square there, but in 1662 he worked only upon the area of the ruined fortifications that he found there and transformed what we would call a brown site into 'urban splendour'. Rue des Fossez became rue Mazarine, and it met the rue de Seine alongside the west pavilion, which had been built on infill, and houses were replaced by the rear facade of the college. Perhaps he modelled the arcade on some more of the engravings of Rome he had been looking at. His plan here involved building sixteen new houses with shops in the gallery to be rented out to add to college revenue and supplement Mazarin's bequest. In spite of the rectors of the Sorbonne objecting to the incorporation of an academy in the scheme according to Mazarin's testament, Le Vau provided for it further along the rue Mazarine, but in the end it was abandoned altogether.[37]

The interior of the college was made up of three courts, one between the chapel and the library, then a large quadrangle behind the teaching staff's accommodation with different proportions from the front court. The scholars' study bedrooms, the classrooms and dining area were to be on four floors surmounted by an attic with lucarnes, the vertical surfaces given depth by shallow projections known as *avant corps*. The triple full-centred arches that were Le Vau's trademark provide the entrance from the front court, deceptive because there is only a single *porte cochère* on the library/chapel side.

This rather bleak quadrangle is a far cry from Vaux-le-Vicomte, but its purpose was basic accommodation for sixty adolescents, and, as the rules for the day-to-day running of the college will show, they were not intended to live in luxury! Their daily austere programme is represented by this extract from the rules imposed by the college directors at the foundation:

At a quarter to nine, prayers.
   After prayers, each pupil shall go up to his room in silence, followed by the assistant master on duty who shall assure that the domestics are at their posts, and whether the rooms are open and the candles lit.
   At a quarter past nine the candles should be put out, the assistant master on duty should do his rounds at that time, and see that everything is locked up.
   Note: In this circumstance, it is a great inconvenience for the master and the children if a domestic has drunk too much.[38]

However, the Sorbonne faculty liked the spaciousness of the quadrangle with its 'good air'.[39] To the rear again of this was another court for kitchens and services, following the straight if diagonal line of the rue Mazarine alongside an equally well-proportioned garden.

On the left-hand side of the front court as you go in is the building that houses Mazarin's transplanted library, which Le Vau adapted to a rather smaller space than it had in the rue de Richelieu site. Mazarin had bequeathed all its elaborate woodwork to the college, and Le Vau provided a ceiling with *voussures* to cover the space, but this is no longer visible since in 1739 more bookshelves were necessary and a flat ceiling was provided. Gabriel Naudé, whom Claude Dulong speaks of as the patron saint of librarians, advised Le Vau on the arrangements, though he ignored his recommendation to build the library away from the busy quay.

Indoors, this impressively lit room is built in the shape of an L and occupies the left flank of the building as well as the quayside front. It was intended for the use of the members of the college and for the bona fide public on two days a week, an arrangement respected by the 1789 revolutionaries. For this latter purpose, Le Vau provided an entrance on the street side where would-be readers were to be vetted with discretion by a porter upon entry. It took until 1692 before this arrangement was up and running as planned. Christopher Wren used it as a model for his library at Trinity College, Cambridge.[40]

On his ground-floor plan of 13 August 1662,[41] since there was no specific use left in Mazarin's will to which the curved wings and the end pavilions could be assigned, Le Vau made his own specifications for them. The west pavilion would house four academies relating to the arts: architecture (though it did not come into being until 1671, the year after his death), mathematics, painting and sculpture, and for military engineering. There were four rooms for their members to meet in upstairs and a room for the general director. These ideas were circulating in Colbert's circle at the time and Le Vau was offering them a space in which to operate. The arts and related disciplines were missing from the list of academies that Colbert wanted to found – *belles lettres*, history, philosophy and mathematics – and Le Vau supplemented them with his own suggestions, with mathematics overlapping into both sets of proposals. His intention was not fulfilled, however, and college staff made use of the rooms.[42]

The downstairs arcades would house shops of a prestigious artistic nature as was done in the Grande Galerie of the Louvre. The twenty-seven shops in the arcades of the college buildings, in contrast to what was often done with shops alongside Parisian churches like Saint-Paul-Saint-Louis in the rue Saint-Antoine, were given all the nobility of orders and decorative mouldings by Le Vau that united them with the church itself. He explained what he intended in a memorandum of 1662:

> The buildings, with the library on one side and the four academies of the arts on the other produce the beauty of the square, provide a public embellishment and a beautiful view from the Louvre, while artisans and

merchants will bring convenience to the college and beauty to the place Mazarine because it will always be filled with masters of the arts.'[43]

It was luxury crafts he was talking about, the ones that Colbert was very concerned to rebuild. Craftsmen such as jewellers, clockmakers, cabinetmakers, tapestry weavers, bookbinders and booksellers who could afford higher rents would make up for the deficiencies in funding from Mazarin's bequest that were emerging. What Le Vau had fashioned for luxury at Vaux-le-Vicomte for Fouquet gave him the experience to apply opposite his south front of the Louvre. There are beautiful views in both directions.

When we come to the church the luxuriant theme continues. This was to be the Mazarin family mausoleum and only the best materials would do. As Alexandre Cojannot has shown, a memorandum in Le Vau's handwriting shows how interested he was in the importation of marble for his constructions here at the college, in the Louvre and at Versailles, all of which sites held his attention concurrently.[44] The marble he used came from Rance in Hainault, red diffused with grey, and he discusses the best means of transporting this heavy material to Paris, whether by sea, by roads, or by rivers and favouring the latter as less expensive, especially as the pieces included those the length of the columns he wanted to use. The man who would provide them was the *marbrier* Jean Le Grue who, even during the Fronde, had delivered the marbles for the chapel of the Sorbonne, ordered by Jacques Lemercier though they were not cut as altars until the 1680s. Le Grue continued to deliver them even though a state of war existed with Spain in whose provinces Hainault was found. But Mazarin had concluded the war in 1659, so that when these designs for his memorial chapel were being drawn up, easier conditions prevailed.

The provision of marble is not to be found in the general contract for masonry in the chapel of 13 August 1662, but in a subsequent document that has not survived, signed at the beginning of 1664. Le Vau made a note in a bill for work completed that was submitted on 17 February of that year: 'There is a contract with Le Gru for some marbles to be delivered for the columns and altars.' Contracts were also drawn up with river transport specialists François and Jean Fillette to bring the pieces, already prepared at the quarry, from Pontavert to Paris.[45]

Le Vau, in his autodidact fashion, depended heavily upon the inspiration he had gained from his reading of Palladio's *Four Books on Architecture*, which he possessed in an Italian version, not Fréart de Chambray's translation. He made frequent use of the colossal order from the days of building the Lambert mansion on the Île Saint-Louis onwards, and put large and small pilasters together on one facade just as Palladio had. His temple front for the chapel owes much to Palladio.[46]

As Hilary Ballon points out, a college of sixty students did not need a dome and there were only three churches in the capital that had domes over them: Saint-Paul, the Sorbonne and Val de Grâce. But a dome was necessary if the college were to hold its head up to the Louvre and to provide a monument appropriate for Jules Mazarin. This dome is remarkable for its being nearly circular in its exterior but oval inside, with its orientation corresponding to the main axis of the church. This was an innovation because the other churches' axes were at right angles to their structures. Le Vau developed the oval form for himself from Vaux into his mature work. Once it had been decided not to have Mazarin's tomb in the middle of the chapel, the building became, like the chapel of the Invalides hospital further down the river on the same bank, 'an extension of the crown's claim on Paris'.[47]

All the disputes and negotiations about land and buildings and the need to agree the college's constitution before it was up and running, besides all the changes made in the design between 1662, Le Vau's death, and the completion of the whole structure with its decorative features under his protégé François d'Orbay, involved huge delays. In 1674 d'Orbay worked on laying the pavements and on a drawing of the cardinal's mausoleum together with the altars. The sculptures were delayed for a long time: those of the large statues of the four evangelists and eight Latin and Greek fathers of the church by Martin Desjardins, Etienne Le Hongre and others were not in place on the facade of the chapel until 1677. D'Orbay finished the church itself and the scholars' lodgings by 1674. He built the shops under the arcades, and, in spite of Le Vau's intentions for them, they were in fact let to small-scale craftsmen, who did a good deal of damage to the fabric. There was a constant need for redecoration, repair and finding new tenants.[48]

The King had decided that the foundation would be called the Collège Mazarin, to perpetuate his first minister's name and the executors had made a contract with the society of the Sorbonne by which they would take over all the teaching. So it was that one of the doctors of the Sorbonne came to make an inspection of the buildings without prior notice in 1688, and what he found in them put him into such a state that he wrote a letter to Colbert about it in which he spoke of his 'shame'.

Taking advantage of the disputes and delays occurring after the buildings were complete, squatters had moved in on the basis of dubious rights or no rights at all. Moreover, certain members of the cardinal's family had allocated certain lodgings to themselves within the college, which had never been intended. But there were all sorts of forms of life that the doctor from the Sorbonne found there. Workmen of various trades had remained on the premises and were camping in the attics in the spaces under the roof beams, doing their cooking there and risking setting the whole place on fire. The doctor listed others whom he found lodging there. A gentleman called Lartille, a poor hack writer, had established himself with his valet in five bedrooms on the top floor on the rue Mazarine side. A water carrier and his wife had taken over a little room under the library staircase. M. Soullier, a priest from Gascony, occupied four bedrooms, an office and a gallery over one of the sundials and sub-let part of this apartment in an attic to two 'demoiselles', who claimed to be mother and daughter. M. Sanguin, described as a '*medecin chymique*', had obtained the keys of twelve rooms, where he lived with five members of his family and, for his own convenience, he claimed the right to a carriage entrance (*porte cochère*) which he kept locked to prevent the college becoming a public passage.

But the most serious case was that of M. Milleti. He came from Italy and occupied four bedrooms and a reception room where he harboured someone called Le Vigne, a tailor of women's dresses, with several boys as his cutters. The good Sorbonne doctor said that this meant that there was 'a great deal of coming and going by girls and women in the college, under the pretext of clothing themselves'. And this was to be the moment when the first pupils were to arrive to be instructed in 'the purity of religion, good conduct and manners and the rules of self- discipline!' Colbert chased all these people out, but not without difficulty.[49]

The problems were not over even when the sixty boarders on free places had been established and teaching had begun. Disputes continued right up to the time of the Revolution. The curé of Saint-André-des-Arts claimed that the college was in his parish, and so did the Abbot of Saint-Germain-des-Prés. They both claimed they had rights of way through the college and they both demanded payment, which the college refused them. This dispute dragged on for fifteen years until settled by decree in 1694.[50] Other colleges in the universities tried to drown the new one, jealous of its royal privileges and its apparent opulence. It was a lot less poor than it claimed because, although the revenues of the foundation were whittled away, the executors managed to find new ones. They took in day boys, some of whose parents paid fees, and this provoked acrimonious law suits with a good deal of sharp practice.

The court is a peaceful place now for the members of the Institut de France and the researchers in the library, but it was a school yard in its time and one day the young Jacques-Louis David received a stone full in his cheek that disfigured him for life. During the Terror, he was imprisoned in his old school for a while – the boys' rooms lent themselves very well as prison cells – and drew exquisite little portraits of fellow inmates such as Bernard de Saintes. The revolutionaries appreciated that the library had been open to use by the public twice a week, and kept it as such, adding books to it from other collections – notably royal ones – that they took over.

Perhaps one reason why no continuous narrative of Louis le Vau's life has been published before now is that providing his career with any kind of continuity, particularly in his later years is very (*vachement*, as they say) hard to bring about. There is so much going on. He was at work on the Louvre Palace, on the Versailles *enveloppe*, on this college. And he had taken on a project in a village in the Nivernais called Beaumont-la-Ferrière that involved him in a good deal of travelling time and much financial anxiety.

Chapter 9

A Metallurgical Disaster

The large canvas for this study has been the urbanisation of Paris and its intensification under Louis XIV. Yet there was another significant development at the same time: the proto-industrialisation in many parts of France, which was becoming as important to the economy as agriculture had always been. The man in charge of it, under the King's authority in 'the administrative monarchy',[1] was Jean-Baptiste Colbert.

Having emerged from the tutelage of Cardinal Mazarin, Colbert appeared after 1661 as the King's principal confidential agent and instituted a programme of national economic policy. This was effective in many spheres of creative activity, from tapestry at the Gobelins factory or rivalling Venice in manufacturing glass for mirrors, to those items necessary for the enlargement of the navy to protect mercantile and colonial expansion that the dockyard facilities at Rochefort, Nantes and Toulon came to represent. This meant the expansion of French metallurgy for the provision of armaments for that navy.

'Colbert's industrial strategy ... was inspired by a vision, by a sense of overall strategy. He therefore set on foot the collection of the first industrial statistics in 1664 ... The statistics which Colbert thus acquired were of high quality. In the localities, the effect was completed by the creation of a corps of industrial inspectors .... very much the personal brain-child of Louis XIV's appointed collaborator.'[2]

Colbert developed his system, which had had a period of gestation even before he became Controller-General of the Finances in 1665. Once Superintendent Fouquet had been overthrown as a result of his own determined efforts, he began to establish his system of nepotistic wheeling and dealing. As opposed to his defeated rival, he appreciated the difference between the realities of power and their appearances. He later had his own chateau at Sceaux, but it was achieved with discretion and did not challenge the King in any way. He put the experience he had acquired in the Mazarin years at the King's disposal, flattering the young sovereign, attributing to him capabilities he did not actually have, letting him think that all the initiatives were his own, when they were, in reality, from Colbert.

'The restoration of justice, of royal primacy, the reform of the finances (or what passed for such) were Colbert's achievements, but he transferred the credit for it to the King. All across his letters, it is remarkable that, from September 1661, he managed the finances, the economy, the navy, the colonies, the *beaux-arts*, and the reform of institutions! He managed it all … without any ministerial portfolio.'

He achieved his control over national economic policy by means of networking in the appointments held by his relations, as well as by his power over the navy, both military and commercial, in the ports and over the taxable salt resources of the Atlantic coastline.[3] A rising population needed employment. The revived navy and the new ports he was planning could, according to his calculations, create employment for two million people. Agriculture existed to provide a reasonably priced food supply, keeping the wage bill from increasing so as to allow manufacture to be carried on without excessive costs. Agriculture was to be relied upon to produce such items as would provide the raw materials for industry: hemp, linen, silk, wool, madder. Horses were always needed for the army. He argued this in spite of the fact that certain French provinces had suffered from scarcity: *disette* is one stage short of *famine*. His arguments were by no means conclusive, but he had the power to implement them in the new system being established once the King was independent of his regents.

The emphasis was to be on national self-sufficiency achieved primarily through manufacturing. This applied particularly to what could be provided by wood from the forests and from metallurgy, where the state was the principal owner of the land on which there were forests and in places where mining could be developed. Trees were needed for shipbuilding and metal for cannon and ammunition, lead for roof coverings at the Louvre and the pipes in the gardens of Versailles, marble for the chateau and the Trianon, and copper for the foundries at Toulouse. The emphasis was to be upon providing all these commodities from within the kingdom of France, not importing them from elsewhere. The economy was to be devoted to the grandeur of the monarch and of the state, and Colbert himself expressed this himself in terms of a *guerre d'argent*:

> It is the same quantity of money which circulates in the whole of Europe. In order to increase the 150 million livres that circulate in a population of 20, 30, 50 millions, funds have to be taken from neighbouring states, and this can only be produced by commerce.

Isn't that in itself a definition of mercantilism, the dominant economic ideology of the age?

After Colbert had succeeded in bringing about the arrest of Nicolas Fouquet on 5 September 1661, there had been no need to wait for his eventual condemnation and imprisonment in perpetuity to set financial changes in hand. After no more than ten days, the King established his Council of Finances to meet regularly on three days every week, and there would be no more superintendents. When Colbert's position became official in 1665 in relation to national finances, his title was to be that of Controller. Colbert fed the lines to the King. He let all concerned – and the King himself – believe that the new conditions of gathering and spending revenue, apparently free of corruption, were the King's own idea.

Colbert had made himself indispensable in the new order of things that has been labelled as absolute monarchy. The Council of Finances went hand in hand with the Council of Justice – the body that would eventually decide on Fouquet's guilt.[4] It may have given the appearance that things had been put into committee, but the committee was in essence advisory and the decision had to be the King's own after taking advice from its members. The same was true of the small *Conseil en haut* – the one that met upstairs at Versailles once government had been permanently established there.

* * *

For the purposes of this study of Le Vau as a manufacturer, we focus on one application of all this in a small area in the Nivernais province, centred on the lordship of Beaumont-la-Ferrière. The years of Colbert's ascendancy in the finances were contemporary with the years of Le Vau's most prominent achievements as the King's First Architect. Those in Colbert's circle, as Le Vau was, were bound to be involved in the implications of the new conditions.

The replacement of expensive lead as a roofing material by tinplated iron was a serious project for Le Vau. He tried his hand at manufacturing it in Normandy after he made the only journey of his life beyond the borders of the kingdom of France to Saxony in the early 1650s to examine techniques for beating and whitening iron. When he returned, he set up forges and furnaces in the forest of Conches in 1653 under the borrowed name of Antoine Champion, which was the actual name of the manager he put in overall charge of the undertaking. Le Vau had his preoccupations as Lemercier's associate in the King's buildings at the Louvre, and subsequently as the King's First Architect from 1654, and could not devote enough attention to the enterprise to make it successful.

However, on 16 February 1665, Louis XIV established the manufacture of tinplate by his edict, and the preamble to the edict – which is worth quoting – shows how closely Le Vau was associated with the royal project from the outset:

our dear and faithful secretary Le Vau, first architect of our buildings, informed ... our dear and well-beloved, *le sieur* Colbert ... [who was] making researches with much application into all those who have acquired a reputation for excellence and have some acquaintance or particular secret concerning manufactures, that from the year 1650 onwards, having informed himself about the techniques with which the Germans [i.e., Bohemians and Saxons] beat and whiten iron, and wanting to make experiments in this field, had to this end had forges and furnaces built where he set Antoine Champion to work for a period of three years near the forest of Conches in our province of Normandy, and that he had so much applied himself and became expert in these works that he had discovered the art of making a better, larger, and thicker [product] than those which they make in Germany, and which could serve for the joints and other places in roofing where it is ordinarily necessary to put lead. However, warfare having ruined this establishment, and the said Le Vau being otherwise completely committed by our orders to design and direction of the buildings in our Louvre and our other royal houses, this work had to be completely set aside ...[5]

This same edict of 1665 set up a royal factory for tinplate in the Nivernais at Beaumont-la-Ferrière: a richly wooded area good for supplying charcoal, and with watercourses to drive the machinery. The director was to be Antoine Champion, the borrowed name [*prête-nom*] for Le Vau himself.[6] Use of such names in the contemporary business world was not unusual and there does not seem to have been anything suspicious about it, though the practice did offer a certain legal protection. It would be easy to psychologise on Louis Le Vau's use of this name either as an expression of self-confidence or a cover for diffidence. That would be in order if it was an invented name, but Antoine Champion was a real industrialist who agreed to lend his name for the Nivernais enterprise in a declaration made on 6 March 1665.[7] He may have been related to the British Champion family of metallurgists active in zinc and brass smelting later in the century, and the whole process pre-dates what would be happening in England from 1708 onwards under the direction of Abraham Darby at Coalbrookdale in Shropshire.

Colbert had proposed to the King that Le Vau should direct the enterprise, encouraged by advantageous conditions: an important royal loan, the privilege of sole production for thirty years and the title of Royal Factory. By 1665, the national economy was back on its feet after the end of hostilities with Spain six years before, and Colbert was looking for ways to encourage the development of industrial projects by attracting the best specialists from at home and abroad. He chose the Nivernais for the first French manufacture of tinplate on the basis of a tour he made of the area in 1659–60 on Mazarin's account, during which he had recognised its potential, with its open-cast coal and iron ore mines,[8] its woods, watercourses and lakes. Furnaces and forges had already been established there for iron production in the fifteenth century, particularly at Beaumont.[9]

The region was not unknown to Louis Le Vau since his brother, François, had been working for *La Grande Mademoiselle*, Gaston d'Orléans's daughter, since 1652 in transforming her Château de Saint-Fargeau while she was exiled from court as punishment for her active part in the Fronde of the nobility.[10] François was also known to have been there at the time in his capacity as an inspector of bridges and highways. There was also an idea that Le Vau's family had roots in the Nivernais from previous generations. Nicole Bourdel, in an enthralling local newspaper article,[11] reports having found in the *Bibliothèque nationale* the genealogy of part of the family living there in the fifteenth century. A neighbouring village, Grénant, was the home of Nicolas Le Vau, held by local tradition to be Louis's grandfather.

Le Vau gathered the funds advanced by Colbert and repaired the manor house at Beaumont to live in whenever he was there. On 30 March 1665, Dame Françoise de la Chatre, separated wife of Henri de la Grange, chevalier, Marquis of Arquien, sold the lands of the *seigneurie* for 40,000 livres to Antoine Champion.[12] With the house, Le Vau also bought the lordship. The house was less than a mile away from the buildings to be used for the manufactures in the village on a stream and by the Vauvégny lake. The lake has dried up, but the watercourses are still visible. The workmen's cottages were grouped round about it.

The nineteenth-century schoolmaster in the village reproduced a watercolour of the house that Le Vau occupied in his monograph about the commune.[13] It has the appearance of being built between two medieval turrets with conical roofs, with the high *combles* of the living accommodation between them. The *corps de logis* has a ground floor, a first floor, and an attic with three windows, topped off with more space under the roof beams lit by diminutive apertures. Behind the house, on the side of the new chateau's garden, is a two-storeyed service building that is still there.

A visit to Beaumont by the author in September 2020 confirmed that there are indeed twin turrets with conical roofs inside the gates of the more recent chateau, and the house shown in Gauthier's illustration that, he tells us, was demolished in 1883, could have occupied the space between them. Some local opinion, however, calls in question what Gauthier claimed. There were three buildings designated as chateaux at Beaumont: this one with the turrets, another, known as *Les Sauvages*, a little way out of the village to the south-west (subsequently enlarged), which is surrounded with vestiges of earlier activity of an industrial nature, and another in the centre of the village that has been replaced by a bourgeois mansion. However, the two turrets remain at the entrance to the new chateau (the present property of Mr and Mrs Robert Whitaker), which replaced the one cited by Gauthier, and they are near the Vauvégny stream – a tributary of the Nievre – which supplied motive power for at least one of the furnaces set up by Le Vau. These features tend to maintain that he did, indeed, live there, a little way to the north of the village centre, as shown in the nineteenth-century Cassini map that Gauthier could have known and used.

* * *

Colbert had offered to bring in German ironmasters, but Le Vau refused on 5 November in one of his rare extant letters: 'Two forges have been up and running for three months and have worked well enough … there are three others ready to start working at the end of the year … we know the process of whitening iron as well as they do in Germany …' He announced to Colbert that he would also be setting up the manufacture of weapons, something that he had in mind since 1660, in the Beaumont area: muskets, cannon and projectiles for the navy, easily transportable on the Loire to Nantes and thence to the new military dockyard that Colbert was establishing at Rochefort at the mouth of the Charente.

On 12 March 1666, Louis XIV confirmed fairs and markets at Beaumont that dated back to Henri II's time 'to our friend and faithful councillor, secretary to our household, the crown of France and our finances, and first architect of our buildings, seigneur of Beaumont-la-Ferrière, in our country of Nivernais … desiring to gratify him and treat him favourably, in consideration of the services which he renders us daily and of which we have entire satisfaction …'. These letters patent were read out in the parish churches around Beaumont on 28 November. Le Vau made friendly approaches to other *seigneurs* in the vicinity, being godparent to the church bell on 19 September 1667 and paying for wall paintings that were still to be seen in 1797.[14]

His privileged position granted by the King was precise and detailed. Anyone who copied the factory's products would have his property confiscated. Any foreign workmen taken on would be accorded French nationality straight away, and there were tax benefits for working at Beaumont and in the villages around. Colbert nominated ten of Champion's (i.e. Le Vau's) workmen who would be taught the secrets of the manufacture of the tinplate, and they were licensed to work for themselves elsewhere. The King himself lent 60,000 livres to Le Vau to help with the start-up, half of it without interest and the other half regarded as a gift provided that, at the end of each subsequent year for three years, the required amount of finished metal should have been manufactured according to national requirements. The accounts of the *Bâtiments du Roi* for March and May 1665 mention a payment of another 60,000 livres to Antoine Champion, half of which was for buying building plots at Beaumont and half as an interest-free float for six years.

Le Vau set about building industrial plant around and about on his manor, where he took up residence during frequent visits, and this included a series of furnaces and forges in nearby villages and others rented from the prior of La Charité and the Duke of Nevers. It has to be remembered that Le Vau was working on the Versailles *enveloppe*, the Louvre frontages and Mazarin's college at the same time, and that the round journey to Nevers from Paris and back was 600 miles in seventeenth-century road conditions: dust in summer and deep mud in winter.

Iron ore had to be mined or bought from established miners in the area to be 'roasted' in blast furnaces using charcoal made from local timber. The furnaces would have been square stone structures with three or four hearths, which could have been big enough for casting cannon, situated by a fast-flowing stream where the water was harnessed by a wheel to drive the bellows to fan the fires. The lakes then in the area would be the source of these artificially constructed streams. Le Vau produced a head of water by means of a pond, the *etang de la Carrière*, 'which drew upon the same hydraulics as André Le Nôtre's gardens at Vaux and Versailles – a phenomenon that helped to develop technology on which the country's industrial infrastructure was based'.[15] Le Vau developed machines such as these in 1662 in company with the engineer Denis Joly to bring water from the Clagny Lake up the hill to the reservoir at Versailles that was later turned into the Grotto of Thetis.[16]

Then came the smelting process: ore heated to beyond the melting point and altered chemically by interacting with charcoal:

> Although the integrity of the cannon depended on the alloy, the chemistry of metal was then unknown [...] only an experienced smelter knew how to mix the alloys to achieve the proper density and purity that kept a cannon from exploding under pressure and determined the ballistics of a ball. [...] Le Vau created a substantial operation to judge by the list of assets in 1667; there were stockpiles of ore and charcoal furnaces and at least seven forges, a battery mill where tinplate was hammered, warehouses, carriages to transport materials and workers' housing dispersed in and around Beaumont.[17]

There was also a refinery and a slitting mill for cutting rods into bars and nails.

Colbert instructed the abbé de Grivel, the French ambassador to Frankfurt, to recruit German workers in tinplate who knew the secrets. But they were doing well where they were and could not be persuaded to take such a risk. When Colbert told Le Vau this, his reply was that they were already up and running at Beaumont without foreign help. All that was lacking was sufficient hammerers (*marteleurs*) to get the work done quicker than it could be without them. Nevertheless, as he told Colbert, he had already branched out into the manufacture of muskets and cannon using immigrant workers and he added in the same letter that he had made a contract with 'the best cannon founder in the kingdom' to supply the necessary materials and moulds.[18]

Soon there was trouble over the direction. Antoine Champion refused to continue at the helm in November 1666 and had to be replaced by Antoine Picquet for hands-on direction at a crucial time in setting up the enterprise, by letters patent of 10 November 1666.[19] Then too few labourers were found in 1667–68 and recruiters were sent to the German mines again. It was realised that transport costs were too high on account of the distance between the furnaces. Le Vau started borrowing capital, first within his own family and then from one of Colbert's relations, François Berthelot,[20] the commissioner-general for gunpowder. Besides that, the costs for manufacturing the tinplate, let alone the cannon, turned out to be much greater than foreseen. They amounted to 350,000 livres in advance, of which 140,000 livres were spent on buildings, 100,000 on materials and 100,000 livres on the start-up costs. That did not include wages, coal or equipment.[21] Le Vau and his brother, who was now inspector of the manufacture of cannon and muskets in the Nivernais, and his wife's brother, the abbé Laisné, had a prominent part in the management of the enterprise and the future looked precarious for them.[22]

In 1959, Guy Thuiller found and published a memorandum from the *Bibliothèque nationale*, undated but revelatory,[23] 'devilishly written and perhaps in Le Vau's own hand' in note form, which proposes a change of direction in the way the enterprise was to be run. 'It is a remarkable example of economic calculation in a very modern tone.' The company's problem was identified as lack of invested capital, so the document proposes that the necessities for production of tinplate should not be manufactured on site but bought in – bar iron, coal and other substances – to avoid errors in calculating prices in advance and the inflated charges that were being paid. The enterprise ought to be carried on through sub-contractors at fixed prices, 'otherwise, the costs of administration, caused by stockage and the hold-ups in production will devour all the profit'. This was the manner in which the forges of the French navy worked in the dockyards such as Toulon and Rochefort under Colbert's direction, so why should it be different at Beaumont?[24]

This memorandum smells of the midnight oil, something written by a sleepless, worried man. It goes on:

> There are three ways of helping to maintain this business: two by the company and one by a pure and simple loan taking interest from the traders with the sureties of a special mortgage on the land, forges, forests, equipment, merchandise, property and so on …
>
> The first way, of the company taking over all the expenses and charges, would be to my mind very difficult. These expenses, these buildings, and false costs would be suspect to anyone who is conscientious and, as the order of payments has not been observed in the proper forms, it would be almost impossible to raise these great expenses […].
>
> For the second way it would be very easy and advantageous for those who choose to take part in this business, to make advances upon it, *which will have to be considerable.*[25]
>
> Firstly, we have to separate out what we are manufacturing and look at it in two ways: one way is to make ordinary beaten iron ready in bars, which is work entirely detached from the manufacture of tinplate and which demands greater and more difficult labour. A distance of between twenty-one and twenty-four miles, according to how far the furnaces and forges are set apart from one another, and the great accumulation of mines, coal, workmen, equipment, carts and utensils which are needed for this work being at present the cause of the greater part of all the charges and great expenses which have been paid up to the present, to the extent that, without entering into discussion of these great expenses and false charges, nor of the paraphernalia of all the forges and furnaces, we will make the bar iron necessary for ordinary sale.
>
> Tin is bought from the traders at ordinary prices.
>
> The forgemen's and whiteners' work is paid for by the barrel and the price for the coal is set in the market (literally: 'under the awning').
>
> There will be the hiring, repair and maintenance of the hammering shop, furnaces and whitening shops with the shops and lodgings for the workmen to enable them to work efficiently […].
>
> No need to count all the expenses met in the past in acquisition as much as in buildings and provisions made and still to make. The company shall exist only to manufacture tinplate … the iron for which shall be provided in the same way as it is for manufacture of cannon and muskets for which a company had been formed with M. Bertholet. The money

which will be advanced shall carry interest according to the ordinance right up to the time of the actual repayment and profit shall be made on the sale of merchandise in proposition to the amount admitted and shall be solely the expenses from the sum of 30,000 livres repaid in proportion to the expense.

Clerks and controllers shall be taken on to keep general registers and to produce accounts upon demand.

What happened is difficult to assess. In June 1668 the cannon manufacturing part of the business passed into the hands, not of Bertholet, but of a Swedish engineer called Abraham de Bresch, who arrived from Wallonia and had been made responsible by Colbert for the inspection of mines and forges in the Nivernais and the Languedoc, which held the monopoly of cannon manufacture throughout the kingdom. To keep up his position he had been granted land worth 40,000 livres by the King.[26] Le Vau and Berthelot were to receive 12,000 livres each from the *Batiments du Roi* fund in compensation for loss of business to de Bresch, so now they had no more than the tinplate business to preoccupy them at Beaumont.

Just when the stream might have started to flow clear again, Dalliez de la Tour turned up to muddy the waters; someone else with 'a grand appetite for profit'. He was the Receiver-General of Finances in the Dauphiné, a speculator on a grand scale, who had, in spite of de Bresch's monopoly, two cannon factories, one in Dauphiné at Vienne and the other in Burgundy at Perrecy. He wanted to set up a tinplate factory in Dauphiné (probably after hearing what Le Vau was up to at Beaumont) but Colbert blocked his application. Dalliez, in a 'smarmy' (*pateline*) response on 11 August 1665, said that he only wanted to be useful to M. Le Vau who held the monopoly and to make his own contribution to the development of a product advantageous to the kingdom and from which it was no more than just that he should make something on account of being the first to have had the idea.[27]

Five days later, he tried unsuccessfully again. But then we find him associated with de Bresch at the cannon foundry and then, all of a sudden, ordered by Colbert to inspect Le Vau's undertakings at Beaumont with a possible view towards reorganisation of them. He had it in mind to regroup the cannon foundries of Beaumont and Burgundy under the same directors.[28]

Colbert visited the Nivernais in April 1669 – just after he become head of the navy department – and brusquely arranged that Dalliez and Le Vau should work together. Then Dalliez went to nearby Cosne-sur-Loire, where Le Vau still had a workshop for making muskets, and reported to Colbert that conditions for production were ideal, but the potential had not been developed sufficiently: there was nothing more there than an accumulation of workmen gathered at hazard and without any clearly conceived intention. Dalliez proposed the manufacture of muskets for use in the navy, and imposing discipline upon the workers at Cosne with the help of better trained artisans brought from Saint-Étienne.

He also reported that de Bresch had succeeded in making steel at Beaumont as good as any being currently made in Germany. It could be used for cannon, for cutlasses and all sorts of weapons with blades. He also reported to Colbert that the root cause of Le Vau's failure to get the enterprise off the ground was his difficulties with his German tradesmen. Dalliez suggested paying them for piecework rather than a daily wage.

Le Vau had agreed after all to a few ironmasters being brought in from Germany to improve production of tinplate, but they had died at Beaumont from bad water and malaria, so the apprentices were not being trained and were disorderly and, without supervision, left to do whatever they liked. The journeymen only worked when it suited them, and they were wasting the coal and iron. They had produced no barrels of tinplate worth more than 300 livres, and even that was badly made.

Dalliez went on to say that he and Le Vau had chosen new masters from out of the better workmen and claimed to have set up two hammering plants with the more reasonable German workers on the same contractual basis as the masters who had died, employed on the same terms as they would have had at home. But they had not co-operated and made insolent replies to the offers that were made. Their demands were ridiculous. All they wanted to do was return home, and the last ones to arrive at Beaumont had done nothing but incite the others to discontentment. It is worth quoting Dalliez's report directly:

> Since a gentler approach, Monseigneur, far from bringing them to order, has seemed up to now to authorise more insolence from them, we have decided, Monsieur Le Vau and I, to commit two of the most mutinous ones to prison as an example to make the others wiser. But, Monseigneur, it is important to bring from Germany only good ironmasters. We have only too many companion-workers and, having only just brought them here, it is hoped that we shall be able to draw up contracts with them which they will undertake to carry out here, for this sort of work can only be done for a price, and to pay to keep them only on a daily rate is to ask for failure and to fall back into the ruinous confusions of the past.
>
> There is one hammering plant run by Frenchmen about which I am happy enough: their sheets of tinplate are perfect but the waste of material is too great. It is to be hoped that experience will give them more

skill. They could perhaps accomplish that if they were on better contracts. [...] Every day, two cannon are poured, but, if there were two forges here like the ones we have in Burgundy, things would advance more quickly. But, at last, there are a hundred and fifty of them ready to be dispatched. We pray you that an agent will come and take them, because we fear that the water levels on the river [Loire] will soon be too low to have them taken to Nantes. We will send a hundred barrels of tinplate and iron bars as well. M. Le Vau, for his own part, is getting carts ready with 300,000 round and square shot for the Navy and 100,000 bullets.[29]

Dalliez put things in order for the company. 'Our Germans,' he said, 'have at last decided to work at prices set by the barrel.' He now had some reliable foremen whom he names – almost all of them young men with whom he holds consultations about the work to be done.

He says that M. Le Vau had M. l'abbé Laisné, his brother-in-law, to help him and that he had the intelligence and capacity for action to manage this type of transactions. Dalliez went back to Vienne at the end of April, leaving behind a deputy called Legoux, with whom he kept in close touch by letter. One missing piece of information in all this is how much time Le Vau actually spent in the *seigneurie* that he bought for himself, bearing in mind all his other commitments 300 miles away. On Colbert's orders, de Bresch, Dalliez and Le Vau shared responsibility for the direction of the *Compagnie de Nivernais*, which had been re-established.

Colbert had the German ironmaster Heinrich Geissel's letter of 17 May 1669 translated into French and sent on to Dalliez.[30] It contained the complaints he had received from him as one of those who had been brought to Beaumont to work: that the workmen believed that they had been exiled to Beaumont, finding no consolation in the place, and French workers had been forced to go there too. Beaumont was situated in the midst of woods and marshland and was unhealthy as a place to live and work.

Le Vau held a letter of credit from 'M. Paul the *blanchisseur*', the only one able to interpret between him and the Germans, and he provoked the painful wrangles of which Geissel complained. However, with regard to bad treatment, on the contrary, Geissel said they were left to their own devices far too much and were over-indulged. Some 40,000 *écus* unaccounted for represented the amounts that they had been paid. Geissel claimed that the Germans 'were loud in their manners and always complained with no justification'. He had seen this for himself in those whose job it was to cast ships' anchors, who perpetrated new misdemeanours every day. On the other hand, he agreed with them when they said that it was not possible to make tinplate at the same marketable prices in Beaumont as it had been in Saxony. The iron was sharp and harder to beat and you had to heat it up more often, so you used a lot more coal. The tin was much dearer when it came from local sources. Above all, the hammering plants had to cease working too often on account of there not being enough water in the streams. That meant a lot of idle time for a large part of the year and was the main reason for not being able to produce manufactures at the prices set.

There had also been unsurmountable technical difficulties. Mineral acids were not available at that time. The sheet iron, once made, had to remain for several days in pickling baths and was then plunged into a receptacle containing the melted tin, the surface of which had to be coated with black tallow to avoid oxidation or the iron sticking out of the tin. The tin itself had to be imported, either from Cornwall or from Saxony. Furthermore, the staffing of the various plants was made worse when the Elector of Saxony adopted the protectionist measure of forbidding qualified workmen to leave his territory. The result was that the price of tinplate from Beaumont was three times the price of any from elsewhere, and its quality was not viable because the variety of iron used was too hard to be malleable.[31]

At the same time as Dalliez was making his inspection at Beaumont, Le Vau had been occupied in Versailles on his *enveloppe* for the old chateau. He came back to Beaumont in August 1699, and, in September, the navy commissioner Menessier came to inspect the workshops and carry out tests on the cannon.[32] Le Vau complained to Colbert about the powers that Dalliez had taken to himself while he was at Beaumont, but he got short change from the minister. Even if they did not like each other, they had been working together for many years by now and there was a certain professional give and take between them. This is what he said – 'with some brutality'[33] – in reply to Le Vau:

> I am not writing to you intending to cause you mortification, but only to make you more aware of your obligation to make a success of the manufacture of tinplate. I was not obliged to give you associates, but you asked me to and, so as to help you, I gave you the help of someone who put up with all the loss with the result that all the changes which you complain about only came about to provide you with the assistance which, as I say, I was not obliged to offer you. I also gave you a very advantageous loan for your iron so that it would turn out that you would have the money which the king gave you to buy the land at Beaumont and set up your establishment, that you would receive great help from your associates and a reasonable price for your iron and that, in the end, His Majesty would have his tinplate. You see well that it was not possible.

That is why you have to apply yourself carefully to put this establishment on a proper basis and see that it produces the results according to the assurance that you gave about it by the contract you made with the King.

This cold douche was administered in October 1699.

Louis Le Vau seems to have made his last visit to Beaumont in April 1670. Then he went to his *manoir* at Brévannes near Corbeil. It was an extensive property with a large park and woodland, but no workshops nor the noise of metal being hammered by machines. Neither did it have mosquito-infested ponds. He had gone there often down the years to work in peace and have time with his family.

Then, back in his official apartment in the Hôtel de Longueville, between the construction site of the Louvre Colonnade and the church of Saint-Germain l'Auxerrois, he took to his bed at the beginning of the summer and died, worn out, at the age of fifty-seven, on 11 October 1670, perhaps a victim of the paludism from the lakes and marshes at Beaumont that had carried off the German ironmasters, as much as of the continuous journeying to and fro. He left his heirs burdened with debts and prosecutions.

A document entitled 'Deed for the creditors of Le Vau against the sieur Dalliez and others' relates what we already know, that:

> Le Vau had obtained privilege for the manufacture of tinplate from the king in 1665, and subsequently for that of cannon, ammunition and forged iron for the Navy and had established these manufactures in the province of the Nivernais, and in order to bring them to perfection had used up all his resources, those of his family and of his creditors to the sum of 500,000 livres. After all this excessive expenditure and the work of six whole years, as he was on the point of gathering the fruit of such outgoings and labour, he died … and had left more than 600,000 livres worth of property in the said province.[34]

As a speculator, Le Vau had used capital from one building account to make up for the deficiencies in another that should have been temporary. He naturally intended to refund the first account when the other was beginning to succeed, but the expectation became a precarious gamble for a man getting on for sixty who had over-committed himself both materially and mentally.

* * *

Louis Le Vau's creditors met together on the day after he died and continued to meet for the next fourteen years. The register of their discussions has entries up until 1684.[35] Le Vau's inheritance would not be liquidated until even later in the next century. The affair of the tinplate works was all mixed up in the affairs of Mazarin's college.

The apartment in the Hôtel de Longueville, his tied accommodation, looked as though it was a rich man's home, but there was no money. The inventory of his belongings says it all:

> Mesdames Guichard and Mignon (his married daughters) declared that, while their father was ill, when they represented to him that he owed them several sums in deniers for the continual expenses which they had to settle, and because they had no money to lend him, and even that there was no money in the house, as their father and his agent Blondet had both told them, he spoke to them in these terms: My daughters, take my silver tableware and sell it. I wish there were more, but you will know that I have disposed of the greater part of it.

He had been living on credit for three years by then, and there was a formidable list of Parisian artisans or shopkeepers who wanted paying: a saddler, an upholsterer, a horse feed merchant, butchers, roast meat sellers, a locksmith. Some of them could be sent away because they had no credible papers. Most of them were his associates in the *Bâtiments du Roi*, but the ultimate sadness was that his family could not settle the bills of M. Belestre, *médecin ordinaire du roi*, Jean de Tanquerey, surgeon, and Denis de Vougues, who arranged his funeral in Saint-Germain-l'Auxerrois. They could not afford a tomb in the church, and his body seems to have gone to the charnel house.[36] It was not taken to the church on the Île Saint-Louis, which is not all that far away from where he breathed his last in the rue de Pouillis.

Jeanne Laisné, Louis's widow, renounced her debt-burdened inheritance from him on 11 January 1671 before the notary Lebeuf. The two married daughters did the same five days later. His brother-in-law, the Abbé Henri Laisné, described in the inventory as councillor and chaplain to the King, tried to gain possession of the tinplate works, but all that happened was that he drew attention to himself from the other creditors in these shark-filled waters. The family was divided: Jeanne and her unmarried daughter Hélène on one side and her married daughters, her brother-in-law François Le Vau, her sons-in-law Guichard and Mignon, her sister-in-law, and Thoison's son-in-law, whose name was Breteuil, on the other.

The only course of action left to Le Vau's widow after over two years of conflict with the creditors was to write to Colbert, which she did in January 1673 in the most self-humiliating terms to ask for his protection against them.[37] The outcome of her letter seems not to be known, but what is certain is that the problems resultant upon the financing of the tinplate manufacture became inextricably mixed with those of completing the College of the Four Nations. The problems are recounted in a document in the *Archives nationales* dated 1689.[38] It is in the form of a deed drawn up for the college against Le Vau's creditors.

In 1662 two estimates had been submitted, one for the construction of the college, church and library by Le Vau and his assistant Lambert, and the other for building sixteen houses that would belong to the college by the late M. Thoison, Le Vau's brother-in-law, also an architect, with whom he had shared projects since their days on the Île Saint-Louis. The figure placed on the second estimate was 100,000 *écus*, for the financing of which Thoison committed himself to find the money to pay rent to the college in his own name at the rate of 15,000 a year, whether the houses had been built or not and whether they had been rented out and occupied or not, for four years, 1665 to 1668. Thoison could then recover his expenses by letting the houses himself.

Thoison worked with Lambert on the college and Lambert with Thoison on the sixteen houses. Mazarin's executors appointed Simon Mariage as treasurer and entrusted 2,000,000 livres to him to pay what was to be spent on the buildings. They appointed Le Vau as director (*ordonnateur*) and Autray (d'Orbay?) as controller. By means of the power of attorney that had been given to Mariage, it was his responsibility to pay the builders on Le Vau's instructions. But he had no orders to pay to Le Vau himself anything other than his fees as appointed architect.

When Le Vau began his involvement with the Nivernais tinplate project, he decided to use money from the college on his other enterprise. Concealing his plans, he surprised Mariage by asking for several sums that amounted to 100,000 livres, claiming that this money was to pay the builders and their labourers at the college. He gave receipts to Mariage as treasurer and undertook to provide receipts himself to the building firms. Besides receipted sums that amounted to 97,350 livres, he helped himself to 6,250 livres on 14 April 1666 under the same pretext, but he handed none of it over to the builders. On the same day, he put himself under an obligation to Mariage by which he undertook to hand over the receipts to him or to pay back the 100,000 livres. On 26 May, his wife, Jeanne Laisné, pledged herself in solidarity with him.

Once Louis Le Vau had died, having handed over neither receipts nor money, Mariage produced a bill dated July 1668 that needed to be paid. Given the apparent prosperity in which the Le Vau couple had lived, he did not think it would be difficult to obtain payment and he made his requests to those whom he thought would be in charge of the inventory of the college building site. Le Vau had settled other sums while he was still alive, so Mariage did not expect any problems.

As for the sixteen houses within the college perimeter, Thoison had done no more than to lend his name for their construction to Le Vau, who was the real builder – as had been the case with Antoine Champion at Beaumont – and he had given Thoison 8,000 livres to tide him over. This gave further confidence to Mariage that all would be well. In 1668, when Thoison died, Le Vau had a deed drawn up replacing him in his responsibilities with Lambert. All Mariage thought he had to do was to look up the registers that had been kept by Le Vau's agent, Blondet. But it seemed that these registers had been destroyed by Le Vau himself.[39] Grave accusations were made against François d'Orbay, who had taken over the college project from his late master. Discreet but obvious reference was made to him in the minutes of the college governors up until 1680.

'Le Vau was a gambler, but, like all gamblers, in good faith,' observed Nicole Bourdel.[40] He gambled on using the college money to serve his other project and then pay it all back when Beaumont-la-Ferrière had turned a profit. He lost his bet.

* * *

That all took place in the capital, scene of his achievements, but in the Nivernais, where he had had little success, Dalliez and Paul Legoux soon made their moves to take over the whole enterprise at Beaumont on the authority of a royal council decree administered by the Intendant of the province, Tubeuf. To try to keep some of the Le Vau property from liquidation, the Abbé Laisné joined them there. A lawyer with a dubious reputation, Sallonyer de Nion, was made executor of the inventory to be drawn up.

The minutes of the inquest for the inventory have not survived,[41] but claims were made for the inventory being 'inexact' and for documents concerning the house at Beaumont being suppressed. False and antedated accounts were devised by means of which 200,000 livres worth of bullets, cannon, and finished iron still at the forges and furnaces or in the shops at Cosne and La Charité were bought and paid for as if Le Vau were still alive.

The records of various inventories also seem suspect. The procurator of Nevers, one named Brulant, never left home but signed the documents as if he had taken part in the proceedings at Beaumont. For some of the sites there was no inventory drawn up at all. Dalliez's agent was responsible for having many false statements certified without any basis of fact. Le Vau's children and nephews took action to reclaim 178,000 livres as late as 23 November 1673. Dalliez and twenty-one others were taken to court after another two years, when they were charged with fraud.

Dalliez's accusers were directed by one Vitari, often under a borrowed name, which was usual (and legal) practice as we have seen, with the support of influential office holders in the province. Naturally, Dalliez contested the charges in and out of court and the wrangling on his part went on until 1689 when he handed over the Beaumont enterprises to Leclerc of Grandmaison, who held the office of Extraordinary Treasurer of War. He put an architect of the royal buildings, Grandguillaume, in charge of production – or was this another case of an assumed name? More disputes followed, and by 1692 the enterprise was in an even more parlous state, although Grandmaison renewed his exclusive rights over it for another twenty years. Le Vau's heirs had not given up, however, and the affair could not be called concluded while certain amounts of tinplate still trickled out of Beaumont into the market. The undertaking was wound up in 1724.[42] Joints for roof coverings were still being made from lead.

* * *

Jeanne Laisné, as we have seen, wrote to Colbert and, so as to avoid being liable for the enormous debts her husband was found to have left, had to renounce the community property deed she had signed with him when they married in 1647. She and her single daughter had to leave the Hôtel de Longueville where they had lived in comfort for nearly ten years since it went with her husband's work on the Louvre across the road. They had to cope with the results of Louis Le Vau's 'lifelong tendency to do business on credit and delay repayment'. Some claims on his estate went back to his time on the Île Saint-Louis.[43]

Four out of the many creditors were appointed trustees to draw up a bankruptcy agreement, collect Le Vau's property and sell it for as much as they could get for the estate and then establish a scheme for payment to all the creditors. These men decided that the biggest asset was to be found at Beaumont and began proceedings against Dalliez de La Tour and his manager, Paul Legoux, who had assumed control there, accusing them of asset stripping and preparing false inventories in the house and the workshops while destroying and altering accounts. The Abbé Laisné was implicated in these charges since it was claimed that he had accepted a large bribe to keep quiet about what

Dalliez and Legoux had been up to. Dalliez treated the charges lightly and said that Laisné had done his best to preserve his relations' interests.

Claims went back and forth with the truth always disappearing in what emerged as disclosures. The works at Beaumont did not belong entirely to Le Vau. Colbert had arranged for investors like Dalliez to have a large stake in the proceedings so as not to have to falsify anything. If he had paid money to Laisné, it could have been what he owed him anyway and actions in the Nivernais courts were beginning to resemble the case of Jarndyce vs Jarndyce.

Colbert had ordered Dalliez to keep the company running and thereby approving what he did. Nevertheless, the court handed down verdicts in 1674 and 1675 against Dalliez and Legoux. Legal actions dragged on another dozen years until 1687. Dalliez repaid 30,000 livres to the crown, the amount of the original tax-free loan that he had received in 1665. Nothing was paid to Le Vau's family.[44]

Meanwhile, in the Paris tribunals, the trustees of Le Vau's estate were in conflict with the directors of the College of the Four Nations, and an agreement reached in September 1674 attributed a debt of 100,000 livres to Simon Mariage and then took him to court with the charge that he had conspired with Le Vau to divert funds. Mariage possessed no more than 30,000 livres, which he had to pay in retribution, but, when he died in 1691, what remained of his property was seized by the college together with a further 17,000 livres from the Le Vau estate.

Hilary Ballon's investigations showed that vindictiveness on the part of the college directors was approved by Colbert, who wanted to exact revenge for Le Vau's failure at Beaumont. He certainly risked destroying his reputation as an architect with the charges of embezzlement in his other role of a speculator who would have liked to have been a financier.[45]

Chapter 10

In the Shadow of his Successors

Mud was slung at Louis Le Vau's posthumous reputation for embezzling the funds from Mazarin's college to repay the sums that he lost at his metallurgical establishments in the Nivernais while hoping to live long enough to restore them to where they belonged whenever it might be possible. D'Orbay loyally protected Le Vau's reputation as an innovative architect by bringing his work at Mazarin's college to completion, and supplementing his master's achievements at Versailles with his own provision of the Ambassadors' Staircase as a vehicle for Charles Le Brun's intended decorations. Yet, as time went on, there could be no avoidance of the fact that Le Vau had died in a state of financial disgrace.

Nevertheless, a building of outstanding beauty was to be seen across the Seine from the entrance to the *Cour Carrée* of the Louvre: the dome and elevation of the College of the Four Nations on the left bank, and it was undeniably Le Vau's creation. It had become significant to remember Le Vau as the embezzler of part of the cardinal's fortune, and disassociate that memory from the carefully constructed dome and cupola, complete, at the time, with its statues of the apostles. The ingenious arrangement of the constraints of the awkward site might count for little when the arranger was recognised as a failed risk-taker. It was unlikely that many in the brutal culture of that epoch would have pity on him, on his reputation as an architect, or on his widow and daughters in their impecunious state.

Others in the not-so-distant past, like Dietrich Feldmann, have tried to write Le Vau's biography. Feldmann told a meeting of the Research and Study Centre on Paris and the Île de France in 1983 that he was trying to write such a monograph 'for completion in four or five years'.[1] But he was subsequently able to do no more than add to the wealth of detailed information about the architect – providing no sustained narrative.

Hilary Ballon's books and articles display an intention towards compiling a narrative account of Le Vau's life, but her early death prohibited its accomplishment. Alexandre Cojannot and Alexandre Gady have laboured, both together and alone, to produce encyclopedic work out of the documents that refer to Le Vau in the National Archives and in collections of ground plans and elevations. M. Cojannot's second volume on Le Vau subsequent upon his appointment as First Architect in 1654 remains eagerly awaited. The compilation and publication of precise scientific texts about Le Vau in the tradition of the *École des chartes* does not cease. What few extant papers there are, written in his own perfectly legible, even elegant, handwriting, are all to do with his working life, such as those that concern the obtaining of marble or the production of tinplate, edited by Alexandre Cojannot.

If ever he did allow himself any spare time – and he does seem to emit the wavelengths of the workaholic – there is no apparent evidence of how he used it, nor do there seem to be the essentials for a biography in the form of family letters, or notes left on the hall table to or from Jeanne, his wife, or any of his children. Nicole Bourdel unearthed some valuable nuggets of information in 1956,[2] but there is, apparently, nothing much of a personal nature, or, if there ever was, perhaps it was lost in house removal or deliberately destroyed in the wake of his posthumous financial disgrace. I longed to find a note that says something like, 'Dear Jacques, Do you fancy a weekend's fishing somewhere?' But there can be little hope of doing so.

He had his country estate at Brévannes, and it is known that he went to spend time there *en famille*, particularly during the distressing final months of the experiments in the Nivernais. But it is not said how he occupied his leisure. His books are a collection aimed predominantly at facilitating his preoccupations as an architect. There is nothing of Nicolas Fouquet at Saint-Mandé about him. Who were they whom he regarded as his personal friends? How did he get on with Charles Le Brun or André Le Nôtre when they were not at work at their various corporate projects?

There is a rare anecdote about his relations with the latter that shows that all was not always peaceful co-operation between these two adepts of their professions. They were both working at the palace at Saint-Germain-en-Laye after a dividing wall on the path alongside the main building had crumbled, and the decision had to be made whether to replace it or not. Le Nôtre saw the view of Paris over the Seine valley and was passionate about not obscuring it again. Le Vau was equally passionate about rebuilding the wall. The usually phlegmatic garden designer flew into a rage and appealed to Colbert, who eventually judged in his favour after at first supporting Le Vau's intention to rebuild.[3]

No extant authentic portrait of him exists. In his 1960 biography of François D'Orbay, Albert Laprade claimed that the portrait he had reproduced, previously catalogued as a portrait of an unknown architect, 1662,[4] was of Louis Le Vau because the plan unrolled under the sitter's arm represents the south-west corner of the Square Yard of the Louvre – the Queen Mother's apartment that he rearranged in 1661 – while behind the figure is presented the new gallery for paintings, burned down on 1 February 1661 and rebuilt by Le Vau soon afterwards.[5] However, in 1998 Thierry Bajou identified this same portrait as the *Surintendant des Bâtiments du Roi* Antoine Ratabon by Pierre Rabon (1619–84), which had been in the Gallery of the Academy of Arts, then put in the Louvre in 1798, and subsequently sent to Versailles. It was the masterpiece on the basis of which Rabon was received into the Academy of Arts on 3 July 1660.

So Louis Le Vau is effectively excluded from the visual record of contemporary architects represented in engraved or painted portraits or sculpted busts – François Mansart, Jacques Lemercier, Jules Hardouin-Mansart and, even, Le Vau's pupil and assistant, François d'Orbay. Was there ever a commemorative portrait of him, or, if there was, did his financial disgrace cause its disappearance? Colbert intended that the credit for the design of the completed Louvre and the *enveloppe* of Versailles should be given only to the King. The portraits of Le Brun and Perrault suggest that they are seen only because they are reflected in the glorious rays of the Sun King. Perhaps Kenneth Clark, standing before the Louvre Colonnade in his series on BBC Television in 1969,[6] was right to say, in what appears as a throw-away line, that Louis XIV's buildings were 'the work of civil servants'. There are many portraits of the chief of those *fonctionnaires*, Jean-Baptiste Colbert, at various stages in his lengthy career. The lack of a Le Vau likeness remains remarkable.

Essentially, the national architectural achievements of Louis Le Vau were overshadowed by the King since they were primarily the results of his initiatives. We have seen Colbert trying to elbow the First Architect to one side by competitions to provide designs to replace what he had already proposed for the completion of the Louvre – not presenting him to Bernini during the latter's visit to Paris from Rome in 1665, although they were sometimes in the same room – or for the enlargement of Versailles. It was not a question of personal animosity towards Le Vau on Colbert's part – although there was an element of it – so much as dislike of there being a First Architect existing in the same person for his remaining lifetime after appointment by the King. Colbert, as Superintendent of the King's Buildings, would have preferred to be able to choose an architect with skills appropriate for each project as it was taken in charge and not to be bound to appoint the same one for each and every royal project. As he showed on at least two occasions by arranging competitions for projects between several invited professionals – at the Louvre and for the Versailles *enveloppe* – he resented not having a free choice in such appointments. Once the King's choice of design had been accepted, however,

Colbert got on with the job, reserving his right to criticise and amend Le Vau's designs, but realising that he had no freedom to choose the designer.

André Félibien interpreted the new chateau at Versailles as the King's creation in his description of the *enveloppe*, and he makes no mention of Le Vau in all 121 pages of it.[7] In Henri Sauval's descriptions of Parisian palaces and mansions, Le Vau has his mentions, but even in the case of the Hôtel Lambert, he is vouchsafed a minimal few lines.[8] We could look for malign remarks in Colbert's letters after 1670, but we do not really need to find any. It would soon have got round in polite and cruel high society that it was Le Vau who had misappropriated funds from Mazarin's college to gamble on being able to provide capital for the tinplate project in the Nivernais or the military hardware that Colbert wanted from him, intending to pay the money back after success, except that there was no success and Le Vau died before there could be any. People would connect his admirable public and private buildings with the unfortunate speculator, and the good that he had done was buried with his bones in an unmarked grave.

Such a burial was a humiliation for the King's First Architect, who had left his family to endure impecuniousness after they had salvaged what they could from the sale of his assets and the repayment of his debts. His wife and remaining unmarried daughter had to move out of the comfortable tied apartment in the Hôtel de Longueville and eventually throw themselves upon Colbert's hoped-for charity.

* * *

How can we explain the disaster that had overtaken Le Vau as the result of his involvement with the metallurgical industry on Colbert's initiative? There is something in the psychological make-up of this ambitious man, as Hilary Ballon suggested, that may provide an appropriate indication:

> In seventeenth-century France the financial boundaries between the state and private financiers were rather blurred. Le Vau learned the methods of the financiers, and his personal finances exhibit an analogous erosion between one investment and the next, one pocket and the other. His carelessness was symptomatic of his milieu, but in the end, Le Vau was probably not so much a dishonest man as a compulsive risk-taker.[9]

Distinctive characteristics of this world of financiers in France had become recognisable by the time that Colbert emerged as the controller of pretty well everything under Louis XIV. Le Vau was well known as a provider of living accommodation – whether town house or chateau in the country – for the financiers who had established themselves at the head of bourgeois society. It comes as no surprise to find so many among those who figure in the account of Louis Le Vau's career listed in the ranks of contemporary financiers,[10] nor when it is realised that their manner of doing business had rubbed off on him.

What were the rules of their game? They have been identified as 'secrecy, association and the loan'.[11] The financiers had to exercise discretion in their dealings with each other and with the world at large, and that involved use of borrowed names, as we have already seen Le Vau doing. The names belonged to men of inferior social status to the financiers because searching for more financial resources than they already held was a characteristic of the upper bourgeoisie who had been successful in trade or industry or both. A self-made bourgeois like Le Vau would not have been content with reaching a halfway house in terms of discreet wealth. He, as much as his clients, the Lamberts, the Bordiers and so on, needed to have had his house on the Île Saint-Louis and his little chateau with its park at Brévannes, to say nothing of the *seigneurie* at Beaumont-la-Ferrière. In accepting the risks of his ascent from the building sites to the upper ranks of royal service, he fell victim to his final throw. Secrecy involves pretence – and between pretence and what is not true there falls a thin lace curtain.

Dissimulation had become institutionalised in the seventeenth century among the financiers. Gone were the days when markets were held in churchyards because now nobody felt comfortable being economical with the truth in the presence of his ancestors. Every one of the transactions would involve secrecy, whether it was the acquisition of land for building, the houses that were built, governmental positions that were bought or sold, or the farming out of tax collection. There was discretion about it, but everything was for sale to those who had the money. Nothing was done directly, but such a general practice invited mistrust. Those who signed the deeds for properties were not usually the true owners. Did Dame Françoise de la Chatre really think that Antoine Champion had resources in his own name of 40,000 livres to buy her land at Beaumont? The financiers had found that, if their identities were concealed during monetary transactions, when difficulties subsequently arose out of such dealings, they could keep their distance while questions were asked. The risk on the part of those who lent their names to their social superiors often enough led to their own rise in society and so, for them, the risk was worth it. Where did Antoine Champion get to in the end? He evidently remained discreet!

The second rule to be observed by the financiers was association. They knew that they needed each other, these Sainctots, these Bordiers, these

Tambonneaus, when they bought offices of profit under the crown (to use the English term). There were six of them who held the office of Treasurer-General in Extraordinary of the Wars, and they shared the administration of the different loans and taxes. They could, between them, have more available capital, more knowledge of what would be involved and more skill to be set to work if they acted in concert with one another. Family groupings were ideal for this purpose. In this way closely knit associations were formed, sometimes among recognisable affinities based on Protestantism, for example.

The third game rule was the established method of making loans and taking advantage of them when available. Loans were necessary to buy an office, to acquire land fitting for the status of an office holder, or to provide a daughter with a dowry for a favourable marriage. There was nothing shocking, when confronted with lack of financial liquidity, in approaching others for a loan. Another of Le Vau's clients, Michel-Antoine Tambonneau, President of Accounts, became 'without contest, the greatest creditor among the tax farmers'.[12]

This, then, was Louis Le Vau's world and he thrived in it for a good many years, noticed by the wealthy, employed by the successful, taken on by Mazarin, by Fouquet, then by Colbert and by Louis XIV. His posthumous disgrace did not commend him to posterity. His work at the Louvre was submerged in the claims for the creation of the Colonnade made for Claude Perrault. At Versailles, when one looks for a big name, it is Jules Hardouin-Mansart who leaps to mind, and then there was a propensity for a very short time to let Le Vau's pupil François d'Orbay overshadow him at Mazarin's college.

Given that he was by no means the only contemporary Parisian architect to be derivative, even though he was not born in the circles most likely to produce candidates for crown appointments, and that what money he made was always at risk from his ambition, we can still see him as one of the outstanding achievers of the *Grand Siècle*, with his share in the responsibility for development of a classical French taste in building and design.

* * *

With the foundation of the Royal Academy of Architecture in 1671, the skills of the practitioner were placed on a professional basis, the conspicuous signal of which is the course of architecture published by François Blondel between 1675 and 1683.[13] This scheme of detailed information for those aspiring to become recognised as architects is based principally on classical models found in the ruins of Rome and in the writings of Vitruvius (though examples on French territory, like the bridge over the Charente at Saintes, are also cited), and on examples given by recent moderns, starting with Léon-Battista Alberti in the fifteenth century, and including Scamozzi, Vignola and Palladio, accepted as classical models from Italy. The barley sugar pillars of the baldaccino in Saint Peter's are cited, but not with accreditation to Bernini. Contemporary French models of buildings are rarely given – the exemplary *Corderie royale* (a very long building for the purpose of making ropes for ships' rigging) in Colbert's naval dockyard at Rochefort is cited, but more recent architects, such as Philibert Delorme, were only given a mention if they were theoreticians as well as practitioners. Hands-on designers including François Mansart are not mentioned, so we should not expect Louis Le Vau to be included in the list either, since he was not one to express his principles on paper except in contracts or the few little memoranda that he wrote for himself, such as the ones cited earlier about bringing marble from Flanders or how to make better tinplate in the Nivernais. However, the polymath Claude Perrault is mentioned for his translation of Vitruvius.[14] The publication of the five books of over a thousand pages of close-set type of Blondel's teaching course, complete with its magnificent engravings, marks the coming of age of the architect's profession.

This would be a world in which the self-taught Le Vau, whose training had evolved as he worked with the builders, would have had no part, and Jules Hardouin-Mansart would immediately become the leader of the new age of practitioners, able to promote himself as such, since he soon became the King's own architectural interpreter.

* * *

We have already taken note in previous chapters of how Louis Le Vau's pupil, François D'Orbay, replaced him on his projects at the College of the Four Nations and at the new palace of Versailles in a seamless continuum after his death, just as he had himself replaced Jacques Lemercier in 1654. But the apprentice architect and head of Le Vau's drawing office was never offered the post of First Architect to the King and was brusquely supplanted by Jules Hardouin-Mansart when the latter emerged as the new translator of the King's intentions after his success with the design and construction of the Château de Clagny. His design for that building in its park on a site now dominated by the Rive Droite railway station and the lines towards Paris impressed the King and facilitated his design to give an establishment of their own, hard by Versailles, to the legitimised children born to him by Mme de Montespan, in particular the duc de Maine.

The Ambassadors' Staircase at Versailles, designed by D'Orbay, with its lower steps in Pyrenean marble, its decoration by Le Brun and its being naturally lit from above through crystal that admitted sunlight as had recently been adopted in Italy, was a major feature of the palace until Louis XV had it destroyed when it was seen to be dilapidated beyond the possibility of repair in 1749. The staircase was D'Orbay's own design, which replaced what Le Vau had intended. Yet, on the Left Bank, facing the Louvre on the Right Bank, he faithfully fulfilled Le Vau's project for Mazarin's memorial, and did not attempt to supplant him in any way. He could not be said to have overshadowed Le Vau, but was acknowledged as his continuator on the site.

D'Orbay's career until 1670 displayed significant similarities with, as well as differences from, Le Vau's own. The family of master masons into which he was born in 1634 was considerably higher up in the pecking order than the Le Veaus had been in 1612. His father, François the elder, who qualified as a comfortably off bourgeois, lived in the parish of Saint-Eustache, and held the post of the King's apartment builder from 1661 onwards, when he was working for Monsieur, the King's brother, at the Palais Royal, and also at the Tuileries and Louvre under Louis Le Vau's direction. He appears in the accounts as being paid 30 livres a year as mason in ordinary in the King's buildings. When he had won the contract for the new chancellery at Versailles (recently restored as a hotel opposite the *Lac des Suisses*) to be constructed according to his son's plans in 1673, he began work immediately. François's brother, Jean, who succeeded their father, completed it after 1677. There had also been an ample number of private contracts in the Île de France. His last years were passed as syndic of the Parisian masons, and he worked for the King at the palace of Fontainebleau. He was buried with due ceremony in Saint-Eustache in 1677. François junior was by no means a social thruster and he left the succession to his brother. By then established as an architect – functioning as a roofer (*toiseur*) – he had been in the habit of employing his father, his uncle, his brother and his nephew on the projects of which he had the direction.

Other members of his family became more prominent in their professions than François, who was conspicuous for his modesty. His father entrusted him as an apprentice to Louis Le Vau in 1648 at the time when the latter was becoming established, having completed Parisian *hôtels particulières* for Lambert, Hesselin and Tambonneau. Le Vau's agency was becoming prosperous, and there was certainly enough work to occupy the able young *dessinateur* in the drawing office, which was one of the first of its kind. He was an example of a new breed – soon to be known by a derogatory word for slaves – who translated their masters' architectural ideas into detailed plans and elevations on paper.[15] D'Orbay escorted his own master into prominence when he (the master) was appointed First Architect in 1654. He was responsible for the working drawings issued to the contractors at Vincennes and at Vaux-le-Vicomte. This brought d'Orbay to Mazarin's notice and to Fouquet's and, through them, to the King's.

* * *

The importance of a sojourn in Italy on the part of French pictorial artists had been recognised increasingly since Marie de' Medici's regency. Nicolas Poussin had lived in Rome for years. He was required to come home by Louis XIII but, after two years in a Paris too claustrophobic for him, he went back to the Eternal City and stayed there for the rest of his days. When his rheumaticky hands would no longer permit him to hold a paintbrush, he passed on his artistic insights to his compatriots, who paid him visits and sat at his feet.

The talented young Simon Vouet concluded his artistic journeyings in other European countries and in Turkey, which he had begun at the age of fourteen, by settling for several years in Rome where patrons from among members of the great families competed with each other for works by him for their palaces. Louis XIII called him home to Paris and established him in the Louvre. As well as training apprentices in his workshop there, he accepted commissions to decorate the new mansions being built by court officials, and extended his skills into the designs for the large tapestries to be woven to hang on their walls – works that displayed the influence of his Italian teachers. André Le Nôtre was among the members of his atelier before he decided to return to the family business of garden design, and his future associate Charles Le Brun was among those who received their early training from Vouet over a period of six years, and appreciated his influence.[16]

Le Vau could not have afforded to go to Rome as a young man, and was not a pictorial artist in any case, but he was aware of the value of such a visit and is known to have interested himself in prints of Italian works and understood their significance, as we have seen, importing the initiatives of Italian craftsmen into his own work, not least his Italian alcove bedrooms. Once he had become established as an architect he could not have left his work in progress in other people's hands while he withdrew across the Alps for any length of time and it was no use going for a week of two: you had to soak yourself in Roman culture or it was not worth it. Fréart de Chantelou, who accompanied Bernini in Paris on the King's orders in 1665, had profited from such an extended visit there.

In 1660, in what turned out to be the interim between Le Vau's employment at Vaux and beginning work at Versailles, Le Vau decided to use a sum advanced to him from the royal building accounts to send his gifted and self-effacing apprentice to Rome in order to expand his own understanding by proxy of the classical buildings there. The young man became at least on nodding terms with the Italian masters working there at the time who were profiting from this well-established tradition for French artist-painters and expanding it to include the redesigning of monumental buildings.

We find the meticulous student of antiquity, the twenty-five-year-old D'Orbay, going about on sites like the Forum, or the Temple of Castor and Pollux and among the other monuments that had been described by Vitruvius while they were being constructed, and absorbing his books a good decade before Claude Perrault brought out his French translation. It is known that Le Vau had a folio edition of Vitruvius's work – before Perrault's was issued – on his own shelves, along with other works that dealt with these antique remains. Because he was paying for the visit, Le Vau was entitled to make use of the knowledge that his apprentice gained in this important year: neither Le Vau, nor Hardouin-Mansart after him, were able to make such a visit. By the time the Versailles projects began, we can imagine the conversations between the enthusiastic pupil and his acquisitive master in the drawing office in the rue de Roi de Sicile and then in the Le Vau family's tied apartment in the Hôtel de Longueville, where d'Orbay also had his bachelor's lodgings.

While he was in Rome, d'Orbay submitted a project for a staircase in the Church of the Santissima Trinita dei Monti, part of the Minimes convent established by Charles VIII of France in 1488, where there was a dispute about the choice of Italian or French style going on in which Mazarin had become involved. Mazarin's agent, the Abbé Elpidio Benedetti, mentions a drawing made by d'Orbay, *'jeune Français envoyé par Mr Le Vau pour étudier'*.[17]

There was a competition for this staircase in progress in 1660 during d'Orbay's visit, which involved Bernini and Rainaldi, and he made his own submission, which Benedetti found impractical and too costly. Mazarin's death in the following year and the pope's being opposed to an equestrian statue of Louis XIV being erected in the Spanish Square led to the project being abandoned for seventy years. D'Orbay's drawing was found by his 1960 biographer Albert Laprade, who was to make exaggerated claims for him. (Laprade also assumed that Nicolas Poussin became known to d'Orbay on the basis of his living near this church and the likelihood of having seen him making his measurements in preparation for his submission.) The claim that the young man's visit to Rome in 1660 had serious repercussions in France can be substantiated if it were found that, on his return, Le Vau had been willing to profit from what his young protegé had learned there. When it comes to the dominating features of the design of the College of the Four Nations, that probably was the case.

* * *

As we have seen previously, credit for the creation of the Louvre Colonnade was soon attributed to the gifted polymath Claude Perrault, certainly after the publication in 1673 of his elegant translation of the treatise on architecture by Vitruvius, who had been one of the designers of imperial Rome for the Emperor Augustus.[18] Perrault's translation 'established a rationalist conception of architecture that placed it in the service of absolutism', comparable to Charles Le Brun's exploitation of Ovid's presentation of classical mythology.

'In essence, Perrault reduced a complex and nuanced art to the simplistic application of … increasingly formulaic designs,' and it was Jules Hardouin-Mansart who was 'the first and most successful student of Perrault's precepts' … whose 'buildings are best characterized as the simulacra of classicism, simplified and aggrandized to serve the needs of a monarch who in his maturity was less the leader of a kingdom than he was the figurehead of a vast state bureaucracy.'[19]

Once his brother Charles's *Memoires* had been circulated in the final years of Louis XIV, it seemed to have been accepted by uncritical contemporaries that it was Claude Perrault and not Louis Le Vau who was the first to think of the colonnade as the best expression of majesty for the King's principal dwelling. A variation of it was adapted by Le Vau himself on the garden facade of the new palace at Versailles. By then, he had already used the concept as appropriate embellishment for the interior of the Square Yard at the Louvre when he doubled the *enfilades* to provide more rooms there.

* * *

Soon afterwards, a more intense professional shadow than Perrault's was cast over Le Vau's achievements by the Sun King's rays shining upon Jules Hardouin-Mansart. He was twenty-four years old in the year Louis Le Vau died, and he began work on his first major royal contract only four years later. By then, Athenäis de Montespan had replaced Louise de La Vallière as the King's accredited mistress, and had given him the first two of their six surviving children. Before these two were declared legitimate – an evident exception to the absolute monarch's respect for the requirements of conventional morality – Mme de Montespan had asked the King for suitable accommodation for them not very far from the apartments she had been given at Versailles.

Hardouin-Mansart had already shown what he was capable of by his reconstitution of the Pavilion de Val, another of Louis XIII's creations, close to the royal chateau of Saint-Germain-en-Laye, which served a similar purpose to that of the Porcelain Trianon at Versailles: a retreat for the King and chosen courtiers to relax in a less formal atmosphere than the palace. His methods of design were on display there: reliance on what was there before, already changed into his own architectural idiom. It was the 'archetype of the single-storeyed country residence'[20] often seen dotted about in rural France and was an updated version of the *chinoiserie* that the King was known to favour at the time – especially in association with Mme de Montespan.

But the first reaction on the part of the King – and Colbert – to Mme de Montespan's request was to commission a mansion at the estate at Clagny down the hill from Versailles that he had bought in 1665,[21] and from whose lake water was pumped up to the reservoirs provided by Louis Le Vau and the hydraulic engineers, Denys Joly and the Francini brothers, on the roof of and alongside the Grotto of Thetis that fed Le Nôtre's fountains.[22] The architect chosen was Antoine Le Pautre, who was architect to the King's brother, Philippe, Duke of Orleans and would very soon be working on his patron's chateau at Saint-Cloud. Colbert's interpretation of the commission, always with his eye on economies in royal expenditure wherever possible, required Le Pautre certainly to build a mansion, but one with no frills. It was nearing completion when the King and Athenäis paid it a visit. Her immediate reaction was to tell the King that what he was offering her would be 'fine for a girl in the opera." Her indulgent royal lover's equally immediate response was to order Colbert to have it knocked down.[23]

Jules Hardouin-Mansart did not just arrive from nowhere. He was born in Paris on 16 April 1646, the first surviving son of Raphäel Hardouin, an established artist (*maître-peintre*), and his wife Marie Gaultier, niece of François Mansart, who has already figured large in this narrative, known for his large commissions in a variety of locations and especially in the Paris region. Even in England, we know what a Mansard window is, (erroneously) named for him (and spelt wrongly): one set into an attic built into the slate above the roofline of the top floor of a building.

Raphäel and Marie lived in the parish of Saint-Nicolas-des-Champs, and they chose a member of the de Luynes family, prominent in court circles, as Jules's godfather. Unlike Louis Le Vau, Jules was well on his way up the social ladder from the time of his birth. On both sides of his family he was connected with established sculptors, painters, engravers and master masons, besides his famous great-uncle architect. Jules had a younger brother, Michel, and a cousin, Marie Delisle, who eventually married the architect Jacques IV

Gabriel. François Mansart died in 1666 and, in the following year Jules and Michel added his surname to their own.

Their father, then with the accolade of a painter in ordinary to the King, also died in 1666, by which time Jules had been apprenticed, but apparently not for the full three years as was usual, to another painter, Charles Poerson, who was Rector of the Royal Academy of Painters in 1658, to learn drawing. Then, aged fourteen, he was taken under his great-uncle's wing since he showed more aptitude for designing buildings than the decorative work in which Poerson specialised. François Mansart was then (1660–61) at the high point of his professional life and Jules worked with him on the Chapel of the Visitation, several *hôtels particuliers*, including the one for Louis Phélypeaux de La Vrillière, who was the secretary of state for the Reformed Church, and the Château de Maisons (now Maisons-Lafitte), where some stone gateways are attributed to him. He seems also to have had a hand in the west front of the Minimes' Chapel in Paris.

After Jules's great-uncle died on 23 September 1666, he was working on projects attached to Saint-Germain-en-Laye. At that time Marie Hardouin and her two sons lived in the rue de Charenton, Faubourg Saint-Antoine. With all the men in the preceding generation dying at more or less the same time, Jules and Michel, though still legally minors, achieved a certain independence. Michel married into a dynasty of engravers, who were ready to give Jules publicity for his creations. It was Michel himself who made the first print for him – of the chateau he designed for Clagny. Jules's own marriage on 7 February 1668 to Anne Bodin brought him into contact with more engravers, all well known for their skill. One of their five children married into the Delespine family of masons who also had their associations with Louis Le Vau.[24]

Because he had been his great-uncle's assistant, Jules was assured of continuing work at the sites where he was already engaged, especially at Maisons, for René de Longueil, the president of the Cour des Aides, a prominent *parlementaire*, and on others for the Guénégaud and the de Ponponne families. This led to the first commissions offered him in his own name, among them religious buildings for those of the Jansenist tendency, even at Port-Royal itself, and then to contracts with bishops in the Midi. There were also *hôtels particuliers* at Paris and six of them at Versailles alongside the convergence of the three avenues at the place d'Armes, for conspicuous courtiers and marshals. This brought him to the attention of Colbert and afterwards of Louvois, who had their offices close by. Colbert would send him on missions to build in the provinces, and Louvois would entrust him with the vast building site at Versailles and the prestigious improvements at the Royal Church of the Invalides in Paris. He entered the King's service and never left it.

He was sent into the Languedoc to make improvements to what was being done on the canal that was to join the Atlantic to the Mediterranean (*Canal du Midi*), a journey that allowed the construction of palaces for the bishops of Grignan (where Mme de Sauvigny's daughter lived) and Beziers. He profited from seeing the Pont du Gard and the arenas at Arles – where he designed the famous vaulted ceilings at the Hôtel de Ville – and the *Maison cube* at Nimes, perhaps some recompense for having refused to leave his promising Parisian projects earlier on so as to spend time with the classical remains in Rome. For the architect, the engineer's task was never far below the surface of his professional experience. He then went north to Flanders to oversee the construction of the parliamentary palace at Tournai.

By the mid-1670s, he was by no means unknown in the capital and at court and had become genuinely prosperous, with a carriage, a few servants and enough resources to take on an apprentice, inviting comparison with the young Le Vau, thirty years before, whose income was never enough to provide adequate security for him as he mingled with the financiers. But there was one more important step before he completely found his feet in the royal entourage. Jules Hardouin-Mansart was known in court circles, but not yet to the King himself. That was about to change.

André Le Nôtre was at work on developing the gardens at Clagny for the King to give to Mme de Montespan. He had been trained by François Mansart in the general management of gardens and parks and, knowing the quality of his teacher's great-nephew's work, particularly on the pavilion of Le Val at Saint-Germain-en-Laye,[25] decided to put in a good word for him with the King. We can imagine him meeting the monarch, with whom he was on familiar terms,[26] and making his recommendation for the young architect to design a more cheerful residence for the illegitimate boy about to be elevated to become the Duke of Maine who would ultimately inherit it from his mother.

The King accepted the recommendation.

'The striking success of Clagny, doubtless strengthened by that of the little pavilion at Le Val, caused (Hardouin-) Mansart to be admitted into the limited circle of King's Architects and members of his Academy at the end of 1675, before even having reached the age of thirty, a position which soon permitted him to deploy his talents and to impose himself as the first among them six years later.'[27]

He received his first salary as *Premier Architecte du Roi* on 4 October 1681.[28] François d'Orbay had done the work since Louis Le Vau's death, but he was a reticent person and was content to be a competent technician without the honours that Hardouin-Mansart set out to accumulate. Louis XIV knighted Hardouin-Mansart twice, in 1683 and 1693, and ennobled him as Count of Sagonne in 1702. He was Superintendent of the King's Buildings from 1699 until his death, brought about suddenly in 1708 after he had gorged himself with fresh peas. His rise was recounted by the Count of Saint-Simon, who had no opinion of him, and accused him and the King of bad taste in the buildings they produced together:

> He came to hold a virtual monopoly on construction of any importance in France. His climb, starting with Clagny, was meteoric, followed soon by other royal commissions. He was ruthless in seizing opportunities and he broke with the convention of not claiming credit for royal buildings, while the King recognised in Hardouin-Mansart the almost preternatural ability to translate his vision of royal *gloire* into architecture and entrusted him with projects of unprecedented variety and extent. He reflected his patron and was the first truly modern practitioner of his profession responsible for a distinct architectural style.[29]

There was no further thought by Colbert of putting the design of any royal building into committee. The King and Hardouin-Mansart worked in tandem to accomplish the further enlargement of Versailles when it had been decided to make it the administrative capital of the kingdom in 1682, building the *aisle du Midi*, the *aisle du Nord*, the Royal Chapel, to provide the ministers with apartments and *cabinets* on either side of the *cour d'honneur*, and the *Grand Commun* to make provision of separate apartments and communal kitchens for those who had to right to eat at the King's table.[30]

All this was in a recognisably distinctive style, and the garden facade of Le Vau's new chateau was given a total makeover when the Hall of Mirrors filled the terrace intended by Le Vau for formal gatherings on the first floor. From whatever vantage point you take at the Palace of Versailles you have to know precisely where to look to see what is left of Le Vau's work. The Grotto of Thetis and the reservoirs alongside it were replaced by the north aisle and Le Vau's original orangery was expanded and remodelled. Even Le Nôtre's territory was intruded upon when Hardouin-Mansart built the colonnade in the gardens to provide a setting for the sculpture of Pluto, Proserpine and Ceres, during a period when the garden designer was absent.

Awesome majesty was to be evermore the theme of the second expansion of Versailles: the height and length of the main buildings, the grand and small *écuries* to shelter and exercise the King's horses and garage his carriages, completed by the royal chapel in Hardouin-Mansart's final years, fulfil as much as Louis XIV and Hardouin-Mansart were able to accomplish in their conjoint architectural lifetimes. Le Vau's porcelain Trianon, instead of being repaired after assaults by wind, rain and winter freezes, was replaced by one in marble; but here a certain delicacy was achieved because its main purpose was not to impress the great public and the visitors from abroad but to please the King and a selected number of courtiers on their afternoons of leisure: the King designed part of it himself while his architect was otherwise occupied.

Then there was the chateau at Marly, a short drive in a carriage from Versailles, required by the King as his private retreat where he could be accompanied by several carefully selected courtiers. This was an important construction for several reasons. Firstly, since it was for the King's private use, it was unashamedly Baroque in style, secondly, because it confirms Charles Le Brun in his role as the co-ordinator of all art and design required by the king, and, thirdly, because it makes self-conscientious reference to the literary[31] and archeological[32] tradition of the ancient Roman world. If anyone were to cast a shadow over the memory of Louis Le Vau, it would be Charles Le Brun, and it is worth devoting space in these comments to this close associate of Colbert who dominated the years between 1670, when Le Vau died, and 1683 when the King replaced Colbert with Louvois as Superintendent of the King's Buildings.

The decisive reason for Le Vau's being posthumously overshadowed is, in the end, a relatively simple one, contained in the King's own application of his theory of administrative absolutism for the glory of the French monarchy and his own position within it. There was no need for the French monarchy to adopt a style that was the creation of the Vatican and the nations that owed it allegiance. The French house of Bourbon was superior to any papal family or any monarchy or principality in Italy, the Iberian peninsula or the viceroyalties in the New World in the King's estimation. Louis XIV wanted his own house style, one that would be more impressive than any extravagances of Baroque illusionism. His choice fell upon neo-classicism therefore, suitably dignified to convey his superiority, and impressive enough, in the spirit of Augustus's marble Rome, to overawe all or any visitors. This was to be the *style Louis XIV* so actively recommended by the absolute monarchy in France.

There could be no doubt about whom Colbert chose as the leading spirit in the King's taking back of the trio of Le Brun, Le Vau and Le Nôtre into his service after Fouquet's disgrace in August 1661. Charles Le Brun was to be the innovative spirit, the prolific designer of ceilings and fountains and decorations on a comprehensive scale, while Le Vau remained focused purely on buildings which served as their framework.[33]

Le Brun's career is a story of inexorable rise and incorporation into royal service. His father was no more than a jobbing monumental mason, but his mother was a member of the powerful Le Bé clan in Paris, the menfolk of which were professional designers of styles of lettering for the printing trade and, in some cases, responsible for teaching successive Dauphins, Louis XIII and Louis XIV, how to read. This gave the young Le Brun access to the outer fringes of the peripatetic court at Saint-Germain and Fontainebleau, and, in Paris, the Palais royal and then the Louvre.

Le Brun passed under the tutelage of Fouquet, and then of Colbert (whose patronage was maintained for the two decades during which the latter remained in power), with the blessing of Chancellor Séguier, without denying any loyalty to his former patron who had protected him in Italy and, once more, after his return to Paris.[34] It was thus that he became First Painter to the King, principal designer for Versailles – the creator of countless design drawings for statuary in Le Nôtre's gardens – and responsible for Marly, for the vault of the new Hall of Mirrors at Versailles, for designs for tapestries from the Gobelins manufactory and the diverse pieces of silver furniture from the Savonnerie works that enriched the Sun King's Palace until the necessities provoked by the War against the League of Augsburg subsequent upon 1688 caused it to be melted it down in order to provide *specie* to pay for the purchase of weaponry.

Le Vau worked within the framework that Le Brun created at Colbert's request – the so-called 'Secret Council' for the design of the Colonnade at the Louvre (along with Claude Perrault) so as to give the King all the responsibility. Le Brun himself submitted a drawing to permit the King to make an informed opinion, thereby establishing a reputation for himself as architect as well as *artiste-peintre*.[35]

* * *

Good buildings lead to tourism, as we saw in the case of Sebastiano Locatelli, the young priest from Modena who visited Paris in 1664 with his two aristocratic patrons,[36] and tourism leads to an industry in informed guidebooks. These succeeded one another regularly in the seventeenth and eighteenth centuries and they provide us with some indication of the reputation of the architects who designed the buildings.[37]

Let's start with Germain Brice (1653?–1727) whose book went through several editions between 1684 and 1752.[38] He gives information about the new Royal Academy of Architecture,[39] to which the King appointed Blondel, previously mathematics tutor to the Dauphin, as its first director and professor, resulting in the teaching material upon which we have already remarked. Other members were Daniel Gittard, the first designer at Vaux-le-Vicomte and later architect of Saint-Sulpice; Libéral Bruand, architect of the accommodation for the veterans at Les Invalides;[40] François D'Orbay; Claude Perrault; Pierre Bullet, who built the Portes of Saint-Denis and Saint-Martin for the ville de Paris, and then the Hôtels d'Evreux and Crozat;[41] and André Félibien, who was the Academy's secretary.

Brice's account can be questioned for two reasons: he suggests that Hardouin-Mansart was a founder member as First Architect – which is chronologically impossible – and that, after the foundation of the Academy, two of its members had died: one of whom was Louis Le Vau, but we are well aware that he died during the year before the foundation. The other one, he says, was Antoine Le Pautre, but he is known to have been still a member until he died in 1678.[42] Moreover, Brice does not mention Pierre Mignard as a member. He was not an architect, but a painter, a rival to Charles Le Brun, who decorated the inside of the dome at Val-de-Grace in 1663 and the salon at Saint-Cloud in 1677.[43]

These criticisms suggest that Brice did not take too much trouble over checking his information but, when we come to look at his descriptions of actual buildings, it is a different story. His account of Mazarin's palace is concise, but satisfying in its completeness.[44] He says that there was no building in Paris that contained more curiosities and precious items of furniture than this one. On the side of its court, its facade is in brick and prepared stone with two marble statues at the entrance. A stairway leads to the apartments whose ceilings are richly decorated with gilded stucco and fine paintings. Bernini had a hand in it and this fact is more valuable than the metals that have been used on it. There are tapestries enriched with gold and silver threads in a gallery that also contains *cabinets de curiosité*, and vases made of jasper and alabaster. The gallery floor is covered in a Turkey carpet, 'all in one piece of extraordinary length'. The rooms beneath the gallery are provided with German and Chinese cabinets, and with varnished chests from Japan, which have a lightness of design and an agreeable scent. There are a great number of pieces of expensive Italian statuary, comparable to pieces in the King's own collection. The ceilings are the work of two Giovanni-Francescos: Grimaldi and Romanelli, whom Mazarin brought from Italy between 1649 and 1651. (Brice says 1641, which would date the building's decoration in the middle of the Fronde when Mazarin was in exile.)[45] These two artists had already established their reputations on the walls and ceilings of palaces in Rome. 'In the end,' Brice says, 'I don't know how to recount all that is beautiful and of great value in this magnificent palace.'

After one or two other mansions nearby, Brice comes to describe the Hôtel de Lionne, which Louis Le Vau designed for this secretary of state in 1662.[46] Brice gives the architect his due: 'The exterior of this mansion makes a very fine arrangement, graced with good design, and the rooms inside are ideal. The garden behind gives a very special appearance to it.'

Later on,[47] Brice gives an appreciation of the Hôtel Lambert, Le Vau's early masterpiece:

> This house is magnificent in all it contains; the entrance is large and raised up high, and the iron-work there is absolutely extraordinary; but that is not what makes you really stop. On all four sides the yard is enclosed by admirable building faced with colossal Ionic pilasters which join the base of it to the roof, with vases placed above. The staircase is at the end of the yard, with two ranks of columns, across which the daylight spreads by degrees because it encounters no obstacles ... on the river front; from the garden, there is a view over a distance of six or seven leagues (!) from Paris, which is very pleasing. You see well-painted ceilings in these apartments, the work of Le Sueur who joined the ranks of the great painters at a very young age, equal to what he achieved in his maturity.

A more detailed appreciation follows, concluding with:

> The facade of the apartment on the river front is of the same symmetry and the same style as the yard which gives an air of greatness to this building, seen from far off and which provides a splendid effect when you come into Paris from Charenton. It is Le Vau's design, who has done nothing more well-designed or more beautiful.

Le Vau is also given his due as the first designer of the new church of Saint-Louis on the island, work continued by Le Duc and decorated by Philippe de Champagne, who was also one of the first of its churchwardens.

* * *

The next of these historians of Paris was Henri Sauval, whose work is more substantial than that of Brice. Sauval was an advocate in the Paris *Parlement* who devoted twenty years of his leisure time to his research on the enlargement and the changes in the appearance of certain key monumental buildings in Paris in the mid-seventeenth century. He died in 1676, but his volumes did not appear between covers until 1724.

The anonymous author of the preface to the published work relates that his writing was admired by Colbert as well as by *érudits* like Paul Pellisson, who had achieved status as official historian of the kingdom once restored to royal favour after Fouquet had been sent to Pignerol for life. Several lesser lights also spoke well of Sauval's antiquarian achievement. The preface also renders justice to Claude Bernard Rousseau, King's councillor, the auditor in ordinary of the Paris Chamber of Accounts, who helped Sauval compile his book while adding supplementary material to it after his death, who had privileged access to relevant manuscript documents about buildings found in the royal registers and a rich fund of knowledge that he had accumulated independently.

When Sauval comes to present some of Le Vau's constructions in his second volume, he gives him the credit that was due to him. You have to wait for it, however, since the first mention of Le Vau as the King's First Architect comes where he is commemorated as the designer of the eastern half of the interior of the Square Yard at the Louvre in 1667, work continued by d'Orbay 'who contributed not a little' to it, Sauval says, after Le Vau had died:

> It is to these two excellent architects to whom we must attribute all the glory of the design and the carrying out of this superb edifice, which will doubtless cause admiration in the centuries to come and give a high idea of him who had produced works of such rare and great perfection in spite of everything that has been published to the contrary.[48]

From such a [49] source, these words are genuine recognition of Le Vau's place in the creation of the French classical style of architecture, even if his name does remain coupled with that of his former apprentice.

When Sauval comes to presenting the Hôtel Lambert, he piles up the superlatives, praising all its distinctive features and its use of classical models on the garden front of the *corps du logis*. He asserts that the Hercules gallery 'has little to equal it in France', and concludes for the whole structure that the house 'has an air of greatness and wisdom standing out from a great distance, which gives above all an idea of the splendour and magnificence of the city of Paris to all who approach from the direction of Charenton. Louis Le Veau [*sic*!] First Architect of the King [albeit after another seven years!], provided the designs for this house, and it ought to be agreed that he did not provide a better building than this one.'

So, in hindsight, Le Vau had started as he meant to go on. A few pages later even the Hôtel Bautru, which, purchased by Colbert as his town house, was so vehemently criticised for unsure foundations, is ranked with others by Sauval as 'yielding nothing in terms of gentility or value'.

It comes as something of a surprise to find that one of these histories-cum-guides, that of Antoine-Nicolas Dezallier d'Argenville published in the middle of the eighteenth century, acknowledges Louis Le Vau as the designer of the Louvre Colonnade. After a full description of it in praise of its twenty-eight Corinthian columns, the author concludes with these words: 'The glory of this masterpiece is due, to all appearance, to Le Vau, despite several persons believing those authorities who attribute it to Claude Perrault.'[50]

In his turn, this author reiterates what his predecessors had to say about the Hôtel Lambert, duly attributed to Le Vau, but adds the different conclusion that it was the paintings of Eustache de Sueur that attracted the attention of all the foreign visitors who came to see what the building contained.[51]

* * *

To conclude our appraisal of Le Vau's work, we need to consider the commentaries of more recent historians of art and culture on both sides of the English Channel, starting with Henry Lemonnier in a work published in 1911. He presents a factual but hardly appreciative account of the First Architect's work:

> Le Vau remains to be judged as an artist. He is sometimes heavy-handed, ungainly (*massif*) and without grace. He did not have any justice for proportions, or delicacy in design – the kind of general harmony which is found in Perrault or Mansart. His constructions are lacking in form (*ligne*); the facades are uneven (*heurtés*); he uses columns or pilasters without great care for the beauty of their shapes; his decorations are a little bit brutish. That is particularly noticeable at the Hôtel Lambert.
>
> He improved and even changed himself as he grew older. The Chateau de Vaux is a powerful building; the conception of the College of the Four Nations is original, but his neglect in the use of the (classical) orders could be seen as characteristic of his heavy-handedness. His style, which is in part that of the first part of the century, disappeared, not even with him, but before his death. We have only to compare his design for the facade of the Louvre on the river front (destroyed in 1665–1667) with Perrault's to see that he reached a breaking-point, a crisis, at this juncture. Le Vau sensed it himself, because he adopted a completely different style at Versailles.[52]

There is nothing much positive in any of that! And when we consult the opinion of Sir Reginald Blomfield in England after the Great War we come across even more negativity. We can collect the reprimands as we go along. Blomfield begins by rightly pointing out that Le Vau is typically representative of the age of Mazarin and Colbert. So his working life coincides with the establishment of absolute monarchy. He reviews the urbanisation of the Île Saint-Louis, and asserts that the Hôtel Lambert 'is a heavy, gloomy-looking building outside but redeemed inside by being a showcase for the artists Le Sueur and Le Brun'. Then he adds that 'the absence of a delicate sense of scale and proportion which disfigured all Le Vau's designs is apparent in this, his first authentic work. The plan is commonplace and inconvenient, and it is difficult to understand the admiration with which this building appears to have been regarded from the first.'

Blomfield makes the claim that Le Vau was a good deal happier with his country houses, but concludes that Vaux-le-Vicomte is 'unsatisfactory as a whole', adding the ultimate in put-down lines: 'the whole thing is overdone.'

> The garden front is clumsy ... the great circular [*sic!*] salon projects partially beyond the main front, and the intersection of the dome and the Mansard roof is ugly and out of keeping with the steep-pitched roofs of the pavilions [...] Vaux-le-Vicomte is a good example of the difference between an architect with a real sense of architecture and the mere technician who is replete with details, but who has not the power to combine them in one organic composition. Le Vau had a great opportunity for a great original design and all he could do was to string together other people's ideas. There is no harm in borrowing if the designer is man enough to assimilate the motive [Does he mean *motif?*] and make it so entirely his own that it acquires a new significance, but this is just what Le Vau seems to have been unable to do. [...] Fouquet, however, and the taste of the time were entirely satisfied.

Nevertheless, Le Vau had gained the King's favour and this overrode the consideration that 'he often seems to have been uncertain what to do next'.[53] All these comments come from one who had himself built many a great country house starting from scratch. We have to admit that the man who was designing and supervising the building of Regent Street in London at the same time as he was writing all this knew his onions. Yet he is at fault for not taking seriously the fact that architects in France before the establishment of the Royal Academy of Architecture in the year after Le Vau died were left to make it up as they went along since they had no formal training and worked on the basis of acquired experience of what would work and what would not, together with learning from models offered by their predecessors and contemporaries.

Nevertheless, wiser counsels had prevailed, even before Blomfield and the French commentator Lemonnier (whom he admired and who preceded him). These judged Le Vau by twentieth-century standards and not by those of his own time.

Jean Cordey, the author of a study of Vaux-le-Vicomte published in 1933 whom we cited earlier,[54] appreciated Louis Le Vau's creativity. His extended essay was printed as an annexe to a study of the chateau by Anatole France. France's study first appeared in 1888 as the text accompanying an album of engravings of Vaux-le-Vicomte by Rodolphe Pfnor, which was intended to celebrate the restoration of the estate by Alfred Sommier, with the fortune that his family had made from the revolutionary cultivation and processing of sugar beet. The publishing house Calmann-Levi gave the short book a new edition forty-five years later.

Anatole France, poet, *academicien*, made complimentary remarks about Le Vau as the architect of the Hôtel Lambert:

> in which President de Torigny's bedroom on the second floor is to be admired and which Le Sueur decorated with an elegance which calls to mind the wall-paintings at Herculaneum. This bedroom was referred to as Italian because [...] the beauty of the woodcarving and the rich wainscots took the place normally occupied by tapestries. [...] The life of this man is not well known, though his works are illustrious.

He goes on to list, in tones of warm appreciation, all the other architectural achievements of Le Vau, and while he refers to his burial on the morning after his death on Saturday, 11 October 1670 at Saint-Germain-l'Auxerrois, he does not mention his dying in poverty, but records his appointments as First Architect, King's councillor, Intendant and Co-ordinator-General of the King's Buildings, and Secretary to the King (a title that often led to subsequent significant ennoblement). A lengthy footnote refers to plans that France had found in the National Archives for a sumptuous cathedral at Nantes being designed by Le Vau.[55]

This brings us up to the pre-Second World War years, in which the American Fiske Kimball and the Frenchman Alfred Marie were beginning to co-operate in admiration of Le Vau in their researches concerning the Versailles *enveloppe*, which were realised once hostilities had ceased five years later. Their observations were soon followed by the magisterial work of Anthony Blunt, who, whatever else he may have been as an associate of a spy ring for the

Soviet Union, was an art historian without parallel in the United Kingdom. We have already taken note of his enthusiasm for what Le Vau achieved from a young age and into his maturity. His verdict on his work is that he ranks with Mansart and Lemercier among the architects of the last years before the founding of the Royal Academy of Architecture:

> François Mansart may have been the most subtle architect of his generation, but he was not the most successful. Louis Le Vau seems to have been temperamentally much more suited to the demands of his patrons and, whereas Mansart threw away commissions owing to his obstinacy and arrogance, Le Vau was adaptable enough to fit in with what was demanded of him. He seems to have lacked the scrupulous artistic conscience which was the most marked quality of Mansart. Le Vau is, on the contrary, an artist careless of detail and thinking always of a general effect, inconsistent in his use of the Orders, but brilliant in decoration. Mansart walked alone; Le Vau was the head of a team of craftsmen – painters, sculptors, stucco-workers, gilders – who combined to produce effects which come nearer to the Baroque than any other architectural work in France during this generation.[56]

* * *

Scholarship is based on careful archiving, and in recent days, the librarians at the *Centre de recherche du château de Versailles* have been carrying out a meticulous review of the periodicals in their reserve collection. They have rediscovered a document that bears the date 21 October 1970 concerning an event that commemorated the tercentenary of Louis Le Vau's death, fully praising him both as an architect and as a businessman. The event itself took place under the cupola of the *Institut de France*, and was presided over by the then President of the Academy of Fine Arts, M. Paul Belmondo. It was the showcase for two speeches, one by the then Vice-President of the Academy of Fine Arts, M. Jacques Carlu, and the other by the then President of the Academy of Architecture, M. Guillaume Gillet, followed by a concert of seventeenth-century chamber music under the direction of Mlle Nadine Boulanger. As a photograph shows, it was a full-dress occasion with a full turnout of *Membres de l'Institut de France*.

M. Carlu began unequivocally by speaking of Le Vau's 'brilliant personality seen in the various stages of his prestigious career and his most celebrated architectural achievements'. He was:

without doubt a great architect. One of those who, in the course of different civilisations, had conceived buildings which, whatever the date of their construction, preserved the privilege of an everlasting youth, one of those rare persons in whom we voluntarily discern the title of genius … So it is possible to affirm that, in spite of the crushing shadow of the aesthetic and administrative edifice that Louis XIV and Colbert created from top to bottom, Louis Le Vau occupies, on account of his work, the very first place among the dynasties of great builders of his time and also among the constellation of illustrious artists who shine with such great brightness around the Sun King.

What he achieved was possible because he matched his skill as an architect with his ability to maintain his position among the courtiers and before the King. Unlike many others among his contemporaries, he was able to meet both of these demands.

The fact that the National Convention did not destroy the Collège Mazarine after 1792 bears witness to the respect that the Revolutionaries held for Le Vau's work. They modified it, taking away all its ecclesiastical and royal attributes, but they kept it as a national property, even though the best use they could find for the boys' sixty study bedrooms was as prison cells, with suspects such as David and Bernard de Saintes detained there for a time, or using the chapel as a grain store, although Pierre Samuel de Nemours, the future founder of the US enterprise Dupont, was able for a while to take sanctuary between the cupola and the dome.

Then came First Consul Bonaparte who planned to turn it into the Institute of France, and then, once he became Emperor, had his architect Anoine Vaudoyer refashion it so that it lost its original dimensions – an action Carlu depreciates as 'a massacre'. This defacement lasted for a century and a half until the decision was made in 1962 to remodel the college according to Le Vau's original – though without the ostensibly Baroque apostles' statues – and entrust the work to André Guiton. Carlu's tercentenary commemoration of Le Vau was thus taking place under *'la vraie cupole retrouvée'* with all the excrescences put up by Vaudroyer taken away.

M. Gillet's discourse gives a résumé of Le Vau's career along the lines of what has already been presented in these pages, placing him firmly within the succession of Lescot, the Cerceaus, and the Mansarts, architects and builders at the same time: 'What strikes you in these works is the extreme usefulness of the designs, their variety, their great logic, and the manner – always happy and original – in which they adapt themselves on the most unaccommodating sites and respond so well to the most diverse kinds of programmes that, in these most functional plans, the charm and warmth of their life still palpitates.'

Gillet then traces the urbanisation of Paris from the undertaking to develop the Île Saint-Louis by Christophe Marie,

> with the terracing of the quays above the reach of flooding and currents, and the making of building lots available by Poulletier, by means of a central axis from east to west and five or six parallel minor streets which lead to a peripheric one that allows for the management of traffic and access to the riverside for water traffic. This kind of urbanisation took up the traces of ancient towns and military settlements, even announcing the plan of Manhattan in miniature.

Then came the Hôtels Lambert, Hesselin, and the church of Saint-Louis en l'île, before Le Vau branched out into the dry moats and oval rooms for the financier Bordier at Raincy, before he came to be the King's First Architect at the age of forty-four, and before he worked on the Château de Vincennes for Mazarin, on the Salpetière Hospital, on the transformation of Meudon for Abel Servian, Vaux-le-Vicomte for Fouquet, then joint superintendents of finance, and then the Louvre and Versailles for the ultimate patron. In these works are seen the research of his whole working life. There are his oval salons, his pavilions at the corners of his mansions, with their high roofs. At Vaux, the chateau itself takes up but a small part of the terrain but it dominates the whole site that Le Nôtre made available. He worked in genial co-operation with so many other people – not just, in Pierre de Nolhac's apposite phrase, the 'fraternal genius' shared with Le Nôtre and Le Brun, but also with Molière, La Fontaine, Lully, Tortelli, and the maître d'hôtel Vatel, who controlled the funding for the banquets.

The turning point for everything in the early years of Louis XIV and at the height of Le Vau's career was Mazarin's demise, which saw the culmination of his whole training course offered to his godson during his mother's regency, ushering in the administrative absolutism of the remaining forty-four years of the reign. The King's godfather and Louis Le Vau's father died in the same year, leaving both their pupils free to assert their authority in their respective areas of influence: the state, or the profession of architecture and commerce. The one is represented by repeated victory in battle and the glory of his buildings, and the other in his elaborate signature and the dropping of the letter e from his family name, never mind that that had been done much earlier. The year 1661 saw Le Vau entrusted by the King's *alter ego* Colbert with the Louvre, Versailles and the Collège Mazarine all at the same time.

Gillet was giving his discourse under the cupola of that very college. In it, he could point out all the trademarks of Le Vau's work: the *avant-corps* and the colossal orders, the high roofs, the flaming urns, the concave lines of the facades that contained the shops for luxury goods, features reminiscent of St Agnès Church or the place Navone in Rome provided by Borromini or Bernini. In among these achievements, Le Vau found the time to become master of forges and director of workshops in the Nivernais, and provider of cannon for the navy: 'a gigantic work' in itself.

Gillet's conclusion, like Carlu's opening gambit, is unequivocal: 'Louis Le Vau, abundant, superb, open and generous, indefatigable worker, leader of men and brewer of affairs, should have been – as indeed he was – an architect and businessman.' But on the industrial level he could have become much more. In other times he could have designed new conurbations, factories and airports, he could have had the largest of research institutes. He could have been adviser to the Minister of Equipment for urbanisation and to the Prime Minister for regional development. He would, in our days, have been the centre of reference for many a great discovery.[57]

* * *

From the time of the tercentenary onwards, the absence of a continuous narrative – let alone a biography – began to be noticed by scholars like Dietrich Feldmann and Hilary Ballon, and was acted upon in the first volume of such by Cyril Bordier, leading to the impressive body of extensive, scientific studies by Alexandre Cojannot from his vantage point in charge of the collection of seventeenth-century Parisian solicitors' deeds and contracts in the French National Archives, and the output of Alexandre Gady, who holds a professorial chair in the history of modern architecture. These two Parisian scholars have often worked in tandem to present Le Vau's buildings as innovative and exemplary, as can be seen particularly in their attractive, lavishly illustrated and authoritative exhibition catalogue, which bears the title *Dessiner pour Bâtir*.[58]

The co-proprietor, with his two brothers, of Vaux-le-Vicomte, very active in the chateau's maintenance and development, M. Alexandre de Vogüé, recently presented the building and the estate as a part of a series called *Go Chateau* on YouTube.[59] When someone asked him to give an assessment of Le Vau's construction of the building, he drew attention to the internal design of corridors provided between the state rooms upstairs and downstairs in the *corps de logis*, which he had first adopted at Vincennes for the King's apartments, then extended into the double *enfilade* for the rooms off the Square Yard at the Louvre. Without such structure, Le Brun and his assistants could have painted all the ceilings, *voussures* and wainscots they liked, but they could not have delivered the unified building, as they were able to, without Le Vau's overall vision of its size and shape. Nicolas Fouquet may have overreached his ambitions, but Le Vau did not, in spite of abandoning his brick and stone design in favour of the entirely stone fabric complete with bas-reliefs, which the patron insisted upon for everything but the service buildings.

* * *

What can be finally concluded, then, about Louis Le Vau's achievement, even having to accept that he died prematurely with so many of his important projects still unfinished?

The most important aspect of his professional life is the fact that, to all intents and purposes, he was self-taught. He came from within the building trade. He was surrounded from his earliest years by its practitioners, who did not hold back from sharing with him their knowledge based on experience. He had an innately enquiring mind, and, once his father and his father's colleagues had taught him how to interpret ground plans and elevations, he set about acquiring a body of architectural models that re-emerged, duly altered, into his own buildings. He learned about the importance of Italy at a distance, and then, by working under Mazarin's direction, was associated with the Italian practitioners whom the minister brought across the Alps to work in Paris, men like Romanelli and Vigarani. He energetically devoured the principles set out by Vitruvius long before Claude Perrault began his translation. Palladio's books were always open before him. He admired, he imitated, he interpreted, and early on became the master of how to deal with any awkward constraints on the sites available to him. When protection of intellectual property was not in operation, and no formal training existed for architects, as opposed to site managers on undertakings who had profited from their apprenticeships, he early discovered a certain self-confidence that appealed to his clients, especially since it was tempered by his willingness to listen and act upon what they said they wanted in the buildings they commissioned from him.

He appears to have had a congenial sociability about him, which appealed to people in the highest ranks of contemporary dog-eats-dog society, and, in time, this would mean Louis XIV himself. Colbert was always a fly in Le Vau's ointment, but as we have noticed earlier, the friction between them was occasioned by the resentment that Colbert felt for the office of First Architect, rather than the personality of the holder of that office. What mattered was the King's confidence in Le Vau's ability to interpret what he wanted and to put up with the frequent changes he required even while work was in progress.

The King had finally to admit that, however much he wanted to be a one-man band, he did not know how to get brilliant melodies out of all the instruments at his disposal, and that there were some things that had to be left to specialists. In military matters, the King was a better staff officer than a general and, in artistic concerns, he knew what he wanted but needed others to provide it for him. This was a function that Le Vau was able to fulfil to His Majesty's satisfaction. What we can still see at Vincennes, at the Louvre, across the river at Mazarin's College, and at Versailles – not only the core of the new chateau but the vanished menagerie and the superseded Porcelain Trianon – are representations of the greatness of the monarchy that the King intended to display. In the few years between Bernini's return to Rome and his own demise, Le Vau got it right.

* * *

In the end, what convinced me of Le Vau's artistic mastery has been making drawings from my own photographs of his work. Once I started doing that, I could see – and even feel – what he wanted to achieve in terms of the interplay of light and shade on walls, the load-bearing structures of his arcades, the value of his attic friezes and Corinthian capitals in uniting and lifting a structure, the way in which the colossal orders he used so often give stature and dignified stability to a building.

All this has an amazing consistency, whether it was in the display of an extravagant baroque style at Vaux-le-Vicomte, the dignity of classical restraint shown in Mazarin's library, or the quiet presentation of authority in the interior of the *Cour Carrée* at the Louvre and in the facade behind which the Sun King greeted the day at Versailles. It is in these features of his achievement that Louis Le Vau's genius is to be seen.

A Glossary of Architectural Terms

Arcade, arcading: A row of free-standing, full-centred arches serving as window or door frames or apertures for shops on the ground floor of a building's facade. This originated in Henri IV's urbanisation of Paris at the Place Royale and the Place Dauphine and was adopted by Le Vau at the College of the Four Nations, the interior of the Louvre's Square Yard, and the Versailles *enveloppe*.

Avant-corps: A projection of masonry on the facade of a building on all its floors that uses sunlight to give a *chiaroscuro* effect and thus make the appearance of the building more substantial.

Balustrade: A row of short, individual columns that can be of any length, resting on a base and supporting a stone railing serving to conceal roof tiles from view from ground level or as the base of window frames.

Baroque: A triumphalist style of painting, sculpture and architecture, originating in the Iberian peninsula at the time of the Counter-Reformation, representing exaggerated self-confidence. (*Barocco* is Portuguese for a misshaped pearl.) It was widely adopted in Italy, especially in seventeenth-century Rome, by such architects as Borromeo and Bernini, and was favoured by Mazarin and Anne of Austria in Paris. Eventually it was rejected by the proponents of French classical taste, although Le Vau's work was influenced by it.

Bay: A section of a facade of a building arranged with others to complete the whole. There are twenty-seven of them on the garden facade of the Versailles *enveloppe*.

Chainage: The surrounds in stone for the brick panels in dividing walls. Good examples on the service buildings at Vaux-le-Vicomte.

Colonnade: An arrangement of columns having bases and capitals in succession, as on the eastern facade of the Louvre or in the Trianon at Versailles.

Colossal pilasters: Rectangular, shallow projections on a facade reaching from the ground to rooflines with bases and capitals corresponding to the classical orders. Le Vau used these on the garden facades of the Hôtel Lambert and extensively in the College of the Four Nations.

Combles brisés: Literally, broken eaves. A device to lower the height of a traditional French high roof by bending it halfway up its height. Le Vau used these to advantage on the royal apartments at Vincennes, although he reverted to using a series of high roofs at Vaux-le-Vicomte.

Cornice: A decorated strip of masonry or plaster marking the base of the roofline on a building.

Corps de logis: The rooms in a building set apart as the residence of the owner's family.

Cupola: A small construction surmounting a dome, perhaps housing a bell.

Dado: The lower part of a marble, wood or plaster wall covering, extending upwards from the floor to about waist height. (Fr: *Lambris*).

Drum: The section of a dome that connects it to the roof of a building, often pierced with windows to give light to an interior from above.

Enfilade: The succession of interconnecting rooms in a building. When Le Vau doubled the *enfilades*, as at Vincennes, the Louvre and Vaux-le-Vicomte, he provided the innovation of corridors between the rooms.

Entablature: A series of horizontal, decorative features found above columns and colonnades taking their form according to the order of architecture in use on a particular building. The category includes cornices and friezes. The entablature surrounds and supports the cross-beams of the roof.

Fausse braye: The term used for a dry moat or defensive ditch as used as in the case of the old chateau at Versailles dating from the time of Louis XIII, removed in Le Vau's enlargement of it.

Flaming Urn: A decorative device frequently used by Le Vau for the rooflines of his monumental buildings whether the roofs were high ones, as at Vaux-le-Vicomte, broken eaves as at Vincennes, or invisible, as at Versailles on the garden facade of the *enveloppe*.

Fronton, **Pediment:** A feature, usually triangular in shape, above the principal entrance to buildings, usually filled with sculpture in *bas-relief*, particularly – but not exclusively – on ecclesiastical edifices, based on illustrations of the entrances to temples found in Vitruvius, as Le Vau knew from the edition in his possession years before Claude Perrault published his edition of the Ten Books in 1674. *Frontons*, either triangular or in the form of arcs, sometimes alternating as such, are used as the heads of windows, as in the interior of the Louvre Square Yard.

Full-centred (Fr. *cintré*) Windows: Windows – or doors – with heads in the form of semicircles whose centres are at the top of the rectangular window frames.

Garde-corps: Railing, usually decorative as well as functional, in iron or stone before a balcony.

Greek or Attic Frieze: A purely decorative feature on renaissance and post-renaissance buildings used on the exterior of facades to mark the separation between a building's different storeys or as a cornice. The main decoration is a repeated sequence of three vertical bars, sometimes secured underneath by three nails, representations in stone masonry of the beam ends in timber of floors or the roofs on earlier antique constructions of the ancient Greek era. Le Vau used these early on in his commissions on the Île Saint-Louis.

Grisaille: Term used to denote a painting used as decoration in monochrome rather than colour.

High Roofs: Typically found on roofs of prominent buildings in France before the reign of Louis XIV, but reused by Le Vau at Vaux-le-Vicomte.

Lucarne: A window, smaller than those at a lower storey of a building, and sometimes round in shape (Fr. *œil de bœuf*, Lat. *oculus*) let into a tiled roof space to let light into an attic. Examples are to be seen on the eastern facade of the Versailles *enveloppe* looking on to the *Cour de marbre* above the King's apartments, and in the *corps de logis* at Vaux-le-Vicomte.

Orders of Architecture: These were enumerated and described extensively in the works of Vitruvius in the First Century AD, and of Andrea Palladio in the sixteenth, editions of which are known to have been in Le Vau's own book collection. They can be summarised (from Palladio[1]) as follows:

The Tuscan Order was described by Vitruvius as 'the most simple and plain of all the orders in architecture', being 'deprived of those ornaments that make the others so sightly and beautiful'. It was invented in 'a small noble part' of central Italy. The columns surmount plain pedestals. The five horizontal components of the capitals are executed in total simplicity with no ornament at all.

The Doric Order took its name from 'the Dorians, a Greek nation in Asia'. As with the Tuscan Order, Vitruvius had laid down precise dimensions that Palladio reproduced. Ancient buildings had no pedestal beneath the columns, and the fluted columns rose straight out of the ground. The Doric capital has three horizontal parts above a *collarino* with simple decoration. The architrave, placed above the capitals, carries a frieze along its length complete with equally spaced triglyphs, the spaces between them filled with other decorations – rams' skulls and roundels – and Palladio gave their technical names.

The Ionian Order, from another Greek province in Asia, Ionia. Ionian capitals are formed with volutes on two sides, the ones facing inwards and outwards from the building, which allows for elaborate fine decoration overall. Le Vau used these for the garden front of the Versailles *enveloppe*.

The Corinthian Order was the one most favoured by Le Vau on his constructions. The pillars are to have twenty-four vertical flutes or channels, with pedestals at their bases, a quarter of the height of the columns themselves. As with the other orders, the height of the capital is to be the same as the diameter of the column, but with an extra sixth part of the height added to it. The remaining space is to be filled with acanthus leaves[2] that seem to be supported on stems which diminish in size as they approach the leaves, as they do in nature.

The story that goes with the acanthus leaves in Vitruvius is often rehearsed, but is worth retelling here. A young Corinthian woman died and was buried. Her friends placed some of her favourite plants on her tomb, among them an acanthus, which they covered with a tile. In the spring, the leaves were found encircling the tile, and the sculptor Callimachus passed by. Noticing how the leaves were growing, he imitated them on the capitals he was carving in the city at the time, and so, subsequently, set the pattern for the Corinthian order. This feature is found in the Louvre Square Yard and all over the College of the Four Nations.

The Composite Order is the result of reflection on the elements of all the orders, particularly the Ionian and the Corinthian. Features of them both, the volutes from the one and the leaves from the other, are present in the capitals.

Pavilion: A building on a larger scale than those surrounding it but connected to them, as was the case at the Place Royal under Henri IV. A principal dwelling had pride of place, surrounded by artisanal dwellings and shops behind arcades on the ground floor. The *corps de logis* of Vaux-le-Vicomte was conceived as a series of interrelated pavilions under roofs that were almost independent.

Peristyle: A row of columns derived from Greek and Roman antiquity to provide monumentality for royal buildings, the best example of which for Le Vau's work is the Colonnade on the eastern facade of the Louvre. Evidence that Louis XIV favoured this form is well seen in the Marble Trianon at Versailles, part of which he designed himself in Hardouin-Mansart's absence.

Piano nobile: The first floor above street level was provided for the principal occupant of royal or princely palaces in Italy and France on the model of Palladio's villas in the Venezia, characterised by their windows and ceilings being higher than on other floors. This tradition was perpetuated in Paris into Haussmann's apartment blocks and afterwards.

Portico: A monumental entrance used for royal or temple buildings in antiquity adopted by Italian architects including Borromeo and Bernini and French ones, such as Lemercier at Val de Grace, for the west fronts of churches and cathedrals. Le Vau's entrance to the church at the College of the Four Nations is the conspicuous example of its use in his work.

Rampe: The term used for a banister rail at the side of a monumental staircase, either in stone or ironwork.

Renfort: A decorative device consisting of horizontal incisions between dressed stones on facades to provide the appearance of depth for the walls.

Rustic Pillars: Columns decorated with features of rough stonework (*mouillons*). Le Vau was constrained to use them at the Louvre while Mazarin and Colbert were insisting on the continuing use of precedents set by earlier architects.

Service buildings: These were constructions provided separate from a main *corps de logis* to provide such service as stabling – for horses and carriages – and kitchens. At Vaux-le-Vicomte, however, Le Vau provided the kitchens in an extensive basement under the palace, lit by half-windows at the level of the surrounding platform inside the moats, to enable quick access to the recent device of a separate dining area. At Versailles, the kitchens and stables were modified with an extra storey under high roofs to provide courtiers in residence with accommodation. Their kitchens were later provided in Hardouin-Mansart's *Grand Commun*, now the chateau's administrative centre, and where the *Centre de recherche* is housed under the eaves.

Triple-arched exit or entry: This feature of three linked arches became something of a trademark for Le Vau, frequently used by him on *corps de logis* and service buildings alike.

Trophies: Sculpted representations of armour, weaponry and battle standards taken from defeated enemies used on the roofline at Versailles by Le Vau and the King to complement the flaming urns.

Voussures: painted, stuccoed, arc-shaped structures placed over the right angles between walls and ceilings in interiors.

Acknowledgements

This book came about by means of felicitous chance: an encounter with Mme Sarah Bakkali in the *Librairie des Princes*, the bookshop in the Palace of Versailles, where she was on duty one day in September 2019. I asked her for two biographies, one of André Le Nôtre, architect of garden spaces, and the other of Louis Le Vau, architect of buildings. She replied that the splendid life of the former by Patricia Bouchenot-Déchin was readily available, but the latter was waiting for an author.

Amused and with my tongue in my cheek, I offered my services. Mme Bakkali, a post-graduate student specialising in the sale of art treasures from the palace after 1789, took me seriously. She introduced me to Mme Marie-Laetitia Lachèvre, in charge of the Curators' Library, housed on the third floor of Jules Hardouin-Mansart's imposing *Grand Commun*, which a few years ago became the administrative centre for the chateau. I was given a place at a table in the reading room presided over by Mme Quitterie Pruvost, and access to published monographs on Le Vau by historians of art and architecture in Europe.

I was befriended by M. Gérard Robaut, who was until his retirement *Responsable, Affaires Générales et Bibliothèque* in the *Centre de recherche du château de Versailles* (CRCV). Such privileged conditions have led to what is contained between these covers. Needless to say, any emergent mistakes are my own.

Many people have assisted in the gestation of this work. A fellow researcher in the Curators' Library has been Dr Susan Taylor-Leduc, who has been ready to discuss many aspects of seventeenth-century culture in France with me and provide essential indications about the way things were developing. Henrietta Hopkins has been willing, despite the demands of her professional preoccupations, to read several versions of my text as they emerged and to continue to act as my adviser on style and presentation.

During and after my visit to Beaumont-la-Ferrière in the Nivernais, the Maire of the Commune, M. René Nicard, and members of his staff – in particular Mme Melina Genty – put themselves out to answer my questions. They provided the e-mail address of M. Jean-Michel Canales, who put me in touch with the proprietors of what was Le Vau's manor house, Mr and Mrs Robert Whitaker, who live in the United States of America and are very sensitive towards Le Vau and what he tried to achieve in the last six years of his life. Mrs Whitaker has provided me with photographs of the domain and made exchanges in a friendly correspondence by e-mail. M. Guillaum Pigoury, on whose farmland traces of Le Vau's efforts are to be found, introduced me to his father, M. Guy Pigoury, who generously drove me round the various sites of the mines and forges and offered explanations of their exploitation in Le Vau's time and subsequently. Mme Myriam Bernard-Lavïe, at the *Archives Départmentales* in Nevers, pointed me towards Gaston Gauthier's important monograph on the village dating from 1892 available on the website Gallica of the *Bibliothèque française Nationale*. Thanks are also due to the staff at the *Bibliothèque de l'Hôtel de Ville de Paris* and at the *Archives nationales françaises* for allowing me access to their collections.

The staff at the bookshop in the Château de Vincennes were very ready to answer my question and to offer me several pointers at an early stage in my search for Louis Le Vau. A friendly letter from the co-proprietor of the Château de Vaux-le-Vicomte, M. Alexandre de Vogüé, gave me much encouragement to continue with the project at what could well have been a dead-end time.

I would like to express my gratitude to Dr Antoine Dubray-Vautrin and Dr Sophie Beaucaire-Danel, with their teams under the umbrella of the Marie-Curie Institute in Paris and at Saint-Cloud, who have, by their care and skill during the last four years, made it possible for this octogenarian to complete his book, and perhaps go on afterwards to new literary pasture.

The commissioning editor at Pen and Sword, Dr Lester Crook, has been – as ever – supportive and watchful over my interests, as have Mr Charles Hewitt, the Managing Director of Pen & Sword and all the staff concerned in the stages of the book's production, especially Ms Harriet Fielding, Mr Jon Wilkinson, who designed the book's jacket, and Mr Mat Blurton who designed the book layout and illustration pages.

My dear friend Lucie has been my sternest and most constructive critic, ready to discuss every aspect of the book as it arose across the barrier of language, and to arrange and make possible the necessary visits.

Richard Ballard, Versailles.

Notes

Unless otherwise stated, translations of French texts made in these chapters are by the author.

Articles without an internet reference attached were provided by courtesy of the Conservators' Library at the Château de Versailles housed in the Grand Commun. Those having an internet reference were obtained for the author by the generosity of the librarian.

Preface
1. See below, pp. 173–174.
2. William Doyle, *The Old European Order 1660–1800*, Oxford, 1978, p.86; Claire Goldstein, *Vaux and Versailles, The Appropriations, Erasures and Accidents that made Modern France*, Philadelphia, 2008, pp.4 & 34.
3. Alexandre Cojannot, *Louis Le Vau et les nouveaux ambitions de l'architecture française 1612–1654*, Paris, 2012, p.15.
4. Cyril Bordier, *Louis Le Vau, Architecte. Les immeubles et hôtels particuliers parisiens, Tome I*, Paris, 1998, p.136.
5. Alexandre Gady, *Jacques Lemercier, architecte et ingénieur du Roi*, Paris, 2005, p.88. Alexandre Cojannot and Alexandre Gady, *Les appartements du Louvre au lendemain de la Fronde (1652–1654): de Jacques Lemercier à Louis Le Vau, Revue de l'art*, no. 142, 2003–4, p.17.
6. Hilary Ballon, *Louis Le Vau, Mazarin's College, Colbert's Revenge*, Princeton NJ, 1999, pp.122–126.
7. *London Review of Books*, 27 August 2017.
8. *Art and Architecture in France: 1500–1700*, Second Edition, Harmondsworth, 1970, p.116.

Chapter 1
1. Hilary Ballon, *The Paris of Henri IV, Architecture and Urbanism*, Cambridge MA and London, 1991, p.88.
2. Ibid., pp.68–69.
3. Ibid., p.98.
4. Ibid., p.138.
5. Cyril Bordier, *Louis Le Vau, Tome I, Les immeubles et hôtels particuliers parisiens*, Paris, 1988, p.40.
6. Hilary Ballon, ibid., p.145.
7. Françoise Bayard, *Le monde des financiers au XVIIe siècle*, Paris, 1988, pp.310 & 368.
8. Ibid., p.357.
9. Maurice Dumolin, *Études topographiques parisiennes*, Tome III, Paris, 1931, pp.4–17.

10. Françoise Bayard, *op. cit.*, p.369.
11. AN, CXVII, 494, cited in Cojannot.
12. Cojannot, p.15.
13. See the family tree, Cojannot, p.341.
14. J.-J. Letrait, *La communaute des maitres maçons de Paris au XVIIe et au XVIIIe siècles (Premiere partie), Revue historique de droit française et étranger (1922–), Quatriène série*, Vol. 23, (1943), pp.217–223. Source: Jstor, www.jstor.org/stable/43814201
15. *Histoire et recherches des antiquités de Paris*, Paris 1724, tome III, p.13.
16. Cojannot, p.18.
17. *Manière de bien bastir pour touttes sortes de personnes*, cited in Hilary Ballon, p.162, although it is noted that what he had in his library at his death in 1670 was the second edition of 1647.
18. The notion of intellectual property was unknown at this time, and architects were notorious as imitators of each other's work.
19. Cojannot, p.20.
20. As shown in the first floor plan, Cojannot, p.25.
21. Cojannot, p.28.
22. Hilary Ballon, pp.154 & 156. It would be interesting to know how he got on with writers like Jean de La Fontaine, Jean Pellisson or Madeleine de Scudéry while he was working at Saint-Mandé and Vaux-le-Vicomte for Nicolas Fouquet in the late 1650s.
23. Cojannot, p.36.
24. M. Dumolin, *op. cit.*, p.172. Cojannot, p.37.
25. Cojannot, pp.38–42, with the author's photographs.
26. G. Tallemant des Réaux, *Historiettes*, Paris, éd. 1960–61, tome II, p.737, cited by Cojannot, p.43.
27. Cojannot, pp.48–55.
28. Cojannot, pp.55–60.
29. But see Cyril Bordier, *Louis Le Vau, Tome I, Les immeubles et hôtels particuliers parisiens*, Paris, 1998, p.72. n. 18, where the claim is made that Louis Le Veau bought the title for both his sons.
30. *Dictionnaire françois contenant les mots et les choses, plusieurs nouvelles, remarqes sur la langue françoise, etc*, 2 vols, Genève, 1680. Source: gallica.bnf.fr Cojannot, p.61.
31. Cojannot, pp.61–64.
32. Cojannot, p.69.
33. Cojannot, pp.167–169 & footnotes.

Chapter 2
1. Daniel Dessert, *Le royaume de Monsieur Colbert*, Paris, 2007, p.85.
2. Daniel Dessert, Jean-Louis Journet, *Le lobby Colbert: un royaume ou une affaire de famille?* In : *Annales, Économies, sociétés, civilisations , 30ᵉ année*, No. 6, 1975, p.1303. www.persee.fr/doc/ahess_0395-2649_1975_num_30_6_293680
3. Emmanuel Le Roy Ladurie, *The Ancien Régime, A History of France, 1610–1774*, ET Mark Greengrass, Oxford, 1996, pp.70–73.
4. Françoise Bayard, *Le monde des financiers au XVIIe siècle*, Paris, 1988, pp.104 & 108–114.
5. Ibid., pp.146–154.
6. Ibid., p.156.
7. Ibid., p.276.
8. Reproduced in Cojannot, 2012, as fig.129, p.191.

9. Ibid., pp.187–209.
10. Ibid., p.171.
11. Bayard, 1988, p.305.
12. Ibid., p.339.
13. Ibid., p.345.
14. Ibid., p.372.
15. Ibid., p.397.
16. Ibid., p.401.
17. Cojannot, 2012, p.286.
18. See above, p.
19. Cojannot, 2012, pp.220–225.
20. François de la Maureyre, *Le goût artistique d'un grand financier au XVIIe siècle: Jacques Bordier*, La tribune de l'art.com, vendredi 14 juin 2014.
21. Bayard, 1988, pp.421–436.
22. Cojannot, 2012, p.225.
23. Cyril Bordier, *Louis Le Vau les immeubles et hôtels particuliers parisiens*, Tome I, Paris 1998, p.
24. Bayard, 1988, pp.402–437.
25. Ibid., p.437.
26. Cojannot, 2012, p.171.
27. G,.Patin, *Lettres (1613–1672)*, ed., Paul Triaire, Paris, 1907, pp.449–450, cited by Cojannot, *Louis Le Vau*, p.172.
28. Dietrich Feldmann, *Maison Lambert, Maison Hesselin und anderen Bauten von Louis Le Vau auf der Ils Saint-Louis, thèse polycopiée*, Hamburg, 1976, cited by Cojannot, 2012, p.172.
29. Cojannot, 2012, p.34, n.2.
30. Nicole Bourdel, *Nouveaux documents sur Louis Le Vau premier architecte de Louis XIV 1612 1670, Paris et Ile de France, Mémoires de la fédération des sociétés historiques,* Tome VIII, 1956, bibliofranciscaine.capucins@orange.fr cote Rev. 85 B, pp.223–224.
31. Cojannot, 2012, pp.170–175.
32. Cyril Bordier, *Louis Le Vau, les immeubles et hôtels particuliers parisiens, Tome I*, Paris 1998, p.136.
33. AN, MC, CV – 405, 11 October 1640, cited by Bordier, p.136.
34. Bordier, p.139.
35. *Art and Architecture in France: 1500–1700*, second edition, Harmondsworth 1970, p.136.
36. Bordier, p.147.
37. Dietrich Feldmann, *Jardins suspendus dans quelques hôtels parisiens du XVIIe siècle. Bulletin de la société de l'histoire et de l'art française*, 1992, (1993), pp.1–20.
38. Ibid. It is important to realise that M. Bordier is qualified as an architect as well as a historian.
39. Bordier, pp.153–154.
40. Frédérique Lemerle & Yves Pauwels, *L'architecture au temps du baroque 1600–1750*, Paris, 2008, p.118.
41. Reproduced in Blunt: Plate 104(B).
42. Blunt, Plate 105(A).
43. Ibid., p.138.
44. Bordier, p.182,
45. Cojannot, *Louis Le Vau*, p.104.

46. Like those to be seen in Le Vau's later creation at Vaux-le-Vicomte.
47. Marie-Thérèse Glass-Forest, Grove Art Online, 2003, ad. loc.
48. Alexandre Cojannot, *Le bas-relief à l'antique dans l'architecture parisienne du XVIIe siècle: du Louvre de François Sublet de Noyers à celui de Jean-Baptiste Colbert*, Studiolo, 2002 1, pp.20–40.
49. *Histoire et recherches des antiquités de la ville de Paris*, Tome III, Paris, 1724, p.14.
50. See the reconstructions in Bordier, p.181.
51. Alexandre Gady, *Les hôtels particuliers de Paris du moyen-age à la belle époque*, Paris, 2008, pp.61 & 72.
52. Hautecœur, *Histoire, Tome II*, pp.91–93.
53. Cojannot, p.58.
54. Volume III, p.51, cited in R. de Crèvecœur, *Louis Hesselin, Amateur parisien, Intendant des plaisirs du roi 1600?–1662, Extraît des Mémoires de la Société de l'Histoire de Paris et de l'Île de France*, t. XXII, 1895, pp.6–7. Source: gallica.bnf.fr.
55. Crèvecoeur, p.10.
56. *Mémoires de Mlle de Montpensier, petite-fille de Henri IV collatonnés sur le manuscri authophraphe, avec notes biograpshoques et historiqes par A. Chéruel*, Paris, 1858, Tome II, p.430, Source: gallica.bnf.fr
57. *Gazette*, 26 August 1656.
58. *Relation de ce qui est passé à l'arrivée de la reine Christine de Suède à Essaune ... ensemble le descripton particulière du ballet ... et un panégyrique latin sur l'entrée de cette princesse à Paris ...*, Paris, Robert Ballard, cited by Crèvecœur, pp.16–18.
59. *Mémoires de Mademoiselle de Montpensier, tome 3,* Paris, 1746, p.189 *et suiv.* Cited in Verena von der Heeyden-Rynsch, *Christine de Suède, La souveraine énigmatique*, Paris, 2001, p.128.
60. Louis Hautecœur, *Histoire de l'architecture classique en France*, 9 volumes, Paris, 1943–1957, Volume II, p.89.
61. Crèvecœur, p.19.
62. Crèvecœur, pp.20–21.

Chapter 3

1. François Aubert, *Colbert, La vertu usurpée*, Paris, 2010, pp.46–55.
2. Jean Cordey, *Colbert, Le Vau et la construction du château de Vincennes au XVIIme siècle, Gazette des Beaux-Arts*, 75me année, 6me période, Tome 9me, 1933, pp.273–293. Alain Erlande-Brandenburg and Bertrand Jestac, *Le Château de Vincennes*, Paris, 1989, pp.76–77.
3. Hilary Ballon, *Louis Le Vau, Mazarin's College Colbert's Revenge*, Princeton, 1999, pp.19–23.
4. Cardinal de Retz was kept in the *donjon* after the Fronde until 1654. Spanish prisoners of war would be brought there even later.
5. Alexandre Gady, *Jacques Lemercier, Architecte et ingénieur du roi*, Paris, 2005, p.57, n. 288, citing *A.N., O^{1*} 2387, État des gages des officiers (1605–1656) publiés dans les Nouvelles arcives de l'art français, année 1871 dans forme de liste alphabetique, fol 100*.
6. François de Fossa, *Le château historique de Vincennes à travers les âges, Monographie des bâtiments du château*, Paris, 1908, http://gallica.bnf.fr/ark:/12148/btp63746057, pp.201–202.
7. Alain Erlande-Brandenburg & Bertrand Jestac, *Le château de Vincennes*, Paris, 1989, pp.80–81.
8. Cordey, 1933, p.273.

9. De Fossa, 1908, p.202.
10. Cordey, 1933, p.278.
11. Paris, 1788, t. II, pp.74–106, by courtesy of *Centre de recherche du château de Versailles*.
12. Philip Mansel, *King of the World, the Life of Louis XIV*, London, 2019, p.87.
13. e.g., Philip Mansel, 2019, p.74, and Erlande-Brandenburg/Bertrand Jestac, 1989, pp.97–98.
14. De Fossa, 1908, p.206.
15. Grove Art Online, *ad loc.*
16. De Fossa, 1908, pp.207–210.
17. Jean Cordey, 1933, p.284.
18. Jal., *ad loc.*
19. Nicole Bourdel, *Nouveau documents sur Louis Le Vau Premier architecte de Louis XIV, 1612–1670, Paris et île de France mémoires, Tome VIII*, 1956, p.220.
20. Grove Art Online, *ad loc.*
21. Erlande-Brandenburg/Bertrand Jestac, 1989, pp.111–112.
22. Hilary Ballon, 1999, p.25.
23. Claude Dulong, *Les signes cryptiques sans la correspondance d'Anne d'Autriche avec Mazarin, contribution à l'emblématique du XVIIme siècle, Bibliothèque d'école des chartes, 1982, tome 140, livraison 1*, pp.61–83.
24. De Fossa, 1908, p.220.
25. Jean Cordey, 1933, pp.287–288.
26. They were taken away in the alterations to the ramparts under Louis Philippe between 1831 and 1844, when the glacis was added to the ramparts: See de Fossa, p.257, who also gives an illustration of eight of the statues, p.259.
27. Hilary Ballon, 1999, p.25.
28. This may be additional evidence for ascribing the initial idea for the eastern colonnade of the Louvre to Le Vau's design rather than to Claude Perrault's. See Chapter 6.
29. Mémoires intérressans, t. II, p.139.
30. Jean Cordey, 1933, p.283.
31. Vincent Cronin, *Louis XIV*, London, 1965, p.78.
32. Alexandre Cojannot, *Un sérail pour le Cardina Mazarin, Louis Le Vau et l'adaptation du Serraglio de Leoni de Florence à Vincennes, Annali di architettura*, no. 21, 2009, pp.151–168. halshs-00769262
33. A plan dated 1694 is reproduced in Jean Cordey, 1933, p.291.
34. 2009, p.168. halshs-00769262
35. Alexandre Cojannot, 2009, p.168.

Chapter 4

1. Alexandre Cojannot & Alexandre Gady, *Les appartements du Louvre au lendemain de la Fronde: de Jacques Lemercier et Louis Le Vau, Revue de l'art*. No. 142, 2003/4, pp.13–29.
2. Louis Hautecœur, *Le Louvre et les Tuileries de Louis XIV*, Paris and Brussels, 1927.
3. Cojannot/Gady, *Les appartements*, p 15 gives references.
4. Henri Sauval, *Histoire et recherches des antiquités de la ville de Paris*, 1724, t. ii, p.34.
5. Alexandre Gady, *Jacques Lemercier, Architecte et Ingénieur du roi*, Paris, 2005, pp 67 & 347.
6. Cojannot/Gady, *Les appartements*, n. 50.
7. Ibid., p.13, n. 59.
8. Reproduced in Jennifer Montagu, *The Early Ceiling Decorations of Charles Le Brun*, The Burlington Magazine, 1963, p.401, cited by Cojannot/Gady, n. 70.

9. AN Min. centr., ét XCVI, 62 23 juin 1654 and ét XCVI 63 8 et 14 août 1654, cited by Cojannot/Gady.
10. Ashmolean Museum, Oxford, *Album Cotelle*, fol. 12.
11. Michel Fleury & Venceslas Kruta, *Le Château du Louvre*, Paris, 1989, p.4.
12. Jean-Pierre Babelon, *Les travaux de Henri VI au Louvre et aux Tuileries dans Paris et l'Ile de France, mémoires de la Fédération des sociétés historiques et archéologiques de Paris et de l'Ile de France*, t. 29,1978, pp.50–130. cited by Cojannot, p.133 n. 1.
13. Alexandre Cojannot, *Mazarin et le 'grand dessein' du Louvre, projets et réalisations*, Bibliothèque de l'École des chartes, t. 161, 2003, pp.133–219.
14. Ibid.
15. Cojannot, 2003, p.137 n.18.
16. Cojannot, 2003, nn. 25, 26 & 27.
17. Ibid., n. 28.
18. Ibid., p.140, n. 29.
19. Ibid., n. 30.
20. Alain Merot, *Eustache le Sueur*, Paris 1987, cited by Cojannot, 2003, p.141.
21. Two of Le Brun's preparatory drawings for this have been preserved and exhibited at Versailles in 1963: Jennifer Montagu, *The Early Ceiling Decorations of Charles Le Brun*, The Burlington Magazine, 1963, pp.395–408.
22. Cojannot, 2003, p.143.
23. Madeleine Laurain-Portemer, *Opposition et propagande à Paris en 1654*, in Études mazarines, t.1. Paris, 198, pp.155–174, cited by Cojannot 2000, p.143.
24. Ibid., Letter to Mazarin, July 1654, a sentiment echoed by Henri Sauval in 1724.
25. Ibid., pp.145–146 citing a letter of 1 February from Mazarin to Nicolas Fouquet, n. 46.
26. The famous Turgot Map, made up of detailed drawings of the capital's buildings in 1734–1736, shows that the Hôtel de Longueville was still standing at that late date.
27. Dietrich Feldmann, *Jardins suspendus dans quelques hôtels parisiens du XVIIe siècle*, Bulletin de la Société de l'histoire de l'art française, 1992, p.12 cited by Cojannot.
28. Cojannot, 2003, p.149, n. 72.
29. Ibid., p.152.
30. Poncet de la Grave, *Mémoires interessans pour servir à l'histoire de France ou tableau historique, chronologique, pittoresque ecclesiastique civil et militaire des Maisons royales, Châteaux et Parcs des Rois de France*, t. II, Paris, 1788, pp.90–118.
31. Louis Hautecœur, *Le Louvre et les Tuileries*, 1927, p.102.
32. Cojannot, 2003, p.156.
33. AN Cartes et plans, F21 3567, pièce 8, repr., ibid., p.157 Fig. 4.
34. Cojannot, 2003, p.158 citing AN O1 1669 no. 402.
35. Daniel Dessert, *Le royaume de Monsieur Colbert*, Paris, 2007, pp.171–172.
36. Inès Murat, *Colbert*, p.164. But see R.W. Berger, *A Royal Passion*, Cambridge, 1944, p.20, where it is claimed that Colbert bought the superintendency from Ratabon.
37. Daniel Dessert, *op. cit.*, p.172.

Chapter 5
1. His son's enemies altered this satirically to *Quo non ascendam* (How far won't I climb?).
2. Daniel Dessert, *Fouquet*, Paris, 2015, pp.23–52.
3. Hilary Ballon, *Vaux-le-Vicomte, Le Vau's Ambition*, in Mirka Benes and Dianne Harris, *The Villas and Gardens of Early Modern Italy and France*, Cambridge, 2001, p.274.
4. André Perraud-Charmentier, *Acquisition par Nicolas Fouquet à Mme de Lyonne de l'étang do Vaux,*, Bulletin de l'association des amis de vieux Maincy, 1983, p.135, n. 1.

5. Phrase of Yves-Marie Bercé.
6. Ulysse Robert, *Notice historique dur Saint-Mandé, Nouvelle Edition*, Saint-Mande, 1901, pp.69–72. Source: gallica.bnf.fr.
7. See above, pp.24–29
8. Jean Cordey, *Le château de Vaux-le-Vicomte, étude historique*, Paris, 1933, p.121.
9. André Perraud-Charmentier, 1983, pp.129–131.
10. Jean Cordey, 1933, ibid.
11. Jean Cordey, 1933, pp.118–122.
12. Jennifer Montague, *The Tapestries of Maincy and the Origin of the Gobelins*, Apollo, Vol. 77, 1962, pp.530–535.
13. Hilary Ballon, 2001, p.275.
14. Hilary Ballon, *Louis Le Vau, Mazarin's College, Colbert's Revenge*, pp.102 & 150–174.
15. Jean Cordey, 1933, p.124, author's translation.
16. Ibid.
17. According to the Inventory made after Le Vau's death, 27 November 16, AN S 6506, cited in J.-M. Pérouse de Montclos, *Le château de Vaux-le-Vicomte*, Paris, 1997, p.55, n.10.
18. Hilary Ballon, 2001, p.276.
19. Pérouse de Montclos, 1997, p.66.
20. Jean Cordey, 1933, p.129.
21. Jean Cordey, 1933, p.139.
22. *Vaux-le-Vicomte, Le Vau's Ambition*, in *Villas and Gardens* in *Early Modern Italy and France*, ed., Mirka Benes and Dianne Harris, Cambridge, 2001, pp.292–293. Such a contrast with the disparaging comment made by Sir Reginald Blomfield eighty years before: 'The whole thing is overdone.' *A History of French Architecture from the Death of Mazarin till the Death of Louis XV 1661–1774*, London, 1921, p.58.
23. Inès Murat, *Colbert*, pp.77–78.
24. J.-C. Petitfils, *Fouquet*, p.184.
25. This aspect of Vaux is developed by Perouse de Montclose on pp.32–33 of his book.
26. Jean-Christian Petitfils, *Fouquet*, Paris, 1998, p.172.
27. Jean Cordey, 1933, p.139.
28. Jean Cordey, 1933, p.132.
29. See above, p.. The historian/architect Cyril Bordier provided vivid illustrations of the way in which the oval salon was constructed in a lecture given online in November 2014, *Vaux-le-Vicomte, génése d'un chef d'oeuvre*, www.franceculture.fr/conferences/ecole-national-superieure-d'architecture-paris-val-de-seine/conference-cyril-bordier
30. Yvan Christ, *Le Louvre et les Tuileries, Histoire architecturale d'un double palais*, Paris, 1949, p.69.
31. Claire Goldstein, *Vaux and Versailles, The Appropriations, Erasures and Accidents That Made Modern France*, Philadelphia, 2008, p.21.
32. Andrew Zega and Bernd H. Dams, *Palaces of the Sun King*, New York, 2006, p.23.
33. Hilary Ballon, 2001, pp.289–290. Mrs Ballon had developed her comparison with Maisons in an earlier article, *actes du colloque*, translated into French by Denis Griesmar, in a *Numéro spécial de la revue anuell piblié par la Société des Amis du Château des Maisons, Le Cahier de Maisons*, Nos. 27–28, December 1999, Dir. Iléana de Vogüé, 78600 Maisons-Lafitte.
34. Jennifer Montague, *The Expression of the Passions; the Origin and Influence of Charles Le Brun's Conférence sur l'expression générale et particulière*, New Haven and London, 1994, p.40.

35. Eugene Guédy, 1858, p.5.
36. Andrew Zega and Bernt H. Dams, *op. cit.*, p.23.
37. Bénédicte Gady and Juliette Trey, *La France vue du grand siècle. Dessins d'Israël Silvestre (1621–1691)*, Paris 2018, pp.11–15 and 70–75.
38. Hilary Ballon, 2001, p.278.
39. Eugène Grésy, *Documents sur les artistes, peintre, sculpteurs tapissiers et autres qui ont travaillé au château de Vau le Vicomte pour le surintandant Fouquet, d'aprés les registres de la paroisse de Maincy*, in *Archives de l'art français, recueil de documents inédits relatifs à l'histoire des arts en France, Tome VI*, 1858, p.7.
40. Was Mme Le Vau there too? Le Vau – for reasons hardly understood – always seems effaced as a character in the story.
41. Jennifer Montague, *The Tapestries of Maincy and the Origin of the Gobelins*, Apollo, Vol. 77, 1962, pp.530–535.
42. Jean Cordey, *La manufacture de tapisseries de Maincy*, Bulletin de la societé de l'art française, 1922, pp.45–47.
43. Colbert's father, like Fouquet's, had chosen to make his armorial device out of a play on words. The *couleuvre* (Latin *colubra*) is a grass snake, not venomous in its French version but with a nasty bite, nevertheless. Daniel Dessert, *Le royaume de Monsieur Colbert*, Paris, 2007, p.84.
44. Claire Goldstein, *Vaux and Versailles, The Appropriations, Erasures and Accidents That Made Modern France*, Philadelphia PA, 2008, pp.65–97.
45. See Gilles Becdelièvre, *Le jeu de la haine*, Paris, 2014.
46. *Mémoires de L'abbé de Choisy, mémoires pour servir à l'histoire de Louis XIV*, ed., Georges Mongrédien, Paris, 1979, pp.91–103.
47. Daniel Dessert, *Le royaume de Monsieur Colbert*, Paris, 2007, pp.24–26.
48. Quoted in Yves-Marie Bercé, *L'affaire Fouquet dans l'opinion de son temps et sous le regard des historiens*, Le Fablier, Revue des amis de Jean de La Fontaine, no. 5, 1993, p.37. www.persee.fr/doc/lefab_09966560_1993_num_5_1_935
49. Ibid.
50. Choisy. p.91.
51. Inès Murat, *Colbert*, Paris, 1980, pp.82–83.
52. Vincent J. Pitts, *Embezzlement and Treason in Louis XIV's France*, Baltimore, 2015, pp.48–49.
53. Inès Murat, *Colbert*, p.84.
54. Ibid., pp.93–99.
55. Daniel Dessert, *Le royaume de Monsieur Colbert*, Paris 2007, pp.122–123.
56. This threat was taken seriously in view of Fouquet's other commercial interests and military potential. He had invested in port facilities on the Île d'Yeu, and at Concarnet as well as Belle-Île. He maintained a fishing fleet in the waters off Newfoundland, had trading ventures in the Orient, and his Atlantic activities were not limited to the French Caribbean islands. He had interests in Canada. All these were private, not national, enterprises. He was also accused of planning an armed rebellion in Brittany in case of his arrest. Bercé, *op. cit.*, p.41.
57. R.W. Berger, *A Royal Passion, Louis XIV as Patron of Architecture*, Cambridge, 1994, p.18.
58. *Oeuvres complètes de La Fontaine, Tome II*, Paris 1875, p.387, cited by Chares Drazin, *The Man who Outshone the Sun King, the Rise and Fall of Nicolas Fouquet*, London, 2008, p.224.
59. Choisy, p.95.
60. Brienne, ed.,1828, Tome II, p.208.

61. Brienne, ed.,1828, Tome II, p.208.
62. Ibid., pp.38 & 39.
63. Georges Bordonove, *Foucquet, Coupable ou victime?*, Paris, 1976, p.287.
64. Loménie de Brienne, *Mémoires*, pp.203–213.
65. Bercé, *op. cit.*, p.42.

Chapter 6
1. Yvan Christ, *Le Louvre et les Tuileries, histoire architecturale e'un double palais*, Paris, 1949.
2. Lucien Bély, *1661 la prise de pouvoir par Louis XIV, La rupture de 1661*, in *Actes de la XVIIIe session du Centre d'Etudes historiques*, Neuves Maisons, 2011, p.18.
3. Daniel Dessert, *Le Royaume de Monsieur Colbert (1661–1683)*. Paris, 2007, p.222, his italics.
4. Françoise Bayard, *Le monde des financiers au XVIIe siècle,* Paris, 1988, p.271.
5. Inès Murat, *Colbert*, Paris, 1980, pp.58–60. Daniel Dessert, *Royaume*, pp.205–22.
6. Robert W. Berger, *A Royal Passion, Louis XIV as Patron of Architecture*, Cambridge, 1994, p.40.
7. Louis XV had this destroyed to allow the provision of some small rooms for his own use.
8. Berger *op. cit.*, p.41.
9. Alain Erlande-Brandenburg, *Les foules du Louvre dt les projets de Le Vau, La Vie urbaine*, December 1964, fasciscule 4. p.263.
10. Louis Hautecœur, *L'histoire des châteaux du Louvre et des Tuileries*, Paris & Brussels, 1927, pp.143–164, & Mary Whiteley and Allan Braham, *Louis Le Vau's Projects for the Louvre and the Colonnade, Gazette des Beaux-Arts,* t. 64, 1964, p.286.
11. Reproduced as Fig. 26 of R.W. Berger, *A Royal Passion*, p.39, and exhibited in situ.
12. Anthony Blunt, *Art and Architecture in France 1500–1700*, Second Edition, Harmondsworth, 1970, p.198, n. 9, following M. Dumolin, Études topographiques parisiennes, Paris, 1931, t. II, p.194.
13. Chantelou, *Journal de voyage du Cavalier Bernin en France*, ed., Milovan Slanić, Paris, 2001, p.218.
14. Alexandre Cojannot, *Antonio Maurizio Valperga, architecte du Cardinal Mazarin à Paris, Paris et Île de France,* t. 54, 2003, pp.33–60.
15. Rudolf Wittkower, *Gian Lorenzo Bernini, The Sculptor of the Roman Baroque*, London, 1966, pp.30–31.
16. *L'histoire des châteaux*, p.155.
17. Chantelou, *Journal de voyage*, ed Milovan Stanić, 2001, p.45.
18. Chantelou, 2001, pp.388–389.
19. Ibid., pp.127–128.
20. Ibid., p.229. Cruder translations of the Italian for this have been suggested involving the French word *décrotter*.
21. *E bello, c'è abbondanza senza confusione, Journal de voyage, du cavalier Bernin en France,* ed., Milovan Stanić, Paris, 2001, p.248, n. 1, p.337. Fouquet's arrest prevented the design being carried out, and the interior of the dome remained and remains blank.
22. Chantelou's *Journal* is well supplied with Bernini's remarks against these, his opponents, who would, in the end, be themselves the providers of the Louvre Colonnade on Colbert's own instructions.
23. *Voyage de France, mœurs et coutumes françaises (1664–1665) traduit sur les manuscrits autographes et publiés avec un introduction et desnotes par Adolphe Vautier,* Pris, 1905, pp.124–127.

24. He claimed its name was derived from '*L'Œuvre*', because it would take until the end of the world to finish it. It really referred to the wolves who were still about in Philippe Auguste's reign.
25. Phrase evidently in use by this Italian voyager in France 250 years before Rudyard Kipling's elephant received its trunk.
26. Chantelou, 2001, pp.97–99.
27. Ibid., pp.149–150.
28. AV Luke 23,12. The nuncio, of course, quoted from the Vulgate.
29. Alexandre Maral, *Le Roi Soleil et Dieu*, Paris, 2012, p.129. This conclusion will be discussed later in connection with the Versailles *enveloppe*.
30. Ibid., p.164.
31. Louis-Alexandre de Bourbon, son of Louis XIV and Mme de Montespan, born 1678 at Versailles, and legitimised as comte de Toulouse in 1681.
32. *Description historique de la ville de Paris, 1765, t.* II, pp.252–264.
33. As excavations showed in 1964, these new foundations were inside those that Le Vau had laid in 1664 and which Bernini found fault with: Alain Erlande Brandenburg, *Les fouilles du Louvre et les projets de Le Vau, La vie urbaine, décembre 1964, fascicule 4*.
34. Louis Hautecœur, *L'auteur de la colonnade du Louvre, Gazette des Beaux-Arts, 66me année, 5me période, tome 9me*, 1924, pp.167–168.
35. *Louis Le Vau's Projects for the Louvre and the Colonnade, Gazatte des Beaux-Arts, t.* 64, 1964, II, pp.347, 354 & 358–359.
36. The opinion persists into Philip Mansel's *King of the World, The Life of Louis XIV*, London, 2019, p.135.
37. Anthony Blunt expressed his agreement with the judgement made by Whiteley and Braham in his second edition of *Art and Architecture in France* (1970), p.198, n.22.
38. Whiteley and Braham, 1964, p.360.
39. See below, Chapter 11.
40. *Les Contes de ma mère L'Oye* (Tales of Mother Goose), 1697.
    As this book was nearing completion, the fascinating work by Christopher Tadgell, *The Louvre and Versailles, The Evolution of the Proto-typical Palace in the Age of Absolutism*, Abingdon, 2020, was brought to my notice by the librarians at the *Centre de Recherche du Château de Versailles*. Mr Tadgell asserts that, at this juncture in the design and construction of the Louvre (pp.133–143), there was major input concerning the interior of the eastern front, once it had been doubled with an *enfilade* by Louis Le Vau – while Louis was still involved though often absent from 1668 onwards – by his younger brother François, who would be a leading light in the Academy of Architecture founded four years later.

Chapter 7

1. R.W. Berger, *Versailles, the Château of Louis XIV*, Philadelphia and London, 1985, p.1.
2. Jean-Marie Pérouse de Montclos, *Histoire de l'architecture française: de la Renaissance à la Revolution*, Paris, 1996, pp.271–301.
3. As, for instance, in *Versailles, Architectures revées, 1660–1815*, an exhibition at the Château, 2019. See also, Alexandre Gady *(sous la direction de), Jules Hardouin-Mansart: Le Chantier infini, Actes du colloque international Jules Hardouin-Mansart*, Paris, 2019.
4. Pérouse de Montclos, *Ibid.*, p.272.
5. Joan Pieragnou, *La Ménagerie de Versailles (1662–1789)*, Versalia, 2010, pp.173–195.
6. See Stephen Fry, *Mythos, the Greek Myths Retold*, London, 2018, pp.244–246.
7. Andrew Zega and Bernd H. Dams, *Palaces of the Sun King*, New York, 2006, pp.23–32.

8. Ibid.
9. Louis Hautecœur, *Louis XIV, Roi Soleil*, Paris, 1953, p.35.
10. Zega and Dams, *op. cit.*, p.26.
11. Ibid.
12. *Promenade de Versailles*, Paris, 1669, 95. Source: gallica.bnf.fr
13. Ibid., p.180.
14. Bernd H. Dams et Andrew Zega, *La Ménagerie de Versailles et le Trianon de Porcelain*, Versalia, No. 2, 1999, p.67.
15. Gérard Mabille, *La Menagerie de Versailles*, Gazette des Beaux-Arts, Supplēment 15, Chron., A.J.83 (1974), pp.5–23.
16. Béatrix Saule, *Trois aspects du premier ameublement du château de Versailles (Colloque Versailles*, September–October, 1985).
17. Lucy Norton, *The Sun King and his Loves*, London 1982, p.23.
18. Annick Heitzmann, Justine Vorenger et Julien Treuillot, *Fouilles archéologiques de la Grille royale du château de Versailles (2006)*, Versailles (CRCV), pp.2–5. http://doi.org/10.4000/crcv.10041
19. As seen in Patel's bird's-eye view painting of 1668.
20. Alfred Marie, *Le premier château de Versailles construit par Le Vau en 1664–65*, Bulletin de la société de l'histoire de l'art française, année 1952, p.52. For the Tallin Collection dating from cultural exchanges during the reign of Queen Christina, see https://ehne.fr/en/node/12221
21. Fiske Kimball, *The Genesis of the Château Neuf at Versailles 1668–1671, I, The Initial Project of Le Vau*, Gazette de Beaux-Arts 6e période, Tome xxxv, 91e année, 1949, pp.354–355. See also Robert W. Berger, *A Royal Passion, Louis XIV as Patron of Architecture*, Cambridge, 1994, p.64.
22. R.W. Berger, *Versailles, the Château of Louis XI*, Philadelphia & London, 1985, pp.2–3.
23. *La promenade de Versailles*, Paris, 1669.
24. Pérouse de Montclos, 1996, pp.273–276.
25. *Memoires de ma vie*, Paris, 1993, Appendix VI, p.259.
26. Kevin Orlin Johnson, *Il n'y a plus de Pyrenées. The iconography of the first Versailles of Louis XIV*, Bulletin monumental, tome 166, No. 4, année 2008, pp.305–313.
27. Pérouse de Montclos, 1996, p.275.
28. P. Clément, *Lettres Tome* v, no. 23 '*raisons générales*'.
29. Ibid.
30. Ibid., *Tome* v, No. 38.
31. Pérouse de Montclos, p.273. M. de Montclos asserts that, when Colbert had written to Bernini after his visit to Paris in 1665 to refuse his project for that work, he had told him that the King might have a future project in mind that might interest him, and asks whether this might have referred to Versailles. This would justify his '*pourquoi pas?*'
32. The other architects' submissions were lost in the fire at the Louvre in 1871.
33. Berger, *Versailles*, p.19.
34. Philippe Beaussant, *Louis XIV, Artiste*, Paris, 1999, pp.176–179.
35. Berger, *Versailles*, p.3.
36. Jean-Claude Le Guillou, *Le château neuf ou enveloppe de Versailles, conception et évolution du projet autonome 1668*–été 1670, Versalia, 2005, pp.112–133.
37. André Félibien, *Description sommaire du Chateau de Versailles*, Paris 1674, pp.21–32. Source: gallica.bnf.fr
38. Arch. Nat., H₃ 2845 presented by Alexandre Cojannot, À l'origine de l'*architecture de marbre sous Louis XIV: les projets de Louis Le Vau pour le collège Mazarin, le Louvre et Versailles (1662-1663)*, Revue de l'art, No. 169, 3me trimestre 2010, © CRCV.

39. J.-C. Le Guillou, *Avant la galerie des glaces: un project méconnu de Versailles*, Versalia, 2009, pp.97–112, esp., p.107, Fig. 12.
40. Félibien, *op. cit.*, p.97.
41. Pierre de Nolhac, *Histoire du Château de Versailles sous Louis XIV, Tome Premier*, Paris, 1911, pp.113–114.
42. Ibid., p.118.
43. The Gobelins was established by letters patent issued to Le Brun on 8 November 1663 as the *Manufacture des meubles de la Couronne*. Confirmation on a permanent basis was made in a royal edict subsequent to a visit by the King to the building in Paris on 15 October 1667. Le Brun designed a tapestry to commemorate the event.
44. Fiske Kimball, *The Genesis of the Château Neuf at Versailles 1668–1671 II*, contradicts Pierre de Nolhac's assertion that d'Orbay faithfully executed Le Vau's design inherited from him in the form of a sketch.
45. Albert Laprade, *François, D'Orbay*, Paris, 1960, p.130. Reviewed by Louis Hautecœur, *François d'Orbay*, in Journal des savants, 1960, p.61, www.persee.fr/doc/jds_0021-8103_1960_num_2_1_981
46. See Chapter 9, below.
47. Frédéric Tiberghien, *Versailles, le chantier de Louis XIV*, Paris, 2002 & 2006, pp.44–45.
48. 'Not unequal to many'. When a slogan was needed for the Hall of Mirrors, the King insisted that 'The King rules by himself' should be in French for all to read.
49. Pierre de Nolhac, pp.126–139.
50. Zega and Dams *op. cit.*, p.26 (cited above, pp.7–8) & 83.
51. Anthony Blunt, *Art and Architecture in France: 1500–1700*, Harmondsworth, second edition, 1970, p.201.
52. Alexandre Gady, *Versailles: la fabrique du chef d'oeuvre*, Paris, 2011, pp.41–42.
53. Pierre de Nolhac, *Histoire du Château de Versailles: Versailles sous Louis XIV, Tome Premier*, Paris, 1911, p.100.
54. Pierre de Nolhac, *op. cit.*, pp.106–108.
55. *La grotte de Thétis et le premier Versailles de Louis Le Vau, Art de France*, 1961, pp.133–148.
56. Daniel Dessert, *Fouquet*, p.308.
57. Guy Walton, *Versailles*, Harmondsworth, 1986, p.60.
58. Robert Graves, *The Twelve Caesars, Suetonius*, Harmondsworth, 1957, p.285. I am indebted to my friend Kenneth R. Hughes for this comment.
59. Claire Goldstein, *Vaux and Versailles, The Appropriations, Erasures and Accidents that made Modern France*, Philadelphia, 2008, pp.182–200.
60. Daniel Dessert, *Fouquet*, Paris, 2015, pp.131–144 & 188–189.
61. Ibid., p.144.
62. Claire Goldstein, *op. cit.*, p.182.
63. Ibid., p.189.
64. André Félibien, *Déscription de la grotte de Versailles*, Paris, 1672,, pp.6–7. Source: gallica.bnf.fr. Goldstein's translation, p.195.
65. Claire Goldstein, *op. cit.*, pp.200–203.
66. Robert W. Berger, *A Royal Passion*, p.69. See also, Jean-Marie Pérouse de Montclos, *De la Renaissance à la Révolution*, note beneath Fig. 327, p.295.
67. Alfred Marie, *Les Châteaux des rois de France*, Paris, 1954, p.25.
68. Zega and Dams, *op. cit.*, p.91.
69. Ibid., p.93.

Chapter 8

1. Inès Murat, Colbert, Paris, 1980, pp.85–86.
2. Poncet de La Grave, *Mémoires intéressans pour servir à l'histoire de France, Tome II*, Paris, 1788, pp.107–115. Source, *Bibliothèque de la Conservation du Château de Versailles*.
3. Hilary Ballon, *Louis Le Vau, Mazarin's College Colbert's Revenge*, Princeton NJ, 1999, pp.8–9.
4. Claude Dulong, *Les signes cryptiques dans la correspondance d'Anne d'Autriche avec Mazarin; contribution à l'emblèmatique du XVIIe siecle, Bibliothèque d'école des chartes*,1982, tome 140, *livraison* 1. Anne used to take Mazarin's letters to read in her oratory since that was the only place where she was not accompanied by her escort. Once, one of the letters was intercepted and read out in the *Parlement*, but, luckily, its content was purely political. In other letters, phrases such as 'yours to my last breath' were common enough (p.65).
5. Mme de Motteville, *Mémoires t. V*, p.101, Source: gallica.bnf.fr. W.H. Lewis, *Louis XIV, An Informal Portrait*, London, 1959, p.41.
6. Daniel Dessert, *Pouvoir et finance au XVIIe siècle: la fortune du Cardinal Mazarin Revue d'histoire moderne et contemporaine tome XXIII avril–juin 1976*, pp.164–165. Source: gallica.bnf.fr.
7. Ballon, *Louis Le Vau*, p.12.
8. Claude Dulong, *La Fortune de Mazarin*, Paris, 1990, pp.14–17.
9. Ibid., p.99.
10. Ibid., pp.57–62.
11. Claude Dulong, *Les origines du Collège des Quatre-Nations, Revue des sciences morales et politiques (Séance du lundi 13 mai 1996)*, p.247.
12. In his *Défences*, p.11, (Source: gallica.bnf.fr). Written while waiting for his trial, Nicolas Fouquet described Colbert pejoratively as Mazarin's '*domestique*', the word used for house servants.
13. Ballon, *Louis Le Vau*, p.14.
14. Ibid., pp.16–19.
15. Claude Dulong, *Les origines*, pp.149–250.
16. Ballon, *Louis Le Vau*, p.38, citing AN MM 462, fol 56v. 29 July 1662.
17. Ibid., p.39.
18. Alfred Franklin, *Recherches historiques sur le Collège de Quatre-Nations d'après des socuments entièrement inédits*, Paris, 1862, p.21 & n. 3. Source: gallica.bnf.fr.
19. Ballon, *Louis Le Vau*, pp.41–42.
20. Alfred Franklin, *Recherches historiques*, pp.18–24.
21. Ibid., pp.24–25.
22. These nieces were the daughters of Mazarin's sister, Girolama, who had been widowed in 1650. One of them had been the young Marie whose love match with the King was ended by her uncle before the Spanish marriage; another was Hortenzia, who married the son of Marshal de Meilleraye and nephew of Cardinal Richelieu, Armand de La Porte. He inherited from Mazarin the dukedom, which the King had granted him along with the revenues of Alsace. The King made the duchy hereditary in his line upon his marriage to Hortenzia when he agreed to take Mazarin's name. He also received the salt revenues from the province of Aunis, the hinterland of La Rochelle, and a large sum in cash from the fortune Mazarin had recouped after the Fronde. Daniel Dessert, *Le Royaume de Monsieur Colbert*, Paris, 2007, p.41.
23. Ballon, *op. cit.*, p.110.
24. Ibid.

25. AN MM 462 pp.48–59, quoted by Franklin, *Recherches historiques*, p.39.
26. Louis Hautecœur, *Histoire de l'architecture classique en France, Tome II*, Paris, 1947, p.261.
27. Franklin, *Recherches historiques*, p.42.
28. Ballon, *Louis Le Vau*, p.45.
29. Jean-Pierre Babelon, *Louis le Vau au Collège Mazarin: Rome à Paris, Communication à l'Académie des Beaux-Arts le 25 avril 2001 [publication électronique], 2001.*
30. AN Min centr, étude XCVI, cited in Nicole Bourdel, *Nouveau documents sur Louis Le Vau, Premier architecte de Louis XIV 1612–1670, Paris et Ile de France mémoires, Tome VII*, 1956, p.221–222.
31. Hautecœur, *Histoire*, pp.261–262.
32. Ibid.
33. Ballon, *Louis Le Vau*, p.43.
34. Hautecœur, *Histoire*, p.263.
35. Margaret Whinney, *Sir Chrisopher Wren's visit to Paris, Gazette de Beaux-Arts, 51, avril 1958*, p.235.
36. Ballon, Ibid.
37. Ibid.
38. Franklin, *Recherches historiques*, pp.178–179.
39. Ballon, p.51.
40. Ibid., pp.53–55,
41. AN NIII Seine 710, n. 4.
42. Ballon, pp.55–56.
43. Ibid., pp.56–57 and n. 57.
44. À l'origine de l'architecture en marbre sous Louis XIV: les projets de Louis Le Vau pour le collège Mazarin, Revue de l'art, no. 169. 3e trimestre, 2010, pp.11–23. *Mémoire util pour les marbres* [2nd semestre 1662] AN H3 2845.
45. Alexandre Cojannot, À l'origine de l'architecture de marbre sous Louis XIV: les projets de Louis Le Vau pour le collège Mazarin, le Louvre et Versailles (1662–1663), *Revue de l'art no. 169, 3e semestre* 2010, pp.11–23 and notes.
46. Ballon, *Louis Le Vau*, p.60.
47. Ibid., p.71.
48. Nicole Folkay, *Louis Le Vau, architecte créateur, en L'institut et la monnaie: 2 palais sur 1 quai, Délégation artistique de la ville de Paris, Société historique du Vie arrondissement, sos la direction de Géneviève Gille et Maurice Berry*, pp.57–62.
49. Dulong, *Les origines*, pp.253–254 citing BnF, 1⁰ Fm 311 pièce 13018.
50. BnF Fol, Fm 17424, Dulong p.254.

Chapter 9
1. Alexandre Maral, *Louis XIV, Un règne de grandeur*, Paris, 2011, p.17.
2. Emmanuel Le Roy Ladurie, *The Ancien Régime, A History of France, 1610–1774*, ET, Mark Greengrass, Oxford, 1998, p.175.
3. Daniel Dessert, *Le royaume de Monsieur Colbert*, Paris, 2007, pp.168–170 & 178–180.
4. Daniel Dessert, *Le royaume*, pp.129–138.
5. Bibl. Nat., F 5001 (236), quoted in Nicole Bourdel, *Nouveaux documents sur Louis Le Vau, premier architecte de Louis XIV (1612–1670), Paris et Ile de France mémoires, Tome VIII*, 1956, p.232.
6. Ibid.
7. Ballon, *Louis Le Vau*, pp.210–211, n. 42, referring to the inventory made after Le Vau's death AN Min cent. LXXXV 198, fol. 22, 27 November 1670, No. 25.

8. These remained viable until the development of deep mines in north-eastern France in the mid-nineteenth century.
9. Nicole Bourdel, *Nivernais-Morvan* (newspaper article) February 1954.
10. *Mémoires de Mme de Montpensier, petite -fille de Henri IV, collationés sur le manuscrit autographe avec notes biographiques er historiques par A. Chéruel*, 6 Vols, Paris, 1858, Vol. II, p.308. Source: gallica.bnf.fr
11. Bourdel, February 1954.
12. Bourdel, *Nouveaux documents*, p.124.
13. Gaston Gauthier, *Monographe de la Commune de Beaumont-la-Ferrière*, Nevers, 1892, facing p.118.
14. Gauthier and *Nouveaux documents*, p.225.
15. Hilary Ballon, *Le Vau*, p.119.
16. Liliane Lange, *La grotte de Thétis et le premier Versailles de Louis XIV, Art de France*, 1961, p.138.
17. Hilary Ballon, Ibid., pp.119–120.
18. Guy Thuillier, *Les spéculations malheureuses de l'architecte Louis Le Vau, à Beaumont-la-Ferrière (1665–1670), Mémoires de la Société Académique du Nivernais, 1959*, p.25 and n. 7 & p.26.
19. Ibid., n. 18. Ballon, p.211, gives the reference: BN MS fr. 21789 fols. 359–360, 10 Nov 1666. The letters patent were necessary because the original grant had been personal to Champion.
20. Daniel Dessert, *Le royaume de Monsieur Colbert, 1661–1683*, Paris, 2007, p.211.
21. Thuillier, p.26, n. 21.
22. Ibid.
23. Ibid., p.27, n. 24 B.N. Ms 21789.
24. Ibid., n. 25.
25. My italics.
26. Thuillier, p.28, n. 26.
27. Ibid., pp.28–29.
28. Ibid., p.29, n. 29.
29. Thuillier, pp.29–30.
30. Ibid., p.31, n. 32.
31. Raymond Robin, *Forges et forgerons du Berry et du Nivernais*, Paris, 1983, p.117. This book was recommended to me by M. Guy Pigoury, whose agricultural land includes some of Le Vau's factory sites – of which he, generous with his time, provided me with a tour during my visit in September 2020.
32. Bourdel, ibid.
33. Ibid., p.31.
34. *Bibl. Nat,. Nouv acq. fr. 2440 fol. 254*, cited in *Bourdel, Nouvelles documents*, p.233.
35. *AN, Minutier central, étude LXXXVI, liasse 199*, cited, Bourdel, p.234.
36. Bourdel, *Nouveaux documents*, pp.234–235.
37. *Bibl. Nat., Mél Colbert, 166 fol 1*, cited ibid., p.216.
38. *AN, M 174*, cited ibid., pp.228–229.
39. Bourdel, *Nouveax Documents*, p.231.
40. Bibl., Institut, ms. 368 cited Bourdel, *Nouvelles documents*, p.231.
41. Thuillier, p.32 and n. 34.
42. Ibid., p.33.
43. Ballon, *Louis Le Vau*, pp.123–124.

44. Ibid., p.216.
45. Ibid., p.125.

Chapter 10
1. *Le Vau et l'architecture parisienne au XVIIe siècle, Centre de recherches et études sur Paris et l'île de France, Tome 1, avril 1983*, pp.191–196.
2. *Nouveaux documents sur Louis Le Vau, Premier Architecte de Louis XIV, 1612–1670, Paris et île de France Mémoires, Tome VIII*, 1956, pp.214–235.
3. Eric Orsenna, *Portrait d'un homme heureux, André Le Nôtre, 1613–1700*, Paris, 2000, pp.124–126.
4. *Musée de Versailles, M V 4346*.
5. Albert Laprade, *François d'Orbay, avec la collaboration de Nicole Bourdel et Jean Lafond et l'aide de la Recherche scientifique*, Paris, 1960, p.65.
6. *Civilisation, A Personal View*, Episode 7, *Grandeur and Obedience*.
7. André Félibien, *Description sommaire du Chateau de Versailles*, Paris, 1674,
8. *Histoire et recherche des antiquités de la ville de Paris, Tome II*, p.238. Paris, 1724.
9. *Louis Le Vau, Mazarin's College, Colbert's Revenge*, Princeton and Chichester, 1999, p.125.
10. Françoise Bayard, *Le monde des financiers au XVIIe siècle*, Paris, 1988, pp.267–277.
11. Ibid., p.267.
12. Ibid., p.276.
13. *Cours d'architecture enseigné dans l'Academie royal d'architecture par M. François Blondel*, Paris, 1675–1683. Source: gallica.bnf.fr
14. Ibid., p.761.
15. Alexandre Cojannot, Alexandre Gady, *Dessiner pour bâtir, le meter d'architecte au XVIIe siècle*, Paris, 2017, p.173.
16. Érik Orsenna, *Portrait d'un homme heureux, André Le Notre, 1613–1700*, Paris, 2000, pp.39–40
17. Albert Laprade, *op. cit.*, pp.109–114.
18. Vitruve, *Les dix livres d'architecture, traduction intégrale de Claude Perrault, 1673, revue et corrigée sur les textes latins et présentée par André Dalmas*, Paris, 1965.
19. Zega and Dams, *Palaces of the Sun King*, New York, 2006, p.147.
20. Despite all their previous claims for Le Vau's lack of creativity, Zega and Dams claim that Hardouin-Mansart paid a certain homage to him at Le Val.
21. Coincidentally, this estate had been owned earlier by Pierre Lescot, architect of the Louvre under Henri II, François II and Henri III. He was commendatory abbot of Notre-Dame, near Le Mans, which was too far away as a residence to allow him to work for long periods in Paris. You did not have to be a monk to be a commendatory abbot. Such offices were used by successive monarchs to provide substantial incomes for prominent royal employees. Henri Sauval, in his *Histoire et recherches des antiquités de Paris*, Paris, 1724, pp.24–51, refers to Lescot as Clagny *tout court*.
22. Lilian Lange, *La Grotte de Thétis et le premier Versailles de Louis XIV, Art de France*, 1961, © CRCV, pp.142–143.
23. Robert W. Berger, *Antoine Le Pautre, A French Architect of the Era of Louis XIV*, New York, 1969, pp.77–83, & Fig. 97.
24. Mireille Rambaud, *Une famille d'architectes: Les Delespine, Archives de l'Art française, nouvelle période, tome.xxiii*, 1968, p.28.
25. Anthony Blunt, *Art and Architecture in France, 1500–1700*, Harmondsworth 2nd edition, 1970, p.204.

26. Le Nôtre was on terms of *bonhomie* with the King, who, it is said, once offered to ennoble him, and he had jokingly refused such advancement, suggesting that his escutcheon would be 'three slugs crowned with cabbages, a spade and a rake'. Nicole Garnier-Pelle, *André Le Notre et les jardins de Chantilly*, Paris, 2000, p.8.
27. Alexandre Gady *(sous la direction du), Jules Hardouin-Mansart 1646–1708*, Paris, 2013, pp.11–18.
28. Ibid., p.20 n. 74.
29. Zega and Dams, *op. cit.*, pp.143–144.
30. Though not *with* the King, for he ate on his own, watched by those who would, and his own food was prepared within the security of the palace itself, not just across the road. His own kitchen and the communal ones were not far apart, however, because it was at the south-west corner of the palace that the water from a spring was purest for cooking. This information was generously provided to me by M. Gérard Robaut, *Résponsable, Affaires Générales et Bibliothèque, CRCV.*
31. This was particularly true in its iconographical borrowings from Ovid's *Metamorphoses* of the myth of Apollo for the bassins and the Grotto of Thetis at Versailles, designed by Le Brun and executed by sculptors like the Marsy brothers, Tuby and Coysevox. And also the *trompe l'oeil* frescoes on the facades of the pavilions at Marly, also by Le Brun, incorporating the idea of the Palace of Jupiter, surrounded by the twelve pavilions of principal deities. Gérard Sabatier, *The Illusions of Marly*, in Ed., Barbara Arciszewska, *The Baroque Villa, Suburban and Country Residences c.1600–1800*, Wilanov, 2009, p.53.
32. The excavations of a century before at Hadrian's villa d'Este at Tivoli incorporated the plan for a circus building including several *bassins*. Hardouin-Mansart used these ground plans for the basis of his pavilions at Marly. Sabatier, Ibid., p.55.
33. Zega and Dams, *op. cit.*, p.26.
34. Bénédicte Gady, 2010, pp.214–221.
35. Wolf Burchard, *The Sovereign Artist, Charles Le Brun and the image of Louis XIV*, London, 2016, p.83.
36. See above.
37. Laurent Portes, https:gallica.bnf.fr/blog/18042018/les-premiers-historiens-de-paris?mode=desktop
38. *Description nouvelle de ce qu'il y a de plus remarquable and la ville de Paris, 2e édition augmentée de plusieurs recherches très curieuses, par M. Brice*, Paris, 1697. Source: gallica.bnf.fr
39. Ibid.
40. Anthony Blunt, *op. cit.*, p.207.
41. Ibid., pp.227–230.
42. R.W. Berger, *Antoine Le Pautre*, New York, 1969, p.5.
43. Anthony Blunt, *op. cit.*, p.212.
44. Brice. *op. cit.*, pp.101–104.
45. Grove Art Online, *ad loc.*
46. Brice *op. cit.*, pp.104–105. Cyril Bordier, *Louis Le Vau, architecte, les immeubles et hôtels particuliers parisiens, Tome I*, Paris, 1998, p.230.
47. Brice, ibid., pp.236–238.
48. *Histoire et recherches de la ville de Paris, tome 2*, Paris, 1724, p.62. To avoid any sense of ambiguity in this statement, it is worth noting what Sauval's French text says: '*C'est à ces deux excellens Architectes qui on doit attribuer toute la gloire du dessein, et de l'exécution de ce superbe édifice; malgré tout ce que l'on a publié de contraire; lequel causera sans doute de*

l'admiration aux siècles à venir, & leur donnera une haute idée de celui qui aura produit des ouvrages d'une si rare & si grande perfection.'
49. Ibid., pp.222–224.
50. *Voyage pittoresque de Paris, ou indication de tout ce qu'il y a de plus beau dans cette grande Ville en peinture, Sculpture, et Architecture, seconde édition*, Paris, 1752, p.36.
51. Ibid., p.193.
52. *L'Art française au temps de Louis XIV (1661–1699)*, Paris, 1911, pp.80–81.
53. *A History of French Architecture from the Death of Mazarin til the Death of Louis XV 1661–1774*, Vol. I, London, 1921, pp.56–61.
54. See above, p.74.
55. Anatole France, *Le Château de Vaux-le-Vicomte*, Paris, 1933, pp.94–96.
56. Anthony Blunt, *op. cit.*, p.134.
57. *Célébration du troisième centenaire de la mort de Louis Le Vau (1612–1670) Institut de France, Académie des Beaux-arts*, Paris, 1970. pp.2–24.
58. Paris, 2017.
59. First aired on 6 March 2021.

Glossary
1. Andrea Palladio, *The Four Books of Architecture*, with a new introduction by Adolf K. Placzek, New York, 1965, 2020, pp.14–25.
2. Vitruvius identifies the plant as such, *Les dix livres d'architecture, Traduction intégrale de Claude Perrault, 1673, revue et corrigé par André Dalmas*, Paris, 1963, p.115.

Select Bibliography

Books in English
Ed., ARCISEWSKA, Barbara, *The Baroque Villa, Suburban and Country Residences c.1600–1800*, Wilanov, 2009.
BALLON, Hilary, *The Paris of Henri IV, Architecture and Urbanism*, Cambridge MA & London, 1991.
—— *Louis Le Vau, Mazarin's College Colbert's Revenge*, Princeton NJ, 1999.
—— *Vaux-le-Vicomte, Le Vau's Ambition*, in *Villas and Gardens in Early Modern Italy and France*, ed., Mirka Benes and Dianne Harris, Cambridge, 2001, pp.292–293.
BERGER, Robert W., *Versailles, The Chateau of Louis XIV*, Philadelphia & London, 1985.
—— *A Royal Passion, Louis XIV as Patron of Architecture*, Cambridge, 1994.
—— *Antoine Le Pautre*, New York, 1969.
BLANNING, T.C.W., *The Culture of Power and the Power of Culture, Old Regime Europe, 1660–1789*, Oxford, 2002.
BLUNT, Anthony, *Art and Architecture in France 1500–1700*, Harmondsworth 2nd edition, 1973.
BURCHARD, Wolf, *The Sovereign Artist, Charles Le Brun and the image of Louis XIV*, London, 2016.
DOYLE, William, *The Old European Order 1660–1800*, Oxford, 1978.
GOLDSTEIN, Claire, *Vaux and Versailles, The Appropriations, Erasures and Accidents that made Modern France*, Philadelphia, 2008.
GROVE Art Online, *ad loc.* www.oxfordartonline.com/groveart
LE ROY LADURIE, Emmanuel, *The Ancien régime, A History of France, 1610–1774*, ET Mark Greengrass, Oxford, 1996.
LEWIS, W.H., *Louis XIV, An Informal Portrait*, London, 1959.
MANSEL, Philip, *King of the World: The Life of Louis XIV*, London, 2019.
MONTAGUE, Jennifer, *The Expression of the Passions; the Origin and Influence of Charles Le Brun's Conférence sur l'expression générale et particulière*, New Haven and London, 1994.
PALLADIO, Andrea, *The Four Books of Architecture*, New York, 1965.
PITTS, Vincent J., *Henri IV of France, His Reign and Age*, Baltimore, 2009.
—— *Embezzlement and High Treason in Louis XIV's France*, Baltimore, 2015.
TADGELL, Christopher, *The Louvre and Versailles: The Evolution of the Proto-typical Palace in the Age of Absolutism*, London and New York, 2020.
TREASURE, Geoffrey, *Mazarin: the Crisis of Absolutism in France*, London & New York, 1995.
TURNER, Jane, ed., *The Dictionary of Art*, 34 Vols; Vol. 18, BAJOU Thierry, J-B Lambert.
WITTKOWER, Rudolf, *Art and Architecture in Italy*, Harmondsworth, 1958.
—— *Gian Lorenzo Bernini, The Sculptor of the Roman Baroque*, London, 1966.
—— *Architectural Principles in the Age of Humanism*, New York, 1962, 1971.
ZEGA, Andrew and DAMS, Bernd H., *Palaces of the Sun King*, New York, 2006.

Books in French
AUBERT, François d', *Colbert, La vertu usurpée*, Paris, 2010.
BABELON, Jean-Pierre, *Demeures parisiens sous Henri IV et Louis XIII*, Paris, 1991.
BAJOU, Thierry, *Le peinture de Versailles, XVIIe siècle*, Paris, 1998.
BAUCHAL, Charles, *Nouveau dictionnaire biographique et critiquedes architectes français*, Paris, 1887.
BAYARD, Françoise, *Le monde des financiers au XVIIe siècle*, Paris, 1988.
BECDELIÈVRE, Gilles, *Le jeu de la haine*, Paris, 2014.
BERTY, Adolphe, *Topographie historique de vieux Paris, Région du Louvre etr des Tuileries, continuée par H. Legrand, 2 tomes*, Paris, 1885, Source: gallica.bnf.fr
BLIN, Maxime, et BLIN, Émilie, *Le Château de Versailles en chantiers*, Paris, 2018.
BLONDEL, Jacques-François, *Architecture françoise ou receuil des plans, élévations, coupes et profiles des églises palais, hôtels et édifices . . . . 4 tomes*, Paris, 1752–1756. Source: gallica.bnf.fr
BORDIER, Cyril, *Louis Le Vau, architecte, les immeubles et hôtels particuliers parisiens, Tome I*, Paris, 1998.
—— *Vaux-Le-Vicomte, génèse d'un chef-d'œuvre*, Paris, 2014
BORDONOVE, Georges, *Foucquet, Coupable ou victime?*, Paris, 1976.
BOUCHENOT-DÉCHIN, Patricia, *André Le Nôtre*, Paris, 2013.
CHANTELOU, Paul Fréart de, *Journal de voyage du Cavalier Bernin en France, Édition de Milovan Stavič*, Paris 2001.
—— *Notice de Ludovic Lalianne, original edition 1885. Notes pour le journa de Bernin, par Jean-Paul Guibbert*, Paris, 1981.
CLÉMENTI, Pierre, Ed., *Lettres, Instructions et Mémoires de Colbert*, 9 Vols, Paris, 1867. Source gallica.bnf.fr/BnF
COJANNOT, Alexandre, *Louis Le Vau et les nouvelles ambitions de l'architecture française, 1612–1654*, Paris, 2012.
COLBERT, Jean-Baptiste, *Lettres, Instructions et Mémoires Tome 7, éd.*, Pierre Clementi, Paris, 1861–1873. Source: gallica.bnf.fr
DE ANDIA, Béatrice et COURTIN Nicolas, Dir., *L'Île Saint-Louis*, Paris, 1997.
CORDEY, Jean, *Le chateau de Vaux-le-Vicomte, étude historique*, Paris, 1933 (attached to an essay by Anatole France).
D'AUBERT, François, *Colbert, La vertu usurpée*, Paris, 2010.
DESSERT, Daniel, *Fouquet*, Paris, 2015.
—— *Le royaume de monsieur Colbert 1661–1683*, Paris, 2007.
DUMOLIN, Maurice, *Études topographiques parisiennes, 3 tomes*, Paris, 1930. Source: Bibliothèque de l'Hôtel de Ville, Paris.
ERLANDE-BRANDENBURG, Alain, & JESTAZ, Bertrand, *Le Château de Vincennes*, Paris, 1989.
FÉLIBIEN, André, *Conférences de l'Académie royale de peinture et de sculpture pendant l'année 1667*, Paris, 1668. Source: gallica.bnf.fr
FLEURY, Michel, *Almanach de Paris, des origines à 1789*, Paris, 1990.
FRANKLIN, Alfred, *Recherches historiques sur le collège des Quatre Nations d'après des documents entièrement inédits*, Paris, 1862, pp.141–184 (the Deed of Foundation, including the rules by which the college was to be run). Source gallica.bnf.fr/BnF
GADY, Alexandre, *Versailles: la fabrique d'un chef-d'œuvre*, Paris, 2011.
—— *Les Hôtels particuliers de Paris du moyen-âge à la belle-époque*, Paris, 2008.
—— *Jacques Lemercier architecte et ingénieur du roi*, Paris, 2005.
—— *et COJANNOT, Alexandre, Les appartements du Louvre au lendemain de la Fronde: de Jacques Lemercier et Louis Le Vau, Revue de l'art*, No. 142, 2003/4. ©CRCV.

—— et COJANNOT, Alexandre, *Dessiner pour bâtir, le métier de l'architecture du XVIIe siècle*, Paris, 2017. See also, https://scribeaccroupi.fr/entretien-alexandre-gady-pour-le-prix-chateau-de-versailles-du-livre-d-histoire

GADY, Bénédicte, et MILOVANOVIC, Nicolas, *Charles Le Brun 1619–1690*, Paris, 2016.

GADY, Bénédicte, *L'ascension de Charles Le Brun, Liens sociaux et procuction artistique*, Paris, 2010.

GAUTHIER, Gaston, *Monographe de la commune de Beaumont-le-Ferrière (Nièvre)*, Nevers, 1892. Source: gallica.bnf.fr

HAUTECOEUR, Louis, *Histoire de l'architecture classique en France*, Tome II, Paris, 1943–1948.

—— *L'histoire des châteaux du Louvre et des Tuileries*, Paris et Bruxelles, 1927.

JAL, Auguste, *Dictionnaire critique de biographie et d'histoire*, Paris, 1872.

LAPRADE, Albert avec le collaboration de Nicole Bourdel et de Jean Lafond et l'aide de la recherche scientifique, *François d'Orbay*, Paris, 1960.

LE GUILLOU, Jean-Claude, *Versailles avant Versailles*, Paris, 2011.

LOCATELLI, Sebastiano, *Voyage de France, mœurs et coutûmes françaises (1664–1665) traduit sur les manuscrits autographes et publiée avec une introduction et de notes par Asolphe Vautier*, Paris, 1905. Source: gallica.bnf.fr.

MAISONNIER, Elisabeth, Dir., *Versailles: architectures rêvées 1660–1815*, Versailles, 2019.

MARAL, Alexandre, *Girardon*, Paris, 2015.

—— Louis XIV, *Un règne de grandeur*, Paris, 2011.

—— et alii, *Versailles disparu de Louis XIV*, Versailles, 2009.

MEROT, Alain, *Eustache Le Sueur 1616–1655*, Paris, 1987, 2000.

MICHELET, Jules, *Histoire de France*, Paris, 1884 edition, *tome* 15.

MIGNOT, Claude, *François Mansart, un architecte artiste au siècle de Louis XII et de Louis XIV*, Paris.

MONTPENSIER, *Mémoires de Mlle de, petite-fille de Henri IV collationnés sur le manuscrit authographe, avec notes biographoques et historiques par A. Chéruel*, Paris, 1858, 6 Tomes. Source: gallica.bnf.fr

MOTTEVILLE, Mme de, *Chronique de la Fronde*, ed., Jean-Michel Delacomptée, Paris, 2003.

MURAT, Inès, *Colbert*, Paris, 2008.

ORSENNA, Erik, *Portrait d'un homme heureux, André Le Nôtre*, Paris, 2000.

PÉROUSE DE MONTCLOS, Jean-Marie, *Vaux-Le-Vicomte, une galanterie refusée par Louis XIV*, Paris, 1997.

—— *L'art de France de la renaissance au siècle de lumières 1450–1770*, Paris, 2004.

PICON, Antoine, *Claude Perrault, ou La Curiosité d'un classique*, Paris, 1998.

—— *Un moderne paradoxal* : Introduction to Charles Perrault, *Mémoires de ma vie*, Paris, 1993.

PIGANIOL DE LA FORCE, Jean-Aimar, *Description historique de la ville de Paris*, Tome II, Paris, 1765. Source: gallica.bnf.fr

SAUVAL, Henri, *Histoire et recherches des antiquités de la ville de Paris,* 3 Vols, Paris, 1724, Source: gallica.bnf.fr.

SCHNAPPER, Antoine, *Le métier de pentre au Grand Siècle*, Paris, 2004.

TIBERGHIEN, Frédéric, *Versailles, le chantier de Louis XIV*, Paris, 2002 & 2006.

VERLET, Pierre, *Le Château de Versailles*, Paris, 1961, 1985.

VITRUVE, *Les dix livres d'architecture, traduction intégrale de Claude Perrault, 1673, revue et corrigée sur les textes latins et présentée par André Dalmas*, Paris, 1965.

Index

Aix-la-Chapelle, Peace of, 1668, 50, 114, 116, 118
Alberti, Léon-Battista, 178
Alexander VII, Pope, 94
Alps, 18
Alsace, 138
Ambassadors, Gallery, Louvre, 90
Ambassadors' Staircase, Versailles, 124, 172, 179
Amboise, 114
America, Viceroy of, 130
Androuet de Cerceau, Baptiste, 2
  Jacques II, 2
  Jean, 7
Anne of Austria, Queen, Regent of France, then Queen Mother, 19, 24–5, 59–63, 96, 104, 106, 128, 132, 135–6, 173
Anne of Brittany, Queen of France, 114
Angers, 66, 85
Anguier, Michel d', 72
Arceuil, 65
Archives nationales, 103, 117
Arsenal, 42
Artois, 111, 138
Aumont, Duke of, 96
Austria, John of, 73

Ballon, Hilary, xi, 72, 77, 137–8, 143, 150, 171–2, 198
Bajou, Thierry, 174
Barbier, Louis de, 10
Baroque, 19, 33, 70, 75, 101, 104, 112, 116, 124, 187
Barricades, Days of the, 25
Barrois, Claude, 57
  Louis, 57
Bastille, La, 10, 85–6
Bautru, Guillaume, 10, 13, 15, 17
Bayard, Françoise, 27
Beaumont-la-Ferrière, 29, 124, 152, 155–9, 163–5, 166, 169, 171, 176
Beauvais, 8, 34
Beauvais, Pierre de, 63
Belgium, 120

Belle-île, xi, 68–9, 82–3
Bellier, Catherine Henriette, 63
Benedetti, Abbé Elpidio, 91, 93
Berger, Robert W., 112
Bergerat, Claude, 56
Bergeron, Antoine, 43, 65, 71, 99
Bernini, Gian Lorenzo, x, 10, 75, 101, 108, 114, 116, 126
  Visit to Paris, 16, 65, 93–100, 146, 174
  Pietro Filippo, 95
Bertel, Liénard, 12
Berthelot, François, 160–2
Bibliothèque Nationale, 70, 103, 135
Birzi, lion tamer, 53
Bissaro, Angelo, 136
Blanchard, Jacques, 18, 34, 36
Blandy, 69
Blondel, Jacques-François, x, 178
Blois, 92, 114
Blomfield, Sir Reginald, 192–3
Blondet (Le Vau's agent at his death), 169
Blunt, Anthony, xii, 30–1, 33, 125, 194–5
Boboli Gardens, 54
Bohemia, 156
Bonaparte, Napoleon, 16
Bonsi, *Abbé* Pietro, 51–3
Bordeaux, 78, 81
Bordier, Cyril, ix, 31, 198
Bois de Boulogne, 15
Boulogne, Valentin de, 26
Bourdel, Nicole, 157, 169, 173
Bresch, Abraham de, 162–4
Brévannes, 28, 166, 173, 176
Brice, Germain, 188–90
Brienne, Henri-Auguste, 80
  Louis-Henri de Loménie de, 63, 80, 84–6
Brulant, Procurator of Nevers, 169
Burgundy, 164

Carlu, Jacques, 195–6
Cerizier, Jeanne, 19
Chambrai, Roland Fréart de, 18
Champion, Antoine, 155–8, 160, 176

Chantelou, Paul Fréart de, 94–5, 97, 99, 146, 180
Charles I, King of England, 1
Charles V, King of France, 42, 47, 52
Charles IX, King of France, 2
Chatre, Dame François de la, 176
Chavigny, Bouthillier de, 39
Choisy, François-Timoléon, 80, 84
Clagny, 159, 178
Clark, Kenneth, 174
Clermont College (Jesuits), 67, 71
Coalbrookdale, 156
Coislin, Marquis de, 143
Cojannot, Alexandre, xi, 26, 53, 149, 172–3, 198
Colbert, Jean-Baptiste, x, 10, 13, 22, 33, 40–2, 45, 49, 52, 58, 61, 63, 65, 67, 73, 76–7, 79–83, 86–94, 96–102, 107–12, 114–16, 118–19, 122, 124, 127–8, 131, 134–5, 137, 139–41, 150–1, 153, 155–8, 161–3, 165, 168, 171, 173–4
Colbert, Nicolas, 21,
Colbert de Terron, 81–2
Colosseum, 54
Comans d'Astry, Thomas de, 34, 36
Combles brisés, 14,
Compagnie des Indes, 108
Compagnie de Nivernais, 164
Conches, Forest of, 155–6
Condé, Prince of, 69, 73
Conflans, 138
Conti, Princess of, 5
  Prince of, 60
Cordey, Jean, 54, 74, 194
Cornwall, 165
Cortona, Pietro di, 93, 106
Cosne-sur-Loire, 9, 162, 169
Cosimo III, Grand Duke of Tuscany, 52, 54
Cotte, Robert de, 4
Cotelle, Jean, 18, 57
Coulanges, Philippe de, 7
Counter-Reformation, 19, 66
Coypel, Noël, 57, 105
Coysevox, Antoine, 125
Créquy, Duke of, 93
Creteil, 12, 28, 71
Cromwell, Oliver, 73
Cucci, Domenico, 123

Dalliez de la Tour, 162–5, 169–71
Darby, Abraham, 156
D'Artagnan, Captain, 84
Dauphiné, 67
David, Jacques-Louis, 151
Delorme, Philibert, 178
Denmark, Prince of, 51

Desgodetz, Antoine, 54, 121
Desjardins, Martin, 150
Desmaretz, Jean, 12–13, 99
Dessert, Daniel, 130
Devolution, War of, 100, 113–14
Dezallier D'Argenville, Antoine-Nicolas, 191–2
Dinan, 119
D'Orbay, François, ix, 57, 90–1, 102–103, 117–19, 121–2, 124, 126, 133, 145, 150, 169, 172–4, 176, 179–82
Dorigny, Michel, 45
D'Orléans, Gaston, 1, 38, 62, 66, 92, 142
D'Ormesson, Olivier, 85
Dublet, Claude, 14, 23, 42, 46, 52, 60
Dulong, Claude, 137, 148
Dumolin, Maurice, xi
Dunes, Battle of, 1658, 73
Dunkirk, 73, 127
Dupré, Pierre, 29
Dutch East India Company. 134

East Indies Company, 134
École des Chartes, 173
Enveloppe, x, 112, 114–15, 120, 122–5, 132, 152, 165, 174, 175
Enfilade, 11, 42, 57
Entrepreneur, 12, 62
Errard, Charles, 57, 105, 109
Essonnes, 37
Evelyn, John, 37

Faubourg Saint-Antoine, 20, 22–3
Faubourg Saint-Germain, 98, 139
Feldmann, Dietrich, 172, 198
Félibien, André, xi, 112, 119–22, 131–2, 134, 175
Ferdinand II, Grand Duke of Tuscany, 51
Feydeau, Antoine, 24
Filles-Dieu Convent, 9
Fillette, François & Jean, River transporters, 149
Financiers, 21–3, 175–7
Flanders, 67, 114, 120, 138
Fleury, René, 10
Florence, 51–2
Florentines, 4
Fontenay-Mareuil, Marquis de, 119
Fontainebleau, 21, 38, 45, 53, 56, 67, 80
Fontrailles, Frondeur, 27
Fossés Jaunes, 10
Fougeu d'Escures, Pierre, 3
Fouquet, Nicolas, 41, 43, 50, 66–9, 71–86, 89, 92, 106–108, 110–11, 129–30, 132, 137–9, 141, 153, 155, 173
  Abbé Louis, 69, 74,
  Bishop of Agde, 82

Fouquet family, 66
Four Nations, College of, ix, 33, 92, 101, 111, 116–17, 120, 124, 138, 167–8, 172
Fourché, Louise (N. Fouquet's first wife), 67
Fourcy, Jean de, 1
Fourrel, Nicolas, 13
France, Anatole, 194
France, Institute of, xi
Francini brothers, 128
Fontainebleau, 21, 38, 40, 55, 67, 77, 84
Franco-Prussian War, 1870–71, 68
François I, King of France, 15, 58, 59
François II, King of France, 2
Frankfurt, 160
Franklin, Alfred, 143
French Neo-Classical Style, 87, 100, 104, 108, 177, 187

Gabriel, Jacques, 116, 124–5
Gady, Alexandre, xi, 172, 198
Gauthier, Gaston, 157
Geissel, Heinrich, 164
Germany, 163
Gillet, Guillaume, 195–8
Girardon, François, 57, 74, 128, 131
Gittard, Daniel, 69–70
Gobelins, 78–9, 123, 129, 153
Gobert, Thomas, 116
Godet, Henri, 39
   Antoine, Viscount, 39
Goldstein, Claire, 129
Gomont, Jean de, 140–1, 146
Gournay-sur-Marne, 11
Gourville, Jean de, 81
Grand Commun, 69
Grandguillaume, 170
Grandmaison. Leclerc de, 170
Grange, Henri de la, 157
Greece, 120
Grénant, 157
Grèves, Marquis de, 84
Grivel, *Abbé* de, 160
Gruin, Magdeleine, 143
Guénégaud, Monsieur de, 143
Guérin, Gilles, 34–7, 57, 128, 131
Guet, Chevalier, 62
Guillemeau, Jean, 28
Guiloni, Francesco, 51–3
Guinon, 82
Guise, Duke of, 38

Hainault, 120, 138, 149
Hardouin-Mansart, Jules, ix, 92, 108, 119, 121, 125–6, 128, 131–2, 134, 174, 176, 178, 182–7

Harlay, *Président du Parlement*, 4, 82
Haro, Luis de, 136
Hautecoeur, Louis, xi, 37, 92, 94, 100
Haye, Martin de La, 30
Hébert, Denis, 42
Hémery, Michel Particelli d', 15
Henri II, King of France, 124, 158
Henri III, King of France, 2, 6
Henri IV, King of France, 1–6, 14, 21, 58, 78–80, 110, 124, 138, 141, 146
Henriet, Israël, 77
Henrietta-Maria, Queen of England, 38, 135
Hesselin, Louis, 16, 34–9, 45
Holland, 82, 127
Hôtel de Balsac, 15
Hôtel de Bautru, 9, 11, 13, 15, 23, 41, 92, 98
Hôtel de Beauvais, 63
Hôtel de Bourbon, 64
Hôtel Chevry, 11
Hôtel Duret, 11
Hôtel d'Épergnon, 91
Hôtel de Frontenac, 99
Hôtel de Gillier, 14
Hôtel Hesselin, 18
Hôtel Lambert, 26, 30, 32–3, 91–2, 123–4, 149
Hôtel de Longueville, 62, 91, 144, 166–7, 170
Hôtel Particulier, x, 3, 5, 7
Hôtel de Pellevé, 12
Hôtel Petit, 15
Hôtel Petit-Luxembourg, 32
Hôtel de Souvré, 62–3
Hôtel de Ville, ix, 8, 12, 61, 67, 139
Hôtel de La Vrillière, 11
Hundred Years War, 49, 67

Ile de la Cité, 3–6, 98
Ile de France, 5, 10, 19, 120, 126
Ile de Notre Dame, 5–6
Ile de Saint-Louis, 5–6, 14, 16, 21, 24, 28, 57, 70–1, 170
Ile des Vaches, 5–6
Institut de France, 142, 151
Invalides, 92
Italy, 2, 18–19, 35, 51, 120, 124, 180
Italian bedrooms (alcoves), 16
Italian influence, tendency, 16, 49, 70–1, 97, 104, 108, 112, 124

Jardin des Plantes, 60, 141
Jean II, King of France, 49
Jesuits, 66, 71
Joly, Denys, 128, 159
Jumeaux, 69

Kimball, Fiske, 111, 116–17, 194
Kircher, Athanasius, 132

La Charité, 159, 169
Laisné, *Abbé* Henri, (Jeanne's uncle), 18
  Abbé Henri (Jeanne's brother), 160, 164, 169, 170
Laisné, Jeanne, 17–18, 167, 170, 173
Lagny, 14
La Fontaine, Jean de, 73, 83, 130, 132
La Fronde, 9, 25, 37, 40, 44, 50, 55, 58–9, 67, 69–70, 73, 81, 98, 106, 135–6, 139
La Grange, 7
Lambert, Nicolas de Thorigny, 19, 28, 45, 71
  Jean-Baptiste de Thorigny, 19, 27
Lambert, (Le Vau's assistant), 168
Lamoignon. Guillaume de, 139
La Motte, de, 98–9
Lange, Lilian, 128
Languedoc, 119, 162
Laon, 120
Laprade, Albert, 173
La Quintinie, 132
Lartille, hack writer, 151
La Vallière, Louise de, 81, 86, 110
La Vrillière, Louis de Phélypeaux de La, 15–16, 29, 33, 71
Le Brun, Charles, ix, 33–7, 56–7, 61, 73–4, 76, 78–9, 91, 97, 99, 101–102, 107, 109, 111, 118, 123, 126, 128, 172–4, 179, 187–8
  Nicolas, 35
  Suzanne, 77
Le Bouteaux, Michel II, 133
Le Camus, Étienne, 57–8, 60
Leclerc, Jean, 12
Leduc, Gabriel, 92, 96
Le Fèvre, Philippe, 127
Legendre, Nicolas, 74
Le Gillier, Melchior, 14
Legoux, Paul, 164, 169–71
Le Grue, Jean, *Marbrier*, 120, 149
Leguay, Estienne, 143
Le Guillou, Jean-Claude, x
Le Hongre, Étienne, 18, 34–5, 56, 122, 150
Le Hongre, Louis, 134
Le Jay, Nicolas, 14
Le Marier, Antoine, 14
Lemercier, Jacques, ix, 1, 11, 16, 18, 41, 55, 63, 88, 118, 120, 155, 174
Lemoigne, Cardinal, 141
Lemonnier, 194
Le Muet, Pierre, 11, 15, 16, 41
Le Nôtre, André, 26, 69–70, 72, 76, 107, 110, 118, 127, 133, 159, 173
Le Paultre, André, 63

Le Pautre, Jean, 130
Le Prebtre, Henri, 12
Le Raincy, 24–7, 68, 76, 112
Le Regattier, François, 6, 29
Le Roy, Philibert, 117
Le Sueur, 26, 33–4, 36, 46, 57, 61
Lescot, Pierre, 2, 37, 55–6, 59, 92
Le Tellier, François Michel at first, then Louvois, Marquis de, 84, 89, 116, 133, 187
Le Tellier, Michel, Chancellor, 105, 139
Le Vau, Louis, viii, xi–x, 1, 5, 10–11, 13, 172–4, 178, 187
  Marie (sister of, twice), 19,
  Anne (sister of), 19,
  François (brother of), 19, 70, 92, 157
  Antoine (brother of), 19–20
  Jeanne (daughter of), 19
  Marie-Marguerite, daughter of), 19
  Marie (daughter of), 19
  Nicolas (son of), 19
  Nicolas (grandfather of). 157
  Early Buildings and Social Ascent, 10–20, 29
  Changed spelling for name, 17
  Working with clients, 21, 23–9, 34, 37–9
  Commissions from the king:
    Vincennes, 41–54
    Louvre, 55–65, 88–103
    Versailles, 104–33
    Beaumont-la-Férrière, 153–71
  Commission from Fouquet: Vaux, 66–87
  Commission from Mazarin's Executors, 101, 135–52
  Evolving assessment of Le Vau: 172–200
Le Veau, Louis, 7–9, 11–13, 17–18
  Anne (daughter), 9
  Louis (son) 9
  Antoine (son), 9
  Claude (sister), 8, 10
  François (son), 10
Levé, François, 42–3
Levigne, *tailleur pour les femmes*, 151
Liège, 119
Ligorio, Pirro, 105
Limay, 28
Lionne, Hugues de, 69, 89
Lionne, Mme de, 69, 99
L'Isle Adam, 12
Livry-en-Brie, 25
Lixein, Princess of, 38
Loire River, 84, 158, 164
Locatelli, Sebastiano, 98–9
Longueil, René de, 76
Longueville family, 62
Lorraine, Marguerite de, 17

Louette, Étiennette, 8
  Charles, 8
  Marin, 8, 11
Louis XIII. King of France, ix, 1–6, 17–18, 21, 23, 26, 41, 58, 66, 89, 104, 115, 118, 124
Louis XIV, King of France, ix, 2, 19, 21, 34, 40, 44, 49, 51, 53, 58, 59, 68, 73–5, 78–80, 85, 88–9, 93–8, 100–101, 104, 106, 108–10, 112–13, 115–16, 118, 120, 123–4, 126–8, 130–2, 135–6, 141–3, 153, 174
Louis XV, King of France, 80, 179
Louis XVI, King of France, 129
Le Tellier, Michel, 84
Louvre Palace, ix, 9, 15, 21, 33, 41, 46, 50, 55–64, 70, 75, 79, 90–104, 106, 108, 110, 114–16, 120, 122–4, 135, 140–2, 144, 146, 148–50, 152, 154, 156, 166, 172–4
Luillier, François, 23
Lully, Jean-Baptiste, 118
Luxembourg Palace, 2, 142
Luxembourg, 138

Madagascar Company, 136
Madiot, 99
Madrid, Château de, 15
Magnier, Laurent, 57
Maincy, 69, 73, 77–8, 129
Maine, Duke of, 178
Maintenon, Françoise d'Aubigné, Mme de, 105
Maison-Rouge, 69
Maisons, 14, 76
Manchole, 45
Mancini, Marie, 136
Mansart, François, 1, 10–11, 14, 16–17, 21, 37, 41, 50, 57, 76, 91–2, 99, 174, 178
Mantua, Prince of, 38
Marais, 14, 22, 24, 26
Marchant, Charles, 3
  Guillaume, 4, 8, 10
  Louis, 6
Margonne, Charles, 24
Margot, Queen of France, 1, 143
Marie, Alfred, 111–12, 116, 194
Marie, Christophe, 5–6, 12, 22, 29
Marie-Thérèse, Queen of France, 44, 68, 78, 109–110, 113–14, 123, 135–6
Mariage, Simon, 168, 171
Marine royale, 87
Marly, 104, 132, 134, 187
Marne, River, 50
Maron, 113
Marot, Jean, x, 10–11, 23, 26, 35–6, 50, 92
Marsy, Gaspard and Balthasar, 123, 128, 131

Martinique, 83
Martinozzi, Laure, 38
Maupeou, Marie de, mother of Nicolas Fouquet, 66
Mayenne, Duke of, 40
Mazarin, Guilio, Cardinal, 13, 19, 22, 25, 33, 36, 38, 40–2, 44–5, 49–51, 53, 55–6, 58–9, 61, 63–4, 67–70, 74–5, 77–81, 86, 88–94, 105–106, 110, 118, 124, 132, 135–7, 139–41, 149–50, 153, 157
Mazarin's College, 172
Mazarinades, 80
Mazarini, Duke of, 51, 53, 139, 142
Mazières, André, 60, 65, 99
Médicis, Catherine de, 1
  Cosimo de, 52
  Marie de, 1–2, 4–5, 142
Melun, 67, 77
Ménagerie at Versailles, 54, 105–109, 111
Menessier, inspector of cannon, 165
Messier, Nicolas, 60
Métezeau, Louis, 2
Meudon, 67–69, 92, 97
Mignon, René, 13
Milleti, M., 151
Mirrors, Hall of, ix, 35, 118, 121, 126
Mitterrand, President François, 88
Modena, Duke of, 38, 96
Modena, 98
Moisenay, 69
Molière, Jean-Baptiste Poquelin, 83
Molin, Nicolas and Toussaint, 105
Mollet, Claude, 56, 60
Monnard, Étienne, 9, 19
Montpensier, Duke of, 5
  Duchess of, *La Grande Mademoiselle*, 9, 38–39, 70, 142, 157
Mons, 120
Montagny-en-Vexin, 8
Montespan, Athenäis, Mme de, 125, 132, 134, 178
Moret, Pierre, 8
  Claude, 8
Morin, Michel, 12
Moroccan ambassadors, 108
Motteville, Mme de, 80
Mulberry Trees, 2
Muret, Marguerite, 12

Namur, 120
Nantes, 1, 66, 80, 83–4, 86, 158
  dockyard at, 153, 164
Naples, 38
Napoleonic Empires, 88
National Archives, 8, 172

Naudé, Gabriel, 148
Nesle Gate, Tower, 141–3
Neufville, 12
Neuilly, 5
Nevers, Duke of, 40, 159
Nièvre, 158
Nivernais, ix, 29, 124, 127, 131, 152, 156–7, 162, 169, 173, 179
Noblet, Michel, 1
Nolhac, Pierre de, 111
Normandy, 111, 155, 156
North Sea Company, 134
Notre-Dame de Paris, 5–7, 98

Obstal, Gérard van, 26, 33–6
Oise, 12
Ondedei, Zongo, 139
Orme, Philibert, de l', 37, 72, 75, 90
Ovid, Ovidian, 13, 106, 107

Papal Curia, 1
Palais-Royal, 10, 55–6
Palais-Richelieu, 11
Palladio, Andrea, 18–19, 32, 70, 76, 134, 149–50, 178
Papal States, 138
Paris, 1, 3, 51, 55, 67–8, 71, 77, 94–6, 113, 120, 139, 140, 142, 149, 153, 173
Parlement de Paris, 5, 67, 89, 135, 139
Parlement de Rennes, 67
Pastel, Jean, 5, 42–3
Patel, Pierre, 33
Paultre, Antoine de, 116
Pecq, 5
Pellisson, Jean, 73, 85
Petit, François, 4, 15
Perrault, Charles, 91–2, 96, 102–103, 109, 111–12, 114, 174
Claude, ix, 50, 93, 97, 101–103, 116, 178, 182
Perrault Brothers, 98–9, 111
Perrier, François, 26, 33
Peter II, King of Portugal, 108
Petit, 127
Pfnor, Rodolphe, 194
Philip IV, King of Spain, 38, 104
Philippe VI, King of France, 49
Philippe II Auguste, King of France, 58
Picart, Bernard, 33
Picquet, Antoine, 160
Piedmontese Alps, 13
Piganiol de la Force, Jean-Aymar, 101–102
Pignerol. Fortress of, 75, 85–6, 107
Pignerol, 138
Pitti Palace, 106

Pius II, Pope, Aeneas Sylvius Piccolomini, 52
Place de La Grève, x, 9
Place Dauphine, 3, 5, 146
Place Maubert, 24
Place Royale, 2–6, 14, 146
Place Turenne, 2
Plessis-Bellière, Mme de, 81
Pliny, 134
Plutarch, 13
Poitiers, 49
Poncet de la Grave, Guillaume, 43–4, 51
Pontavert, 120, 149
Pont des Arts, 143, 146
Pont de La Tournelle, 6
Pont Marie, 6–7, 12, 13
Pont Neuf, 3–4
Pont de Neuilly, 5
Pontheron, Nicolas, 18
    Pierre, 12
Porte Saint-Denis, 9
Portoro, 120
Portugal, 108, 132
Poulletier, Lugles, 6
Poussin, Nicolas, 19, 94, 119, 137, 180
Pré-des-Clercs, 23
Prou, Jacques, 78
Pyrenees, Treaty of, 1659, 63, 78, 104, 138
Pyrenees, 119

Quai d'Anjou (d'Alençon), 12, 14, 17, 19, 30
Quai de Célestins, 6, 13, 17
Quai de Dauphin, (Quai de Béthune), 34
Quai Malaquais (now Voltaire), 143
Quarries, location of, 65

Rabon, Pierre, 109, 174
Racine, Jean, 86
Rainaldi, Carlo, 93
Rambouillet, Marquise de, 15
Rance, 120, 149
Ratabon, Antoine, 57–8, 60, 62–5, 174
Ravaillac, François, 1
Religion, Wars of, 3
Reformed Church, 15
Regnaudin Thomas, 57, 128, 131
Reims, 61
Renouard, Nicolas, 13
Rhine, River, 128
Rhine, Rupert, Prince of the, 38
Ricci, Ottavio, 51–3
Richelieu, Cardinal, 7, 17, 10, 15, 22, 55–6, 66, 86, 106, 127, 130, 136–7
Richelet, César-Pierre, 17
Robaut, Gérard, 121
Robert, Hubert, 129

Rochefort dockyard, 153, 158, 161, 178
Rome, 18–19, 41, 46, 77, 94–5, 97, 147
Romanelli, Giovanni Francesco, 33, 41, 60, 70, 93, 106
Rossi, Mathei de, 95, 100
Rotterdam, 120
Rouen, 120
Rouen, Archbishop of, 89
Royal Academy of Architecture, 9, 100, 105, 119, 177
Royal Academy of Painters and Sculptors, 15, 57, 90, 123, 174
Royal Academy, of Sciences, 108
Rousseau, Jacques, 33
Rue d'Arbre-Sec, 56
Rue de Deux-Ponts, 12
Rue François Miron, 63
Rue Frémenteau, 62–3
Rue de La Bûcherie, 19
Rue de La Fromagerie, 12
Rue de La Mortellerie, 9
Rue Mazarine, 147
Rue Plastrière, 27
Rue Poulettier, 14, 35
Rue des Poulies, 144
Rue de Prouvelles, 6
Rue Neuve Petits-Champs, 10, 64
Rue du Roi de Sicile, 12, 46, 65, 144
Rue Royale, 24
Rue Saint-Antoine, 148
Rue Saint-Jean-en-Grève, 8
Rue de Saint-Louis-en-L'Isle, 17, 30
Rue du Temple, 71
Rue de La Tissanderie, 18
Rue de La Université, 23
Rue de Verbois, 10
Rue Vivienne, 10

Sachet, Guillaume, 143
Sainctot, Pierre, 3
  Nicolas de, 34–6
Saint-André-des-Arts, *M. Le Curé de*, 151
Saint-Anne-La-Royale, Church of, 140
Saint-Cyr, 105
Saint-Cloud, 96, 116
Saint-Étienne, 163
Saint-Fargeau, 9, 70, 157
Saint-Germain-en-Laye, 92, 94, 101, 110, 114, 123–4, 136, 173
Saint-Germain-des-Près, Abbey, 143, 151
Saint-Germain l'Auxerrois, Church of, 62, 91, 96, 98, 101, 144, 166–7
Saint-Gervais, Hospitallers of, 14
Saint-Jean de La Grève, Parish of, 18
Saint-Jean-de-Luz, 44, 78, 79, 81, 135

Saint-Julien, Church of, Versailles, 126
Saint-Louis, Church for the Recollets at Versailles, 127
Saint-Mandé, 50, 52–4, 68, 71, 73, 80, 82, 85, 129, 173
Saint-Michel-en-l'Herm, Abbey of, 139
Saint-Paul-Saint-Louis, Church of, 148, 150
Saint-Sépulcre, 36–7, 92
Saint-Simon, Louis de Rouvroy, Duke of, 105
Saint-Thomas du Louvre, Church of, 91
Saintes, Bernard de, 151
Sallonyer, de Nion, 169
Sarrazin, Jacques, 26–7, 34–5, 37
Sauval, Henri, x, 10, 36, 105, 175, 190–1
Savoy, 75
Saxony, 70, 155–6, 165
Scamotti, Vincenzo, 70, 178
Sceaux, 153
Scudéry, Madeleine de, 73, 108, 113, 129–30, 132
Séguier, Chancellor, 61, 85, 136
Seine, River, ix, 1, 64, 90, 120, 141, 146–7, 172–3
Sens, Archbishop of, 110
Seraglio at Vincennes, 50–4
Serlio, Sebastien, 70
Servien, Abel, 67, 69, 92
Sforza, Galeazzo, 52
Siam, 108
Siamese Ambassadors, 53
Silk Manufacture, 2–3
Silvestre, Israël, x, 26, 37, 41, 56, 77, 118, 122, 132, 146
Sommier family, 74, 194
Sorbonne, 120, 138, 140, 147, 150
Spain, 15, 19, 44, 53, 62, 73, 81, 88, 113–14, 127, 132, 149
Spanish Netherlands, 114
Stanić Milovan, 95
Sanguin, *Médecin physique*, 151
Soullier, 151
Stockholm, 107, 111, 116
Sublet de Noyers, François, 18, 55, 58, 94
Sucy-en-Brie, 25–9
Süe, Louis, 35
Sully, 3–5, 58
Swanevelt, Herman van, 33

Tabouret, Martin, Sieur de Tourny, 39
Tambonneau, Michel-Antoine, 23–4, 177
Terror, The, 151
Tessin, Nicodemus, 107, 111
Thétis, Grotto of, 109, 111, 128–31
Third Republic, 48, 88

Thiriot, Jean, 11, 24
Thirty Years War, 67
Thoison Charles, 9, 19, 23, 46, 52, 168–9
Thuiller, Guy, 160
Tinplated iron, ix, 70, 124, 155, 157, 160, 164, 166–8
Toulon, dockyard, 153, 161
Toulouse, Count of, 101
Toulouse, foundries of, 154
Tours, 85
Trianon de Marbre, 69, 122, 132, 134, 154
   de Porcelaine, 105, 132–4
Trinity College, Cambridge, 148
Troyes, 11, 36
True Cross, 49
Tubeuf, Intendant of the Nivernais, 169
Tuby, Jean-Baptiste, 122–3, 125, 128, 131
Tuileries Palace, 1, 4, 51, 63–4, 75, 79, 90, 100, 124, 135
Turenne, Marechal de, 73
Turgot, Map, 12

United Provinces, 134
University of Paris, 138
Urbanisation, 1–4, 79, 146, 153

Val de Grâce, 56, 92, 150
Valdor, Jean, 60
Vallot, Antoine, 60, 141
Valois Dynasty, 1, 3
Valperga, Antonio Maurizio, 93
Varin, Jean, 100
Varro, 105
Vaux-le-Vicomte, ix, 9, 33, 37, 41, 52, 54, 67, 69, 71, 74–6, 79–80, 83, 87, 91, 97, 99, 104, 106–108, 111, 116, 122–3, 129–30, 132, 138
Vauvégny Lake, 157
Veniat, Guillaume, 18
Venice, 70, 124, 153
Versailles, Palace of, ix, 33, 44–5, 49, 54, 69, 79–80, 86, 92, 101, 104, 108–112, 114–15, 119–24, 126–7, 129–30, 132, 172, 174
Vespasian, Roman Emperor, 130
Vexin, 8
Viart, 113
Vieux-Versailles, 126
Vigarani, Carlo, 93, 100, 110, 116
   Gaspare, 63–4
Vignola, Giacomo Barozzi da, 178
Villedo, Michel, 10, 12–13, 16–17, 26, 28, 32, 43, 71
Villeneuf-sur-Gravois, 9
Villeroy, Maréchal de, 58
Vincennes, 14, 40–54, 61, 64, 68, 77, 82, 84, 104–105, 108, 114, 135–6, 140
Vitruvius, 70, 93, 178
Vogüé, Alexandre de, 198
Vouet, Simon, 34, 180

Wales, Charles, Prince of, 38
Wallonia, 162
West Indies, 130
West Indies Company, 134
Westphalia, Peace of, 1648, 67, 138
Whiteley, Mary, 102
Wren, Sir Christopher, 146, 148